The Jewish Concern for the Church

The Jewish Concern for the Church

How Far Have We Drifted from the One New Humanity the Apostles Envisioned?

Edited by
CHRISTINE GRAEF

WIPF & STOCK · Eugene, Oregon

THE JEWISH CONCERN FOR THE CHURCH
How Far Have We Drifted from the One New Humanity the Apostles Envisioned?

Copyright © 2017 Wipf and Stock Publishers. All rights reserved. Except for brief quotations in critical publications or reviews, no part of this book may be reproduced in any manner without prior written permission from the publisher. Write: Permissions, Wipf and Stock Publishers, 199 W. 8th Ave., Suite 3, Eugene, OR 97401.

Wipf & Stock
An Imprint of Wipf and Stock Publishers
199 W. 8th Ave., Suite 3
Eugene, OR 97401

www.wipfandstock.com

PAPERBACK ISBN: 978-1-5326-0827-8
HARDCOVER ISBN: 978-1-5326-0829-2
EBOOK ISBN: 978-1-5326-0828-5

Manufactured in the U.S.A. FEBRUARY 6, 2017

Taken from the Complete Jewish Bible by David H. Stern. Copyright © 1998. All rights reserved. Used by permission of Messianic Jewish Publishers, 6120 Day Long Lane, Clarksville, MD 21029. www.messianicjewish.net

Taken from the Holy Bible, New International Version®, NIV®. Copyright © 1973, 1978, 1984, 2011 by Biblica, Inc.™ Used by permission of Zondervan. All rights reserved worldwide. www.zondervan.com

Scripture taken from the NEW AMERICAN STANDARD BIBLE®, Copyright © 1960,1962,1963,1968,1971,1972,1973,1975,1977,1995 by The Lockman Foundation. Used by permission.

The ESV® Bible (The Holy Bible, English Standard Version®) copyright © 2001 by Crossway Bibles, a publishing ministry of Good News Publishers. The ESV® text has been reproduced in cooperation with and by permission of Good News Publishers. All rights reserved.

Scripture is taken from GOD'S WORD®, © 1995 God's Word to the Nations. Used by permission of Baker Publishing Group.

In gratitude to all the writers who contributed to this volume and the countless others called out in tireless faith to know the God of Israel.
Todah rabah.
You bring light as we each find our place in the body of the Lord.

His purpose was to create in himself one new humanity out of the two, thus making peace, and in one body to reconcile both of them to God through the cross, by which he put to death their hostility

(Eph 2:15–16).

Contents

Contributors | xi

Beit Tefilah: A House of Prayer

  1   Pesach (Passover) | 3

  2   The Haggadah (The Telling) | 14

        The True Origin of Easter
           by Rabbi Stephen Luft

        Christian Persecution of the Jews
           by Shira Sorko-Ram

        Yom Hashoah
           by Rabbi Stephen Luft

  3   B'Rit Hadashah (The New Covenant) | 25

        Coming Home to My Jewish Messiah
           by Nette Tepe

        Jewish Roots
           by Rabbi Ben Volman

        New Covenant Writings
           by Rabbi Stephen Luft

        Gentiles and Jews Together in Ancient Rome and North African Carthage
           by Dr. Jeffrey L. Seif

Contents

In What Ways Did Jesus Live as a Jew?
by David Sedaca

The Times of the Jews
by Shira Sorko-Ram

Messianic Judaism Gaining Momentum in Israel
by Rabbi Barry Rubin

Understanding Messianic Judaism
by Rabbi Stephen Luft

4   Rosh Hodesh (Head of the Month) | 58

What I Believe and What I Reject
by Rabbi Loren Jacobs

Exposing the Elitist, Sectarian Spirit
by Tom Martincic

Covenant of Salt: You Gotta Serve Somebody
by Chris Suitt

Beit Midrash: A House of Study

5   Shavu'ot (Pentecost) | 77

Shavuot, the Feast of Weeks
by Rabbi Loren Jacobs

Gentiles in the Messianic Movement
by Dr. Bruce H. Stokes

Why All Christians Should Celebrate Pentecost
by Pastor Ross Clark

Inconvenient Truths: The One New Man
by Rabbi Dr. Stuart Dauermann

6   Yeshua HaMashiach (Jesus the Messiah) | 96

Why Shouldn't a Christian Train Jewish People to Say "Jesus Christ"?
by Shira Sorko-Ram

Any Other Name Would Still Be a Jew
by Patricia Pason

A Challenge to Believers
by Geoff Davenport

Contents

   Why Jews Don't Like Evangelicals
    by David Lazarus

7 Talmidim (Disciples) | 106
   The Jewishness of the Gospels
    by Rabbi Frank Lowinger

   A Challenge to Believers
    by Geoff Davenport

   What is the Role of the Church?
    Shalom Messianic Congregation Northern Ireland

   Let Us Reclaim Our Family
    By Rev. Canon Brian Cox

8 Church and Israel | 123
   Other Problems in Semantics
    by Shira Sorko-Ram

   What I Believe and What I Reject
    by Rabbi Loren Jacobs

   Holidays and Festivals
    by Chosen People Ministries

   Paul Employing Leviticus: Same Sex Intercourse Considered Amongst Torah Commandments
    by Dr. Jon C. Olson

   What I Believe and What I Reject
    by Rabbi Loren Jacobs

   The Unique Place of Gentiles in Messianic Jewish Congregational Life
    by Rabbi Dr. Richard C. Nichol

Beit Hallel: A House of Praise

9 Baruch HaShem (Blessed is God) | 143
   The Real Miracle of Chanukkah
    by Rabbi Loren Jacobs

   Keeping a Balance for the Gentile Messianic
    by Pastor Ross Clark

   Gentiles Within the Messianic Jewish Community
    by Rabbi Jeffrey A. Adler

Contents

10 Mikveh (Immersion) | 160
 Baptism
  by Rabbi Stephen Luft
 Shic'zur o t'ciya?—Restoration or Revival?
  by Geoff Davenport

11 Sukkot (Feast of the Ingathering) | 170
 The Meaning of Sukkot
  by Rabbi Stephen Luft
 Sukkot: Messiah and the World to Come
  by Rabbi Joshua Brumbach
 When was Yeshua Born?
  by Rabbi Stephen Luft
 Is Christmas Scriptural?
  by Graeme Purdie
 What I Believe and What I Reject
  by Rabbi Loren Jacobs

12 Tikkun Olam (Repairing the World) | 186
 Tikkun Olam: Repairing the World
  by Stan Meyer
 The Feast of Trumpets
  by Tom Martincic

Bibliography | 199

Contributors

RABBI STEPHEN LUFT

"A common, and I would say majority, view of Pesach by Christians and the church is that of being irrelevant," said Messianic Rabbi Stephen Luft. Views include: Pesach is for the Jewish people only; it has been done away with because it's part of Torah and no longer relevant; it has been fulfilled by Yeshua and we are no longer required to do it. All of these views could not be further from the truth, he said. Rabbi Stephen opened Kehilah Portland, the first Messianic Synagogue in Maine in 2011 because of the need for a faith community where Jewish people can embrace their heritage as believers in Yeshua ha Me and non-Jewish believers are encouraged to join in worshipping the God of Israel. Kehilah Portland is affiliated with the Messianic Jewish Alliance of America and the International Alliance of Messianic Congregations and Synagogues.

SHIRA SORKO-RAM

Shira Sorko-Ram is author of *I Became as a Jew: What Jews and Christians Should Understand About Each Other*, published by Maoz Inc. She and her husband, Ari, are founders of the Maoz Israel Ministries in Tel Aviv. They are pioneers of the modern day Messianic Jewish movement in Israel and founders of a Messianic Jewish congregation, TiferetYeshua (The Glory of Yeshua).

NETTE TEPE

Bounded by the Indian Ocean to the north and west, and the Southern Ocean to the south, the ancient low lands of western Australia witness a growing population of Jewish believers. Celebrate Messiah established Beit HaMashiach (House of Messiah) Messianic Congregation in the heart of the Jewish community of Melbourne-Caulfield, Australia, in October 1998. Celebrate Messiah is an interdenominational evangelistic society dedicated to raising the Messiah of God's people to Australia and beyond through partnership with Chosen People Global Ministries. Nette Tepe is a worshipper at Beit HaMashiach.

RABBI BEN VOLMAN

Chosen People Ministries was founded in Brooklyn, New York, in 1894 by Rabbi Leopold Cohn, a Hungarian Jewish immigrant wanting to share the knowledge of Yeshua the Messiah with God's chosen people. It spread to have ministries around the world. Rabbi Ben Volman serves as the Toronto Director of Ministries for Chosen People Ministries in Canada. He is also the founding Messianic pastor of Kehillat Eytz Chaim / Tree of Life Congregation in North York, Ontario.

DR. JEFFREY L. SEIF

Dr. Jeffrey Seif was awarded the title of University Distinguished Professor of Bible and Jewish Studies at Kings University and served as the pastoral leader at Zola Levitt Ministries. He serves on the faculties of the Messianic Jewish Bible Institute, the Messianic Jewish Theological Institute, the Israel College of the Bible, Christ for the Nations Institute, and teaches at Kings University. In 2012 Dr. Seif gathered with Messianic rabbis and ministry leaders for the Borough Park Symposium in New York organized with the Union of Messianic Jewish Congregations to share compelling thoughts on the Messianic Jewish community and its relationship in the world.

DAVID SEDACA

David Sedaca serves as Vice President of Chosen People Ministries. David and his wife Julia live in New York City and are involved in starting a ministry in Brooklyn, home to the largest concentration of Jewish people in the world outside of Israel.

RABBI BARRY RUBIN

Rabbi Barry Rubin is the president and publisher of Messianic Jewish Publishers and Resources/Jewish New Testament Publications. He is also Rabbi of Emmanuel Messianic Jewish Congregation in Clarksville, Maryland, that began in 1915 as Emmanuel Neighborhood Center to help the new immigrant Jews of east Baltimore.

RABBI LOREN JACOBS

Rabbi Loren Jacobs' great-grandparents lived near Kiev in the Ukraine in early 1900. They migrated to the US during the first decade of the twentieth century when being Jewish was becoming increasingly difficult in Russia and the Ukraine. Rabbi Loren grew up in the Chicago, Illinois, area in the 1960s. He is senior rabbi and founder of Congregation Shema Yisrael (Hear O Israel) in Bloomfield Hills, Michigan, near the Detroit metro area where nearly 80,000 Jewish people live.

TOM MARTINCIC

In Ava, Missouri, Tom Martincic, created the website EliYah.com in 1995 to proclaim the Messiah and create a network of conversation and teaching. EliYah means My Mighty One is Yahweh.

CHRIS SUITT

Torah Class is an independent, non-denominational organization of Gentile Christians and Messianic Jews on Merritt Island, a peninsula on the east coast of Florida. They are part of Seed of Abraham Ministries Inc. and support a variety of ministries to Israel. Torah Class states, "We understand and agree with the desire to celebrate Christ's birth and resurrection. Yet Christmas and Easter are undeniably manmade celebrations that over time have been co-opted by the secular world and so we have chosen different occasions to celebrate the believer's intent of Christmas and Easter. Therefore, while there is no God-ordained biblical feast after which we can model a celebration of Jesus' birth, there is a three part series of God-ordained biblical festivals that precisely speak of his death, entombment, and resurrection: the Biblical Feasts of Passover, Unleavened Bread, and Firstfruits. We celebrate those feasts in lieu of Easter." The salt on the Passover table is significant. Chris Suitt, a teacher at Torah Class, speaks of trusting Jesus even when the result of obedience is not yet clear.

DR. BRUCE H. STOKES

Dr. Bruce H. Stokes is pastor of the Disciple Center in Anaheim Hills, California, formed by Christians committed to the unity of Messianic Jews and Gentiles and of Judeo-Christians and Hebrew Christians. The Center assists denominational churches to understand the unique calling of the Messianic movement in the larger Jewish community. Dr. Stokes serves as the vice president of the Union of Messianic Believers and as an advisor to the Administrative Board to the International Messianic Jewish Alliance. His writing is from an article presented to the International Messianic Jewish Alliance meeting in Puerto Vallarta Mexico in 1997.

PASTOR ROSS CLARK

Bounded by the Indian Ocean to the north and west and the Southern Ocean to the south, the ancient low lands of western Australia witness a growing population of Jewish believers. Perth Messianic Assembly is a congregation of Christian and Messianic believers in Yeshua with a heart to bridge the gap between Jew and Gentile. Pastor Ross Clark has ministered in China, Hong Kong, and the US. He said that in the light of the new dispensation of Yeshua's coming and the New Covenant era, there is a new understanding that was not fully revealed to earlier covenant saints and prophets.

RABBI DR. STUART DAUERMANN

Rabbi Dr. Stuart Dauermann, PhD, is Rabbi Emeritus of Ahavat Zion Messianic Synagogue in Santa Monica, California, and Director of Interfaithfulness, upgrading spirituality and relationships for Jews and Christians around a more Jewish Jesus. His latest book is *Converging Destinies: Jews,*

Christians, and the Mission of God (Wipf and Stock). Current initiatives include developing the HaB'er Havurah Network under the auspices of Interfaithfulness.

PATRICIA PASON

In western New York State, Congregation B'rith Hadoshah was established in the town of Amherst. Men, women, and children gather together to celebrate the Lord's festivals, pursue understanding of God's word, learning in Bible studies during the week, during Shabbat Service and Torah Talk after the service. Scripture is a daily way of life. Member Patricia Pason shares insight.

GEOFF DAVENPORT

In New Zealand there are about half a dozen Messianic congregations listed nationally. Out on a peninsula in northeast New Zealand, framed by the Bay of Plenty in the Pacific Ocean, believers established The Way—Haderech Messianic Community in Mount Maunganui to serve the community with the gifts inherent in everyone. Ministry leader Geoff Davenport says, "If you have given your heart to Yeshua Ha Maschiach (Jesus the Messiah), repented and been forgiven for your sins, and count yourself as part of his Jewish/Gentile Body with a heart for Israel, and look eagerly for His return to the exact spot He departed from 2,000 years ago, Jerusalem, then you are Messianic. Jew and Gentile, two equal united halves of His Body with Yeshua Ha Maschiach as its head."

DAVID LAZARUS

West of Jerusalem on the coast of the Mediterranean Sea, Jaffa is the oldest part of Tel Aviv. An ancient port, it is where the cedars of Lebanon for Solomon's Temple were brought, the place where the prophet Jonah embarked for Tarshish, and where Peter stayed a long time, with a tanner named Simon, and raised Tabitha from the dead. The Catholic armies of the first Crusade occupied Jaffa with terror in 1099. Now, Jaffa is a city of lights and businesses where camels once carried burdens across sandy hills. Living there today, David Lazarus belongs to Beit Immanuel, one of the first congregations of Messianic Jews in modern Israel.

CONTRIBUTORS

SHALOM MESSIANIC CONGREGATION NORTHERN IRELAND

In Belfast, Northern Ireland, the Shalom Messianic Congregation has been meeting since 2007 to re-educate believers in the Hebraic foundation of their faith and expose the false doctrines of Replacement Theology, Calvinism, Two House theology, British Israelism, and Christian/Israelite identity groups.

REV. CANON BRIAN COX

The Toward Jerusalem Council II is directed by a fourteen member International Leadership Council representative of international movements and churches that believe in Yeshua as the Lord and Savior. Seven members are Jewish and seven are non-Jewish, coming together to accomplish the work of the Lord by healing the divisions, unifying the body worldwide, and restoring the Jewish believers to their place in God's plan. Member of the Council, Reverend Canon Brian Cox, is Rector of Christ the King Episcopal Church in Santa Barbara, California, Senior Vice President of the International Center for Religion & Diplomacy in Washington, DC, and Director of the PACIS Project in Faith-Based Diplomacy of the Straus Institute for Dispute Resolution at Pepperdine University School of Law in Malibu, California.

DR. JON C. OLSON

Dr. Jon C. Olson is a Clinical Assistant Professor of Epidemiology at the University of Massachusetts School of Public Health. He is author of *Tailoring Truth: Politicizing the Past and Negotiating Memory in East Germany, 1945–1990*, published in 2015 with Berghahn Books.

RABBI DR. RICHARD C. NICHOL

Rabbi Dr. Richard C. Nichol has served as the Rabbi of Congregation Ruach Israel in Needham, Massachusetts, since 1981. He is Director of the Rabbinical Ordination Institute of the Messianic Jewish Theological Institute in Los Angeles, California. He is also past President of the Union of

Messianic Jewish Congregations and serves as President of the Messianic Jewish Rabbinical Council. Rabbi Richard submitted a paper to the 2012 Borough Park Symposium, a gathering of more than twenty Messianic rabbis and ministry leaders organized with the Union of Messianic Jewish Congregations.

RABBI JEFFREY A. ADLER

In the 2012 Borough Park Symposium, rabbis and ministry leaders shared compelling thoughts on the ongoing dialogue about the Messianic Jews and the church. Among participants who contributed papers was Jeffrey A. Adler, Rabbi of the Messianic Jewish Congregation, Sha'arey Yeshua in Indianapolis, Indiana.

RABBI JOSHUA BRUMBACH

Ahavat Zion Synagogue is a Messianic synagogue founded in 1973 in west Los Angeles, Beverly Hills, California. Rabbi Joshua Brumbach is senior rabbi and president of the Union of Messianic Jewish Congregations. He is author of *Jude: On Faith and the Destructive Influence of Heresy* (Messianic Jewish Publishers).

GRAEME PURDIE

On the eastern shores of northern New Zealand, the Talmedie Yeshua Messianic Ministry of New Zealand established on Hawkes Bay where rivers flow out to the Pacific Ocean. Talmedei Yeshua is a congregation of talmidim (disciples) who meet on Shabbat and maintain the Hebraic expression of their faith in accordance with Scripture. Graeme Purdie is the founder.

STAN MEYER

"Jews for Jesus" is a Messianic Jewish non-profit organization founded in 1973 in San Francisco by Moishe Rosen to share belief that Jesus is the promised Messiah of the Jewish people. Today there are branches all over the world. Stan Meyer is a senior missionary for Jews for Jesus.

BEIT TEFILAH

A House of Prayer

My house will be called a house of prayer for all peoples
(Isa 56:7)

1

Pesach (Passover)

So this day shall be to you a memorial; and you shall keep it as a feast to ADONAI throughout your generations

(EXOD 12:14)

The moon was rising to brighten the streets of Jerusalem as it waxed toward its lunar phase, illuminated by the sun, round and full. The Pesach (Passover) was nearing to celebrate the people's deliverance from bondage in Egypt. It was springtime. Adonai had instructed Moshe (Moses) and Aharon (Aaron) that Nisan would be the first month of the year (Exod 12:1–2), the month of redemption that comes soon after the edge of day and night meet over the equator to bring spring equinox. "Tell all the congregation of Israel that on the tenth day of this month every man shall take a lamb according to their fathers' houses, a lamb for a household" (v4). The lamb would be kept until the fourteenth day of the month, the full moon, and killed at sunset (v6). Called the Feast of Freedom followed by the Feast of Unleavened Bread and the Feast of First Fruits, it is a holiday about the past, present, and future of the Messiah.

As the day approached for the lambs to be sacrificed, the disciples asked Yeshua, "Where do you want us to prepare your Seder?" "Go into the city, to so-and-so," he replied, "and tell him that the Rabbi says, 'My time is near, my talmidim and I are celebrating Pesach at your house.'" The talmidim did as Yeshua directed and prepared the Seder. (Matt 26:17–19).

Beit Tefilah: A House of Prayer

The winter rains had gone, leaving cisterns full with fresh water. The air was scented with the sweet fragrance of soft pink almond blossoms. Narrow dusty streets swelled with people as they traveled to the Holy City, making the long ascent from Jericho, rounding the Mount of Olives and sighting the City of David that would be the joy of all the world (Lam 2:15). The Temple stood high above, built on the center of white stone. Zion, the upper city, stood beyond arched passageways to the west with its marble villas. The lower city was at its south, grouped with limestone houses on roads that sloped down to the Tyropean Valley. From here the sounds of the Temple could be heard, the busy voices and clatter of donkey hooves, and the smell of cooking carried on light breezes. Craftsmen sat at work weaving, dying, baking, or sewing. Carpenters and potters, metalworkers and merchants of food offered their wares on market days. Some had become rich by filling the Temple's need for loaves of bread, priestly vestments, incense, wood for altar fires, and golden vessels. Only on Shabbat and feast days did the streets become quiet and empty.

Crowds of people went up to the Temple, singing the songs of ascent, Psalms 120 to 134, as they climbed the sloping hills to the place that God had chosen to meet with them. The ascent is the story of our journey to the presence of Messiah. "I lift my eyes up to the hills," the travelers sing. "Too long have I lived among those who hate peace." Living in a world of conflict, many feel miles from the presence of God. "Woe to me that I dwell in Meshek," hundreds of miles to the north of Jerusalem between the Black and Caspian seas, or "among the tents of Kedar," hundreds of miles to the south in what became Saudi Arabia. Knowing they were one of God's people, but living among those who did not know the living God, feeling far from his presence for far too long, they sang in yearning anticipation as they climbed toward the place of his presence."I rejoiced with those who said to me, Let us go to the house of the LORD."

The joy as they started on their journey soon turned into the difficulties of a long and arduous distance, driven into the wilderness as Yeshua had been where he was tempted not to continue. Even knowing the destiny will be glorious, the journey becomes tiring. The relief of the ending is still miles away. The psalms sing about praying in hope, sowing in tears, being restored by the rains that plow a path through the deserts that only God brings, turning to hymns that ask God to intervene, with the refreshing Spirit, to help their limitations so that they may sow from strength to strength. They sang about the captives who were as men in a dream when

Pesach (Passover)

they returned to Jerusalem, full of vision, praying that God would pour water on the dry ground of their lives. The psalms of ascent are a story of sorrow and redemption written in every believer's life.

As they arrive and gather in comfort, their thoughts turn toward others with an invitation to share in worship.

May Adonai, the maker of heaven and earth, bless you from Tziyon (Ps 134:3).

As they gathered at the Temple each of their struggles gave way to worship as they heard the past and the future of their own story. The journey is to the city of the living God, heavenly Jerusalem, to thousands of joyful angels, to a community where the mediator of the new covenant, Yeshua, redeemed the firstborn whose names are recorded in heaven (Heb 12:22–24).

A high stone wall circled the city four miles around with gateways at intervals where publicans collected taxes on merchandise entering or leaving the city. Every room of the city was filled with guests. Many found lodging at an inn. Most stayed in tents outside the city where groves of olive trees budded feathery white flowers over the hillsides, providing exports for Jerusalem's farmers. Some found lodging in private homes in the village of Bethany. The travelers brought economy, needing food, lodging, sacrificial animals, and a required tithe to the Temple. Roman soldiers were stationed throughout because of the overcrowding and excitement. To the thousands who made the pilgrimage, there was nowhere on earth like Jerusalem and no thought more near than the Temple.

Preparations were keeping everyone busy. Bridges and roads were reinforced and homes had to be ceremonially cleansed and inspected. On the eve of Pesach the head of the household searched a final time for any leaven, a thorough inspection preparing the heart for the Seder recalling Adonai's powerful hand leading the people from slavery to freedom.

Yeshua came into Jerusalem on the day the lambs without blemish were being selected. In an upstairs room a table had been prepared with the best dishes, cups, silver, and oil lamps for the festival lights. There was a bowl of salt water, three pieces of matzah, and an overflowing cup for Eliyahu (Elijah).

The sun was lowering beyond the Mediterranean Sea and the sky changed to its twilight colors. The shofar sounded from the Temple as a priest signaled the lambs were slain in the Temple's Court of the Priests. Its call stirred the people's souls. It's time to come into Adonai's presence. Women were lighting the oil lamps everywhere.

When the time came, Yeshua and the emissaries reclined at the table, and he said to them, "I have really wanted so much to celebrate this Seder with you before I die!" (Luke 22:14–15).

He and his disciples lifted the first cup of the Pesach—the Cup of Sanctification. Yeshua gave the b'rakhah, saying:

> *Ba-ruch a-ta Adonai, Eh-lo-hay-nu meh-lehch ha-o-lahm, bo-ray p'ree ha-ga-fen. Amain*
>
> Blessed are You O Lord our God, King of the universe, creator of the fruit of the vine. Amain.

Yeshua and his talmidim sipped from their cups.

To prepare to commune with Adonai's presence, Yeshua got up from the table. He was aware that the Father had put everything in his power and he would soon return to heaven. He wrapped a towel around his waist and poured water into a basin. Going around the table he began washing the feet of the talmidim and wiping them dry with the towel. He came to Shim`on Kefa (Simon Peter) who said, "Lord! You are washing my feet?" Yeshua said, "In time you will understand." "You will never wash my feet!" Kefa said, but Yeshua answered, "If I don't wash you, you have no share with me." He explained that he was setting an example so that they could do for each other as he had done for them (John 13:3–15).

Yeshua was preparing his talmidin for a royal priesthood. The practice is held with ritual washing before a priest can enter the Holy of Holies in the Temple, a symbolic act of purification. Who may go up to the mountain of Adonai? Who can stand in his holy place? Those with clean hands and pure hearts, who don't make vanities the purpose of their lives or swear oaths just to deceive (Ps 24:3–4). Aharon and his sons were prepared for service, brought to the entrance of the tent of meeting, washed with water, and anointed for the office of priest (Exod 40:12–15).

Yeshua spoke the b'rakhah:

> *Ba-ruch a-ta Adonai, Ehlohaynu meh-lech ha-o-lahm ah-sher keed-sha-nu beed-va-reh-cha v'tzee-va-noo ahl n'tee-laht ya-da-yeem. Amain.*
>
> Blessed are You O Lord our God, King of the Universe, Who has sanctified us in Your Word and commanded us concerning the washing of hands. Amain.

Adonai is willing to wash our hands and feet. We are clean because he spoke the word to us and we abide in his love (John 15:3). Called *rachatz*, washing hands before a meal is still a custom done with bowls of water on the table in today's Pesach. The hands of the person sitting beside someone are often washed and needed prayer is acknowledged.

The Seder Plate, called a *Ka'arah*, contains maror, a bitter herb such as horseradish, that represents the sorrow that Adonai removed when he delivered Isra'el from Egypt, the land of bondage and the embitterment of the transgressions in every life. A green vegetable is on the plate, such as parsley that is symbolic of spring's new growth and the hyssop used to dip blood to mark the doors in Egypt. The bowl of salt water represents the tears that the Lord turns into joy and the salt of the covenant first mentioned in Leviticus 2:13. Charoset is a mixture of apples, honey, nuts, grapes, and sweet spices such as cinnamon, representing the mortar that was used by the Hebrew slaves to build Egypt. There is a lamb shank bone in remembrance of the Pesach lamb, no longer sacrificed at the Temple. Eliyahu's cup is full, speaking of the future coming of Messiah. Matzah is the bread of redemption. During the first Pesach, the people ate quickly, dressed in their traveling clothes, ready to leave in a hurry. There was no leaven in the breads they baked. Leaven represents sin left behind.

Three unleavened breads are a distinction during Pesach. Other meals offer two. The three unleavened breads are considered to represent the Trinity by Messianic Jews. Matzah that is striped and pierced reminds us that Yeshua was pierced for our transgressions and crushed for our iniquities. The punishment fell on him and by his stripes we are healed. The matzah also reminds that the Messiah was tempted in all ways yet never sinned. Some say the three matzahs represent the three Temples. Two have been destroyed. The third will be built with the Mashiach (Messiah) return.

The unleavened bread in the middle of the stack is taken and broken in half. One half is wrapped in cloth and hidden away. The holy child of God born a few miles southwest of Jerusalem, in a town called Bethlehem, meaning House of Bread, was not recognized by Israel. The Messiah was broken and wrapped in a shroud. The truth was hidden for a time.

"You are to observe the festival of matzah, for on this very day I brought your divisions out of the land of Egypt. Therefore, you are to observe this day from generation to generation by a perpetual regulation" (Exod 12:17). When the children ask what this ceremony means, they are to say, "It is the sacrifice of Adonai's Pesach, because Adonai passed over the houses of the people of Isra'el in Egypt, when he killed the Egyptians but spared our houses."

Beit Tefilah: A House of Prayer

The young at the table chant four questions:

> *Mah nishtanah ha-lahylah ha-zeh mi-kol ha-layloht, mi-kol ha-layloht?*
> *She-b'khol ha-layloht anu okhlin chameytz u-matzah, chameytz u-matzah. Ha-lahylah ha-zeh, ha-lahylah hazeh, kooloh matzah.*
> *She-b'khol ha-layloht anu okhlin sh'ar y'rakot, sh'ar y'rakot. Ha-lahylah ha-zeh, ha-lahylah ha-zeh, maror.*
> *She-b'khol ha-layloht ayn anu mat'bilin afilu pa'am echat, afilu pa'am echat. Ha-lahylah ha-zeh, halahylah ha-zeh, sh'tay p'amim.*
> *She-b'khol ha-layloht anu okhlin bayn yosh'bin u'vayn m'soobin, bayn yosh'bin u'vayn m'soobin. Ha-lahylah ha-zeh, ha-lahylah ha-zeh, koolanu m'soobin.*

Why is this night different from all other nights?
On all other nights, we may eat chametz and matzah. On this night, why do we only eat matzah?
On all other nights, we eat many vegetables. On this night, why do we only eat maror (bitter herbs)?
On all other nights, we do not dip our vegetables even once. On this night, why do we dip twice?
On all other nights, we eat either sitting or reclining, On this night, why do we eat reclining?

By answering, the Pesach story remembers Adonai's eternal mercy for his people and their responsibility toward him.

You are to observe this as a law, you and your descendants forever (Exod 12:24).

The story begins with God giving the promise to Avram (Abram). When Avram was an old man Adonai appeared to him and said to him, "I am El Shaddai [God Almighty]. Walk in my presence and be pure-hearted. I will make my covenant between me and you, and I will increase your numbers greatly." Avram fell on his face, and God continued speaking with him: As for me, this is my covenant with you: you will be the father of many nations. Your name will no longer be Avram [exalted father], but your name will be Avraham father of many, because I have made you the father of many nations (Gen 17:1–5).

When the cry of the people went up to Adonai and he heard how they were being oppressed in Egypt, he sent a child, Moshe, who was pulled out of water in a basket, so that Moshe would pull his people out of slavery.

Pesach (Passover)

Yeshua would later personify God's desire to save and say, "Come to me, all who are heavy laden, and I will give you rest" (Matt 11:28).

Moshe went to Pharaoh, and Adonai spoke through him. "Let my people go so they may worship me in the wilderness." Ten judgments passed over Egypt, the last one striking the first born son of every house unless the blood of the sacred lamb marked their doorway. Death passed over the homes. Egyptian women found their oldest boys dead in their beds or in the fields and heard the cries coming from other homes. The Jewish families and others who chose the blood waited, covered by grace as the wailing filled the streets. There will be a horrendous wailing throughout all the land of Egypt—there has never been another like it, and there never will be again (Exod 11:6).

Then Moshe and the people of Isra'el sang this song to Adonai for the first time: Yah is my strength and my song, and he has become my salvation. This is my God: I will glorify him; my father's God: I will exalt him (Exod 15:2).

The elders respond to the children's questions with a melody. As night fell on Jerusalem, inside the homes the voices echoed through the streets joining the sound of Yeshua's voice as they sang:

> How great is Adonai's goodness to us!!! For each of His acts of mercy and kindness we declare Dayanoo (It would have been enough)
>
> If Adonai had merely rescued us, but not judged the Egyptians,
>> Dayanoo!
>
> If He had only destroyed their gods, but not parted the Red Sea,
>> Dayanoo!
>
> If He had only drowned our enemies, but not provided us with manna in the desert,
>> Dayanoo!
>
> If He had only led us through the desert, but not given us Shabbat,
>> Dayanoo!
>
> If He had given us Shabbat, but had not brought us near to Him at Mount Sinai,
>> Dayanoo!
>
> Had He brought us near to Him at Mount Sinai, but not given us Torah,
>> Dayanoo!
>
> Had He given us Torah, and not brought us into Eretz Yis'rael,
>> Dayanoo!

Beit Tefilah: A House of Prayer

The plate was passed around and Yeshua took a piece of maror, the bitter herb, to dip in the salt water. Moshe was instructed to add salt that God would provide to all the offerings. He gave the kingship of Israel to David and his descendants forever through a covenant of salt (2 Chr 13:5).

They lifted up the herb, remembering the oppression of bondage and how Adonai brought Isra'el into the blessing of being a nation. For you were once darkness, and now are light (Eph 5:8). Yeshua sang the blessing:

> *Ba-ruch a-ta Adonai, Ehlohaynu meh-lech ha-o-lahm ah-sher keed-sha-nu bidevaro v'tzee-va-nu al akhilat maror.*
>
> Blessed are You, O Lord our God, King of the universe, who has set us apart by His Word and commanded us to eat the bitter herbs.

Also, taking a piece of matzah, he made the b'rakhah, broke it, gave it to them and said:

> *Ba-ruch a-ta Adonai, Eh-lo-hay-nu meh-lehch ha-o-lahm, ha-mo-tzee leh-chehm meen ha-a-retz.*
>
> Blessed are You O Lord our God, King of the Universe, Who brings forth bread from the Earth.

The bread was dipped into the charoset, representing the crushing mortar of life in Egypt and the power of God to make all things new every year. As they were eating Yeshua told the disciples that one of them would betray him. They were sorrowful hearing this and each asked if it was them. "He who dips his hand in with me is the one who will betray me," he told them (Matt 26:23).

For each of the ten plagues that God afflicted Egypt with, they dipped their fingers in the cup of wine. Just hours away, Jesus would say, "Father if you are willing, take this cup from me" (Luke 22:40).

The disciples would remember that though they may be despised by the world, oppressed, and suffering, they are a royal priesthood. The deliverance showing up in the form of a sacrificed lamb was telling the people what the work of the Messiah would look like. He would be gentle and approachable. The talmidin had heard Yochanan (John) calling, "Look! God's lamb! The one who is taking away the sin of the world!" (John 1:29). Yeshua was crucified during the Pesach, the blood on the posts of the cross at Calvary marking the door to new life. Perfect, without blemish, his legs were not broken, just like the Pesach lamb (Exod 12:46). The custom was to break the legs of those crucified so they would die quickly because they couldn't push up with their feet to take a breath. But Yeshua had died before this was

Pesach (Passover)

necessary. The believers sharing the Pesach meal recognized Yeshua as the lamb that was symbolically given to them through the generations, whose blood would protect as the shadow of judgment passed over the world. They knew that when Avraham offered his son Isaac on Mount Moriah and Isaac asked where was the lamb for sacrifice, Adonai provided a sacrifice (Gen 22:1–19) where Solomon would later build a Temple. Without atonement, there is no way to approach the presence of God.

The promises in Isaiah 53 were familiar to the disciples who sat at the table. "He was pierced through for our transgressions, He was crushed for our iniquities; The chastening for our well-being fell upon Him, and by His scourging we are healed. All of us like sheep have gone astray. Each of us has turned to his own way; But the LORD has caused the iniquity of us all to fall on Him. He was oppressed and He was afflicted, yet He did not open His mouth; Like a lamb that is led to slaughter, and like a sheep that is silent before its shearers, so He did not open His mouth."

Don't think that I have come to abolish the Torah or the Prophets. I have come not to abolish but to complete (Matt 5:17).

For our Pesach lamb, the Messiah, has been sacrificed (1Cor 5:7).

For the life of a creature is in the blood, and I have given it to you on the altar to make atonement for yourselves; for it is the blood that makes atonement because of the life (Lev 17:11).

The men at the table with Yeshua bowed their heads as he spoke the b'rakhah, the blessing after eating the Pesach meal.

> Blessed are You, O Lord our God, King of the universe, who, because of Your goodness, grace and love, feeds and supports all Your creatures. May Your name be blessed now and throughout eternity!

The bread that was wrapped and hidden was now taken and unwrapped. This bread represents the Lord's resurrected life, unwrapped from his grave clothes. Paul would later write to believers in Corinth to keep the feast, not with old leaven, neither with the leaven of malice and wickedness; but with the unleavened bread of sincerity (1Cor 5:8).

Yeshua took the bread, broke off a piece, and passed it around. He had told them, "I am the bread of life. Whoever comes to me will never go hungry." Now he said, "This is my body, which is for you. Do this as a memorial to me" (1Cor 11:24). And they ate the bread.

Holding up the third cup, the Cup of Redemption, the disciples and Yeshua took a moment to re-consecrate their hearts to Adonai.

"Here, the days are coming," says Adonai, "when I will make a new covenant with the house of Israel and with the house of Y'hudah. It will not be like the covenant I made with their fathers on the day I took them by their hand and brought them out of the land of Egypt; because they, for their part, violated my covenant, even though I, for my part, was a husband to them," says Adonai (Jer 31:31–32). The third cup is the cup of redeeming blood. Wine in Jewish history represents living blood and joy. Moses turned water to blood. Jesus turned water to wine, his first miracle, fulfilling Hebrew expectation.

Yeshua lifted the cup of redemption and proclaimed, "This cup is the New Covenant, ratified by my blood, which is being poured out for you" (Luke 22:20). He confirmed the New Covenant with the cup of redemption with twelve Jews in an upper room.

Yeshua brought the good news that all are covered by his shed blood. All who draw near are forgiven, remaining the gender and nationality they were born to be (Gal 3:28). Scripture would explain to the Gentiles that if some branches were broken off for the wild olive, the Gentile, to be grafted in to share the root of the cultivated olive tree, no one should be arrogant. It is the root that supports all the branches. How much more would the natural branches be able to be grafted back in? (Rom 11:16–24).

Lifting the cup of redemption with his believers at the table, Yeshua said:

> *Ba-ruch a-ta Adonai, Eh-lo-hay-nu meh-lehch ha-o-lahm, bo-ray p'ree ha-ga-fen. Amain.*
> Blessed are You O Lord our God, King of the universe, creator of the fruit of the vine. Amain.

Yeshua and his twelve men from Galilee sipped the cup of redemption.

They lifted the fourth cup of the Pesach, the Cup of Praise, and Yeshua again spoke a blessing.

> *Ba-ruch a-ta Adonai, Eh-lo-hay-nu meh-lehch ha-o-lahm, bo-ray p'ree ha-ga-fen. Amain.*
> Blessed are You O Lord our God, King of the universe, creator of the fruit of the vine. Amain.

"I tell you, I will not drink this fruit of the vine again until the day I drink new wine with you in my Father's Kingdom," he said. (Matt 26:29). In his day, when a young man fell in love with a young lady, the ceremony that secured their commitment involved the man bringing a cup of wine to her. He told her the wine represented his very life's blood and if she drinks it, she'll be wed with him. He's giving her his very life. Yeshua's last Pesach fulfilled the tradition as it presented the marriage of the lamb.

Yeshua linked Passover with the promised banquet of Isaiah 25 that sees the transformation of the entire world when the Messiah returns. A sheltering wall against the arrows of the ruthless, the Lord will prepare a feast of rich foods for all peoples. Tears will be dried on all faces and the disgrace removed from all the earth. We trusted in him and he saved us.

The woman wed to a man did not move in with her husband right away. The betrothal, called *kiddushin* (sanctities), could last more than a year. The man would return to his father's house and build a suitable home for his bride with his father guiding him in what was needed. Her father would bestow a gift on her for her marriage and the man would send his betrothed gifts as they waited so that she would be secure. Then he would go to get her and she would prepare herself to joyously meet him.

They would not drink of the fruit of the wine together until they were reunited. This is why Jesus said, I will not drink of this again until I drink with you. Paul came saying, some who are participating in this communion unworthily are becoming sick or dying because they are not serious in committing to this relationship.

By the time of the last supper, his talmidin understood they were not having just another Pesach. Yeshua was far more than just a man speaking the blessing as they solemnly drank the cups. This was Yeshua ha Mashiach, the long awaited Messiah. After his final Pesach meal was completed and he had told his disciples about the New Covenant, they sang the Hallel, the praises of Psalms 113–118, a tradition that has continued for generations. In Psalm 118 they all sang:

> The very rock that the builders rejected
> has become the cornerstone!
> This has come from ADONAI,
> and in our eyes it is amazing.
> This is the day ADONAI has made,
> a day for us to rejoice and be glad (v22–24)

After singing the Hallel, they walked together out to the Mount of Olives, the full moonlight casting their shadows on the ground.

2

The Haggadah (The Telling)

For that is what Adonai has ordered us to do: "I have set you as a light for the Goyim, to be for deliverance to the ends of the earth."

(Acts 13:47)

The Haggadah (The Telling)

THE TRUE ORIGIN OF EASTER[1]

by Rabbi Stephen Luft

Unfortunately, not everyone gets it right now. But the good thing is that it is changing, yet slowly, but it is changing. You can't force a message. You can't teach a vision. A vision is cast and either embraced or rejected. This is the challenge of today, just as it was 2,000 years ago and every year in-between.

For many of the Messianic believers, representing Yeshua's resurrection as the Easter holiday ignores Scripture and submits to anti-Semitism. Pesach, with the Feast of Unleavened Bread and First Fruits conveying Yeshua's death, burial, and resurrection, is identified sixteen times in the gospels. Unfortunately, it was man who changed the recognition of this Feast of Adonai and replaced it with the adaptation of Easter.

What is the true origin of Easter? Is it the celebration by the church that commemorates the resurrection of Jesus from the grave?

This is what we are led to believe, however, it is not what God instituted. Are you saying that hundreds of millions of people, including church leaders from all over the world, are wrong about Easter.

Yes I am. So, if God did not institute Easter, where does Easter come from and what is it? In our next article we will go into greater detail as to what he did command. This article will focus solely on the origins of Easter.

First, nowhere in the Tenach (Old Testament) or B'rith Hadoshah (New Covenant) will you find mention of a feast ordained by God with pagan origins. What we know as Easter, is not of God or from God. It is of man.

Is Easter mentioned in the Bible? Once in Acts 12:4, in the King James version, it states, "And when he had apprehended him, he put him in prison and delivered him to four quaternions of soldiers to keep him, intending after Easter to bring him forth to the people." We know that this is not actually Easter but Passover from the previous verse (Acts 12:3). And because he saw that it pleased the Jews, he proceeded further to take Peter also (then were the days of unleavened bread). The word translated Easter is the Greek word pascha (derived from the Hebrew word pesach; there is no original Greek word for Passover), and it has only one meaning. It always means Passover.

---

1. Luft, "The True Origin of Easter."

The first church as found in the Book of Acts didn't celebrate Easter, but rather celebrated God's feasts, as he commanded. If this is so, what happened? The answer isn't in God's Word, but rather found in history.

The changes began when the Roman Emperor Constantine assimilated Christianity into the Roman Church. It was common practice for the Roman Church to take a pagan celebration and convert it into a church celebration. This practice enabled the church to influence many pagan nations, making it more palatable and familiar to heathen worshipers, whom the Church was trying to attract.

The Ontario Consultants on Religious Tolerance timeline reports the steady erosion.[2]

- 306: The church Synod of Elvira banned marriages, sexual intercourse and community contacts between Christians and Jews.

- 315: Constantine published the Edict of Milan which extended religious tolerance to Christians. Jews lost many rights with this edict. They were no longer permitted to live in Jerusalem or to proselytize.

- 325: The Council of Nicea decided to separate the celebration of Easter from the Jewish Passover. They stated, "For it is unbecoming beyond measure that on this holiest of festivals we should follow the customs of the Jews. Henceforth let us have nothing in common with this odious people . . . We ought not, therefore, to have anything in common with the Jews . . . our worship follows a . . . more convenient course . . . we desire dearest brethren, to separate ourselves from the detestable company of the Jews . . . How then, could we follow these Jews, who are almost certainly blinded."

- 337: Christian Emperor Constantius created a law which made the marriage of a Jewish man to a Christian punishable by death.

- 339: Converting to Judaism became a criminal offense.

- 343–381: The Laodicean Synod approved Cannon XXVIII: "It is not lawful [for Christians] to receive unleavened bread from the Jews, nor to be partakers of their impiety."

- 367–376: St. Hilary of Poitiers referred to Jews as a perverse people who God has cursed forever. St. Ephroem refers to synagogues as brothels.

2. Ontario Consultants on Religious Tolerance.

- 379–395: Emperor Theodosius the Great permitted the destruction of synagogues if it served a religious purpose. Christianity became the state religion of the Roman Empire at this time.
- 380: The bishop of Milan was responsible for the burning of a synagogue; but referred to it as "an act pleasing to God."

As further explained by historian James George Frazer:

> "Now the death and resurrection of Attis were officially celebrated at Rome on the 24th and 25th of March, the latter being regarded as the spring equinox, and . . . according to an ancient and widespread tradition Christ suffered on the 25th of March . . . the tradition which placed the death of Christ on the 25th of March . . . is all the more remarkable because astronomical considerations prove that it can have had *no historical foundation*. When we remember that the festival of St. George in April has replaced the ancient pagan festival of the Parilia; that the festival of St. John the Baptist in June has succeeded to a heathen Midsummer festival of water; that the festival of the Assumption of the Virgin in August has ousted the festival of Diana; that the feast of All Souls [following Halloween] in November is a continuation of an old heathen feast of the dead; and that the Nativity of Christ himself was assigned to the winter solstice in December because that day was deemed the Nativity of the Sun; we can hardly be thought to be rash or unreasonable in conjecturing that the other cardinal festival of the Christian church—the solemnization of Easter—may have been in like manner, and from like motives of edification, adapted to a similar celebration of the Phyrigian god Attis at the vernal equinox . . . It is a remarkable coincidence . . . that the Christian and the heathen festivals of the divine death and resurrection should have been solemnized at the same season . . . It is difficult to regard the coincidence as purely accidental."

Easter is actually a pagan festival of fertility celebrated to the goddess of spring. In Babylon she was known as Ishtar. The Anglo-Saxon fertility goddess was known as Eostre or Ostara. The goddess of Easter was *one* goddess with *many* names—the goddess of fertility, worshiped in spring when all life was being renewed.

Easter has nothing to do with resurrection . . . it is all about fertility. It was a celebration of renewal in that it was celebrated during spring when plants returned from their dorment winter state and animal reproduced. There is nothing miraculous about this . . . all living creatures (plant and animal) are able to reproduce. Using Easter as a celebration for the resurrection of our Messiah is completely wrong and totally off the mark.

So why would the church use this "holiday?" Again, you have to go back into history. When Rome adopted Christianity, the persecution of believers by the Roman empire ceased, however, their hatred for the Jewish people didn't. Throughout church history, the Jewish people have been known as the ones who killed Christ. Rome wanted nothing to do with a heritage of a people that they hated, even if Jesus was Jewish. Intentional efforts were made to remove the Jewish heritage from the Messiah of the world who was promised to the Jewish people, written of by the Jewish people and was Jewish himself. The adoption of Easter, along with Good Friday, was the church's attempt to replace God's ordained festivals. It is also very conceivable that Satan was the chief deceiver in this plot to destroy the church . . . guiding the church away from being at the center of God's will.

The 1967 edition of *The Catholic Encyclopedia*, when describing the final decision of the Council of Nicaea in A.D. 325, quotes the words of the Emperor Constantine, writing to all the churches:

> At this meeting the question concerning the most holy day of Easter was discussed, and it was resolved by the united judgment of all present that this feast ought to be kept by all and in every place on one and the same day . . . And first of all it appeared an unworthy thing that in the celebration of this most holy feast we should follow the practice of the Jews, who have impiously defiled their hands with enormous sin . . . for we have received from our Saviour a different way . . . And I myself have undertaken that this decision should meet with the approval of your Sagacities in the hope that your Wisdoms will gladly admit that practice which is observed at once in the city of Rome and in Africa, throughout Italy and in Egypt . . . with entire unity of judgment.

Claiming that Jesus provided a "different way" to honor him is completely false and not supported by the scriptures. What does God's Word say about replacing his ways with "man's" traditions? Jesus himself addressed the Pharisees in Mark 7:1–13, regarding putting aside God's commandments for those of man. Not only was this pagan celebration adopted by the church, but so were many of the customs for which you will probably be familiar.

1. Lent-For which you will not find any instruction in the bible, is a forty-day abstinence period was anciently observed in honor of the

pagan gods Osiris, Adonis and Tammuz. According to Johannes Cassianus, who wrote in the fifth century, "Howbeit you should know, that as long as the primitive church retained its perfection unbroken, this observance of Lent did not exist". There is neither biblical nor historical record of Christ, the apostles or the early Church participating in the Lenten season.

2. Easter Eggs-The egg, originated through early European races (pre Christ), first as the symbol of spring. During the church era, the egg became the symbol of the rock tomb for which Jesus emerged from.

3. The Easter Bunny-Nowhere in the Bible will you find mention of the Easter Bunny (rabbit) in relation to Jesus. The rabbit's origins can be traced to that of the symbol of fertility in ancient Egypt. This symbol later found its way into European customs and traditions.

4. Sunrise Service-Unlike the previous three traditions of Easter, the Sunrise service is mentioned in the Bible. Even though it is found in the Bible, God is not all that fond of it. In speaking to Ezekiel in chapter 8, He clearly states His dislike of such an action. God is very specific in His word regarding the worshiping of idols or false gods. Even though the church has wrapped Messiah into a pagan celebration doesn't make it right. Throughout God's Word, he conveys His displeasure for this practice. In Jeremiah chapter 44, Jeremiah conveys from God a message to His people who fled to Egypt during the Babylonian captivity. In Judges 2, Israel had greatly angered God.

What does God think about pagan gods? 1 Samuel 5:1–12 provides us with his displeasure of other gods. I can hear you saying now, "it isn't a big deal, we are not celebrating a pagan holiday, but rather the resurrection of Jesus." That is exactly what Satan wants the church to believe. Let's look at the emphasis of Easter as it is celebrated today.

Now, take a look at the focus of society during Easter. Walk down the aisles of your nearest Wal-mart, Kmart or any story for that matter. What do you see? Easter bunnies, chocolate eggs and candy, greeting cards with bunnies and eggs. Nowhere do you see the mention of our Messiah's name. Maybe that is a good thing, however, Easter has turned into something completely out of control. Many millions celebrate with Easter egg hunts, and going to church (the most attended church day during the year) but fail to know the truth of their true heritage.

As Easter is a pagan holiday, so have the symbols of Easter consumed the thoughts of society. Where in the bible does God's Word ordain Easter? The answer is nowhere. God's word is specific to his feasts . . . for which Easter is not one of them.

There is much sin in the church, for which the celebration of Easter is at the forefront. This issue is a greater deal than you have been lead to believe.

I have great concern for the church as it is today. The great deceiver has done a masterful job in blinding the church of the truth. That has to stop now. The time is at hand where the return of our Messiah is close and can happen at any time. He is coming for his bride—HIS SPOTLESS BRIDE. It is time for the church to remove its spots, and prepare for the coming of its bridegroom.

The Haggadah (The Telling)

CHRISTIAN PERSECUTION OF THE JEWS[3]

by Shira Sorko-Ram

Each Israeli child learns in school that his history is one long, tragic persecution of Jews by Christians. Anti-Semitism has always been present in the Christian world to some extent, but at certain points in history it has been vicious.

The Jews lived peaceably during the time of Moslem rule in Spain. Then in the fifteenth century the Christian King Ferdinand and Queen Isabella united Spain under their throne. The Jews were told, "Kiss the cross and become a Christian" or be deported. Thousands of Jewish people who felt they could not become part of a religion of idolatrous heathen were tortured, killed, or left the country. Those who pledged Christianity were expelled anyway. Russian persecution under Christian czars sent armies into Jewish villages to slaughter and rape the people. Some soldiers and others, knowing the wrongness of this action, warned them before they arrived. Jewish villages all through Russian and eastern Europe were notified that they could no longer live there. The people packed their belongings onto carts and again began down long roads in search of a home. Many of the first Jews to return to the Holy Land in the twenty-first century came from Russia and eastern Europe, when it was still called Palestine. It was preferable to Christendom. Hitler came from a Catholic background. He enlisted thousands of Germans and others who called themselves Christians. They pinned the Crusaders Cross to their Nazi uniforms and herded Jews into death.

Even today, Jewish people in such countries as France rarely discuss with a Gentile the fact that they are Jews. And in the Passover season of 1970, European papers published reports that Jews had been accused (as they have for centuries) of killing Gentile children for their blood to be used at the Passover.

Communism has collapsed. And at this moment, the old line churches—Russian Orthodox in the Soviet Union, Catholic in Poland and Eastern Europe—have come out into the open. Anti-Semitism is again rapidly gaining ground, causing Jews living there to fear for their lives. Anti-semitism is again gaining ground and bringing fear for their lives to Jews around the

---

3. Sorko-Ram, "I Became as a Jew."

world. There is also a visible growth in hatred of the Jews in Catholic and Protestant Western Europe, Scandinavia, Britain, and even parts of the U.S.

Now imagine a sincere, born-again American or European traveling to Israel. He finds himself caught up in the ecstasy of the Reborn Land, with its rich promises of God for Israel, and he asks a Jew, "Wouldn't you like to become a Christian?" The Jew's negative response inevitably leaves both parties puzzled.

Thus the paradox: the positive, but meaningless answer from a Christian Arab, who is glad to tell you he is a Christian, and the extremely negative reaction from a Jew. The Jew understands the question thus: "Would you like to become a part of a Gentile, idolatrous religion which consists of heathen who have tried to exterminate the Jews for nearly 2,000 years?" The Jew, at best, will probably politely answer, "I cannot be a traitor to my people."

The Haggadah (The Telling)

YOM HASHOAH[4]

by Rabbi Stephen Luft

Events that impact our lives, in either a positive or negative way, are typically memorialized through a date that commemorates the event—Veteran's Day on November 11 is only one example. Likewise there are dates that are so profound, the mere mention of them brings to mind the event itself. Dates such as December 7, 1941, November 22, 1963 and September 11, 2001 are so profound and memorable that if you were living could likely recall where you were and what you were doing when you heard the news.

Now, imagine the impact of an event that didn't just happen on one day but for years and directly impacted a large percentage of a people. This event so secretive that once discovered shocked the world. This life changing event was the Holocaust.

In the spring, between Passover and Shavuot is Yom Hashoah, is Holocaust Remembrance Day. A day that has been set aside to remember the six million people who were killed for only one reason—they were Jewish. The rampant anti-Semitism in Europe that was propelled to new levels by the Nazi regime would exterminate two thirds of the Jewish population living in Europe.

This was just one of many attempts over the centuries to eliminate the Jewish people from the face of the earth. One such attempt to eliminate the Jewish people from existence can be found in the book of Esther.

You might be asking . . . what does this mean to me?

What would have happened had the Nazis been successful with what was known as "The Final Solution," that being the elimination of all Jewish people from the face of the earth? As believers and followers in Yeshua there would have been an enormous impact that would have forever changed your lives, which is why continuing to remember such a dire time in history is important. Today, there are people who claim that the Holocaust never really happened. It is important to remember and teach the next generation so history won't be revised or repeated.

A fallacy is that the New Covenant is made with the church, when in all reality it is made with Israel and the Jewish people. Ask yourselves, why has there been so much hatred inflicted upon the Jewish people for centuries. I believe the root of this hatred comes from the adversary—ha satan.

---

4. Luft, "Yom Hashoah."

He knows that without the people for whom the covenant is made with, makes null and void the covenant and therefore the promises. These very promises that include salvation would be eliminated without the people for whom the covenant was made with.

What many pay little attention to is that goyim have been grafted into Israel, not the other way around. The hope of the world rests upon the New Covenant promise that Adonai made with Israel and the Jewish people.

"Here, the days are coming," says Adonai, "when I will make a new covenant with the house of Isra'el and with the house of Y'hudah. It will not be like the covenant I made with their fathers on the day I took them by their hand and brought them out of the land of Egypt; because they, for their part, violated my covenant, even though I, for my part, was a husband to them. For this is the covenant I will make with the house of Isra'el after those days. I will put my Torah within them and write it on their hearts; I will be their God, and they will be my people. No longer will any of them teach his fellow community member or his brother, 'Know Adonai;' for all will know me, from the least of them to the greatest; because I will forgive their wickedness and remember their sins no more" (Jer 31–33).

3

B'Rit Hadashah (The New Covenant)

Nations, hear the word of Adonai! Proclaim it in the coastlands far away. Say: "He who scattered Israel is gathering him, guarding him like a shepherd his flock."

(Jer 31:10)

The Feast of Unleavened Bread begins the evening after the Passover to celebrate Israel being delivered from Egypt (Lev 23:6). The feast lasts seven days. On the last day, the Song of Moses is sung that Moses and the Israelites sang at the victory of Pharaoh's army being drowned in the Sea of Reeds (Exod 15:1–18). It was their first prayer together as a people.

> I will sing to the Lord, for he is highly exalted
> The Lord is my strength and my defense; he has become my salvation
> He is my God and I will praise him, My father's God, and I will exalt him
>   (v1–2)

It is said that the song has all the poetic power of the stars singing at the birth of creation. Referred to by Paul when he said his people were all baptized into the sea with Moses, the singing marked the end of part of Israel's history. Brought from darkness into a new life, a new history was before them. They stepped into the water and were separated from the world around them, leaving behind the idols of others, in awe of God, trusting in God and in his servant Moses. They sang in the spirit as they passed through the waters that would represent the past, present, and future of salvation. The enemy was seized with trembling. The enemy was hurled to the bottom of the sea. It's a victory song of God being a warrior who distinguishes between those covered by the blood of the lamb and those who follow the world's oppressions. God stretched out his hand and the earth swallowed them. He guided his people to his holy habitation. It's a prophetic song. He redeems his people. He leads them. He guards them.

> You will bring them in and plant them on the mountain of your inheritance—the place, LORD, you made for your dwelling, the sanctuary, Lord, your hands established. The LORD reigns for ever and ever (v17–18).

At the end of the song the people have a clear and unshakeable identity. After the victory, after 430 years of living as slaves, as many today live under the darkness of bondage, they were not to turn back to a culture that could not save. Sing and rejoice. Be different than the world until all God's people have crossed. The praise is again sung in unity in Revelation 15:3–4.

> Great and wonderful are the things you have done, ADONAI, God of heaven's armies! Just and true are your ways, king of the nations! ADONAI, who will not fear and glorify your name? because you alone are holy. All nations will come and worship before you, for your righteous deeds have been revealed.

B'Rit Hadashah (The New Covenant)

COMING HOME TO MY JEWISH MESSIAH[1]

by Nette Tepe

I was born in Amsterdam into a loving Jewish family. When Hitler's armies marched into the Netherlands our lives changed forever. We were secretly moved from one house to the next until, on May 31, 1944, my parents were taken by the Nazis into concentration camps. My mother later died in Auschwitz but somehow my father managed to escape from the *Eisenbahnkommando* concentration camp near Landshut in Germany.

After the war, my father remarried a non-Jewish lady who, strangely enough, was very anti-Semitic. She persecuted us children in many drastic ways and tried to deprive us of education. I left home at the age of sixteen and began to search for answers. What does it mean to be Jewish? Where did I belong? Was God real and how can we be the Chosen People in light of what happened in the Holocaust? I was on a mission to find God.

At that time, the local Synagogue where I lived was closed as most of the Jews in our area had been deported and killed. I started to visit a few churches to see if God was there. But the people seemed to be so solemn and void of any joy in their lives. So, I soon gave up. But God did not give up on me!

A Christian friend invited me to her local church. It was not like the others I had visited. The people where so happy and their singing was so joyful. I thought God must be here! It was later, when I had migrated to Australia and was married to my loving husband Peter that I finally came to fully understand that Jesus was God's son, who had left the glory of Heaven to come and save me, a sinner. It is such a joy to know the Lord.

When I finally told my pastor that I was Jewish, he said to me "don't worry, you have now been changed, you are no longer Jewish but a Christian." I was stunned, hurt, and confused. How can one forget their heritage, my mum, my grandparents, my uncles and my extended family—many who died in the Holocaust? From that time on, I kept my Jewishness a secret from everyone, including my children. Only my husband knew I was Jewish.

Many years passed until one day, about fifteen years ago, my eldest daughter Margaret, asked me to come with her to a messianic congregation that she had been attending that was run by Celebrate Messiah. I went with

---

1. Tepe, "Coming Home to My Jewish Messiah."

her to Beit HaMashiach and was so amazed to meet Jewish people who believed in Jesus. They were so happy and they loved the Lord. And the most amazing thing was that they were proud to be Jewish. Finally, I had come home!

I now continue to worship at Beit HaMashiach Messianic Congregation. I feel that it is a safe place for me where I can worship the Lord freely as a Jew who believes in Messiah. I feel at home and don't have to leave my Jewish identity at the door, as I did for so many years in other churches. It has also opened my eyes to God's Word anew, learning about God's covenants and blessings through the feasts and getting to know Yeshua even better. I also have more confidence in sharing about God with my own Jewish people. If only the Jewish people would accept the love of God through his son Yeshua HaMashiach! What a day that would be.

B'Rit Hadashah (The New Covenant)

JEWISH ROOTS[2]

by Rabbi Ben Volman

It's a common misconception of both Christians and Jews that a Jewish person who believes in Yeshua is no longer Jewish. This view has been mistakenly repeated both by Christians and Jews.

In fact, under religious tradition, a Jew is someone who is born to a Jewish mother. (Broader interpretations of Jewish identity now accept that Jewish heritage may also come through a Jewish father.) That person does not cease to be Jewish, no matter what their personal religious choices or disposition.

Another major reason for the misconception that Jewish followers of Jesus are no longer Jewish is a decision by the Israeli Supreme Court in the early 1960s. In 1958 Brother Daniel Rufeison came to Israel. Born Jewish, Rugeison was hiding in a nunnery during the Holocaust and later became a Catholic priest. Upon entering Israel, he claimed his rights under the Law of Return, which normally grants immediate citizenship to Jews.

The original court ruling denied his claim—never claiming to make a religious or final ruling on Jewish identity, but simply citing the prerogative of the State of Israel not to accept Jewish followers of Yeshua. However, under a 2008 Supreme Court ruling, that previous decision can no longer be applied to Messianic Jews who can attribute Jewish identity to a father, if not to themselves, so this is no longer a restriction on immigration.

In previous eras, Jewish followers of Yeshua were compelled to assimilate into Christian cultures to practice their faith. This is no longer needed, although one may choose to do so. The Worldwide Messianic Jewish movement promotes and supports Jewish culture, holidays, traditions, and faithfulness to Jewish identity among its adherents.

A common experience of Jewish people who come to faith in Messiah is that they have never felt as Jewish as after the decision to follow Yeshua. That step of faith brings a rebirth of Jewish identity, not its end.

---

2. Volman, "Jewish Roots."

NEW COVENANT WRITINGS[3]

by Rabbi Stephen Luft

The majority of Bibles divide scripture through the inclusion of a page entitled "New Testament" This page acts like a dam in that it disrupts the flow of Adonai's message. This page has created a distinction that was never intended to happen. Separation of Torah from the New Covenant has led to teachings that are contrary to that of Yeshua.

Let's look at the book of Acts for a minute. This book by Luke recounts what transpired after Yeshua's death, burial, and resurrection. It recounts the development of Yeshua's talmadim who ultimately became the leaders of this movement that would spread throughout the world. Starting in Jerusalem, the first nine chapters are an exclusively Jewish story, with thousands of Jewish people coming to trust in the testimony of people like Kefa, who is known as Peter, and Yochanan, who is known as John. We see 3,000 coming to trust during the time of the feast of Shavuot or what many know as the Feast of Pentecost. Likewise, as recounted in chapter five, 5,000 men alone come to faith in Yeshua as Messiah.

How are they doing this in that they don't have any of the New Covenant writings we have today?

The simple answer is through their practice of relating Yeshua to the Jewish scriptures. Within the first nine chapters of the book of Acts, there are fifty-one direct quotes from the Jewish Bible, used to relate Yeshua to the promises that he is the promised Messiah. It is in this context that they were able to convey these truths as evidence to the people who were familiar with these writings and for many who lived by them.

"On hearing this, they were stung in their hearts; and they said to Kefa and the other emissaries, 'Brothers, what should we do?'" (Acts 2:37).

Throughout the book of Acts, there are a total of seventy-six direct quotes from the Jewish Bible used to convey the Message of Adonai, which is the Good News of Yeshua. Can you be like the emissaries of Messiah and convey the power of the Good News through the Jewish Bible?

The page before the book of Matthew that identifies the beginning of the New Covenant writings creates a division of Adonai's Word, to the point where people justify their actions. "We are no longer under the old covenant or we are no longer under the law but, we are under the new

---

3. Luft, Stephen, New Covenant Writings.

B'Rit Hadashah (The New Covenant)

covenant"—a common statement made by many believers. In all reality, the nations were never under the Mosaic covenant unless they like Ruth chose to become part of Israel, when she said, "Don't press me to leave you and stop following you; for wherever you go, I will go; and wherever you stay, I will stay. Your people will be my people and your God will be my God" (Ruth 1:16).

For men making this decision, physical circumcision was required. People who made this decision are identified as the foreigner and stranger dwelling among Israel. The term foreigner or stranger is found in a total of fifty-three verses in Exodus, Leviticus, Numbers, and Deuteronomy. Even though they were not Israel by birth, they, for lack of another word, converted and followed the God of Israel.

Through the New Covenant made with the house of Israel and the house of Judah, it has been made available to all who come to believe that the blood atonement that ratifies this covenant, being that of Yeshua are welcome. There is still a circumcision that occurs, one of the heart. Within the New Covenant, there are some things that have changed in Torah, but based on Yeshua's own words, there are still expectations, for he says in the Gospel of Yochanan.

"If you love me, you will keep my commands" (John 14:15).

What commandments are Yeshua talking about?

The same commandments that the foreigner and stranger, such as Ruth, desired to do when she said she would accept the God of Israel as her own. Some will say all we are required to do is love Adonai and love one another. This is true, but ask yourself "how do we do this?" The challenge is knowing what applies to whom and in relation to the New Covenant. In earlier episodes we explored Torah. I had stated that Torah offers instructions that are both specific to a certain people, whether the priests, king of Israel, men or women, but that there are also instructions that apply to all people. The ratification of the New Covenant does not change many of these instructions.

When we recognize that the intent of the covenant Adonai made with Israel through Moshe, it was to distinguish a single nation from all other nations. A nation unique in that Adonai identified Israel by placing his name upon them. As the only God and creator of all things, He gave them specific instructions that no other nation had:

"For you are a people set apart as holy for Adonai your God. Adonai your God has chosen you out of all the peoples on the face of the earth to be his own unique treasure" (Deut 7:6). Adonai's own unique treasure. In other words—one of a kind. Ultimately, when more is expected, more is required. The New Covenant does not replace this relationship but adds to it. It isn't about replacing Israel as many will teach, but just as the foreigner and stranger mentioned previously, it is becoming part of a people with whom the covenant is made. Sha'ul reminds the Ephesians of their former state of life:

"Therefore, remember your former state: you Gentiles by birth—called the Uncircumcised by those who, merely because of an operation on their flesh, are called the Circumcised at that time had no Messiah. You were estranged from the national life of Isra'el. You were foreigners to the covenants embodying God's promise. You were in this world without hope and without God" (Eph 2:11–12).

Ultimately, we are not talking about a new entity, but rather the inclusion of a people, the nations, who were once excluded, but now as part of this New Covenant are able to enter without physical circumcision, but rather a circumcised heart.

B'Rit Hadashah (The New Covenant)

GENTILES AND JEWS TOGETHER IN ANCIENT ROME AND NORTH AFRICAN CARTHAGE[4]

by Dr. Jeffrey L. Seif

Josephus observed how many Gentiles were thus inclined and "adopted Jewish customs and manners" (War 2.463). He elsewhere stated that Jews were "constantly attracting to their religious ceremonies multitudes of Greeks" (Wars 7.45). He also said—and perhaps not in hyperbolic fashion: "[t]here is not one [single] city, Greek or barbarian, to which our [Jewish] customs... have not spread" (Against Apion 2.282). Particularly, says he, "... [in] the whole of Syria... each city has its Judaizers" (Italics mine; War 2.262–63). What "Judaizers" meant is another matter. That aside, elsewhere Flavius Josephus notes: "in Damascus [Syria] men noted how 'wives had all become subject to the Jewish religion'" (War 2.559–60). For his part, Dio Cassius said Jews were "converting many of the natives to their [Jewish] ways" (Roman History 57.18.5a). Tacitus similarly spoke of "those who come over to [the Jewish] religion" (Histories 5.5). Lending even more credence to Jewish attractiveness, and speaking perhaps in a disparaging manner with regard to it, Horace said: "we, like Jews, will compel you to join our throng" (Satires 1.4.142–143).

Epigraphic evidence in Asia and Rome speak of "proselytes" in higher echelons who appreciated the Jewish world and ways. Veturia Paula, for example, was remembered as "a proselyte for sixteen years under the name of Sarah, mother [or patroness] of the synagogues of Campus and Voluminus." Julia Severa, was a patroness of the Jewish community, and financed a synagogue in Phrygia. (Her son, L. Servenius Cornutus served in the Senate under Nero in 73 CE and was legate to the proconsul in Asia. Another relative, L. Iulius Severus served as a consul.) According to Josephus, other Jewish-friendly friends in high Roman places include Emperor Nero's mistress Poppaea Sabina who "pleaded on behalf of the Jews." Titus, the elder son of Vespasian—both of whom participated in the "sack" of Jerusalem—took a Jewish woman named Bernice as his mistress with him back to Rome after the war—which would give him a Jewish-friendly voice in the bedroom, at the very least. Lastly in this regard, Professor Magnus Zetterholm, in his The Formation of Christianity in Antioch, alights upon Judaism's presence and influence in culture, by referencing St. Augustine

---

4. Seif, "Gentiles and Jews Together."

in *Civ.* 6.11, citing Seneca who exclaimed: "the customs of the accursed [Jewish] race have gained such influence that they are now received. The vanquished have given laws to the victors."

Valerius Maximus reported in 139 BCE that Jews invoked the ire of Romans and that Cornelius Hispanus/Hispalus (see above) had them expelled from Rome, for "peddling their ancient wisdom" and "for attempting to transfer their sacred rites to the Romans" (Val. Max. 1.3.3). Seneca is on record describing Jews as a most pernicious people (*sceleratissma gens*). Because he nowhere else speaks directly of Jews in his vast writings—save for this extract culled from St. Augustine's City of God—one cannot say that Seneca was particularly obsessed with Jews, and given to their slander. The satirist Juvenal took on Jews for adherence to dietary laws, Sabbath, circumcision, and the like, but construed the practices to be "more laughable than dangerous." For his part, Tacitus was tolerant of Jews, but "angrier at the converts than at the Jews . . . who have disserted their native gods, ancestral traditions, homeland, and families."

That Gentiles were attracted to Jews and Judaism is obvious. Why were they? Though there are various reasons, a few will be considered below.

Jewish and Gentile Interaction in the Ancient Rome.

In his "Diaspora: Jews amidst Greeks and Romans," Dr. Erich S. Gruen, professor emeritus in the Department of History, University of California, says the population of Rome "exploded" in the first and second centuries BCE, resulting in emerging "Jewish communities . . . in the late Republic and early Principate, with modern estimates of a Jewish population ranging from 20,000–60,000" people. After calling for and assessing Gentile views of Jews, in his section "The Jews of Rome" Professor Gruen concludes:

> Romans in the private sphere had little reason to trouble themselves over the Jews. Writers scoffed and laughed. The weird ways of the Jews provided a source of amusement, even amazement. However, they did not lead to bile, and they did not provoke hostilities. The preserved comments, even in the aftermath of the [Jewish] Revolt, convey mockery rather than malignancy.

Though anti-Jewish statements appear in the Roman press, every now and again, Dr. Gruen isn't minded to make too much of it—and rightly so. For, at the street-level, it could be argued that Jewish ideas made headway.

Roman women seem to have been increasingly attracted to Judaism and its daughter religion—Messianic Judaism. "The early church was so especially attractive to [non-Jewish] women," says Professor Rodney Stark, "that in 370 [CE] the emperor Valentinian issued a written order to Pope Damascus I requiring that Christian missionaries cease calling on the homes of pagan women." For reasons that will be unpacked below, Dr. Stark believes "women enjoyed far higher status" in Jewish and Messianic Jewish homes and communities, in Rome as elsewhere, "than did women in the Greco-Roman world at large." For reasons that will become patently obvious, this higher status and consequential better treatment drew non-Jewish women into the Jewish fold and into the Messianic movement's ranks.

Writing around 200 CE, in his "The Roman History: The Reign of Augustus," the Roman historian Dio Cassius noted there was an "extreme shortage of females" in Roman culture. Dr. J.C. Russell concurred and, for his part, posited that there were 131 males for every 100 females in the city of Rome, and 140 males for every 100 in Italy. Why the disparity in numbers and what does this have to do with Jewish attractiveness?

In his "The Ancient World: Manners and Morals," Dr. Jack Lindsay noted how even in large and reasonably wealthy families "more than one daughter was practically never reared." Why not? This diminished number of Roman women, according to Dr. Stark, can only be attributed to some engineering of human life, or of "tampering" with it, as Dr. Lindsay put it. With no offense to culture and morals, many, many baby girls were left to die at birth in Greco-Roman culture—as were males with deformities. Undesired baby girls were left to die at dumps at the edge of Roman cities. Most did; some, however, were picked up and raised as prostitutes.

Seneca regarded the disregarding of unwanted children as "reasonable" and "commonplace." Plato and Aristotle recommended infanticide as a legitimate state policy, and lent their credence to the pagan practice as a result. Torah-minded Jews disdained the murderous practice, and were game to criticize it. In The Histories 5.5, Tacitus construed the Jewish notion that it is "a deadly sin to kill an unwanted child" as one of the Jews' "sinister and revolting" ways of thinking. Testifying to the horrific pagan views, while positioning Jewish practice over and against them, Josephus noted: "The [Jewish] law, moreover, enjoins us to bring up our offspring, and forbids women to cause abortion or to destroy it afterward; and if a woman appears to have done so, she will be a murderer of her child." Torah forbids the murderous brazen disregard for life in the Ten Commandments.

In his "Sentences of Pseudo-Phocylides," an Alexandrian Jew similarly advised: "a woman should not... throw it [i.e. her newborn baby] before dogs and vultures of prey." In his First Apology, Justin Martyr expressed this sentiment with "it is wicked to expose even newly-born children ... [for] we would then be murderers." As noted, Pagans by contrast disregarded their unwanted children—girls particularly—whereas Torah-bound Jews eschewed the immoral practice. Mindful of this, Dr. Rodney Stark surmised: "the views of family ... sustained by Christians revealed the Jewish origins of the movement ... [those views] being "very family oriented" at the core.

Messianic believers' refused to condone female infanticide. Coupled with Judaism and Messianic Judaism's stalwart disparagement of divorce, marital infidelity, fornication, and polygamy, it is not hard to understand how non-Jewish women could and would become attracted to the Jews. Life-loving, loving, and nurturing were accentuated. Fidelity without divorce was held out to be the norm in the Jewish counter-culture, and was expected of every Messianic adherent as well. Not only that, believers' marriages were entered into on better terms than what tended to prevail in the broader culture.

The fortunate Roman girls that made it past the disgraceful abandonment were typically married off to older men before puberty. In his "The Age of Roman Girls at Marriage," in Population Studies, Dr. Keith Hopkins informs through Plutarch: "Romans gave their girls in marriage when they were twelve years old, or even younger," something Plutarch said caused "the hatred and fear of girls forced [into sexual relations] contrary to nature." Dio Cassius said much the same, that "Girls are considered ... to have reached marriageable age by their twelfth year." According to Dr. Hopkins, 10 percent of pagan girls were married by age ten, with 44 percent marrying by age fourteen, most often with men much older and with the unions consummated at once, despite the tender age of the girls. Women in Messiah-believing communities tended to marry later.

Though not particularly respected in the broader Greco-Roman culture, babies, girls, and older women arguably fared much, much better in the Messianic Jewish subculture. Therein, not only were believing men more predisposed to value their marriage partners with exhortations in the Scriptures to "love their wives," but, should women fall upon hard times when untimely death seized their husbands, the Messianic community felt it incumbent to assist the unfortunate widows—their "sisters" in a communal sense. This harks back to James' noting that assisting widows represents religion that is "pure and undefiled before God," and thus at its best.

B'Rit Hadashah (The New Covenant)

Arguably, the valuation of female life in Jewish communities, over and against the devaluation of female life that prevailed in the regnant culture, prompted not a few women to cast their approving gazes toward the Yeshua/Jesus movement. In his "The Body and Society: Men, Women and Sexual Renunciation in Early Christianity," Dr. Peter Brown observed how "'women were prominent among upper class Christians." That women were prominently represented in the believing community's ranks—way in excess of the women that presented in the broader culture where they were outnumbered 140:100 in Italy—created an unanticipated "surplus of women" in the Messianic movement, and at a time when the world was used to there being a "vast surplus of men," not of women. This created something of a problem.

In about 200 CE, Callistus, Bishop of Rome, "upset many of his fellow clerics" when he ruled that Christian women could live in just concubinage, "without entering into marriage"—what we would call fornication. Why would a bishop provide a mechanism for such things? Professor Harnack opines "[t]hese circumstances arose from the ... problem[s] facing upper-class women whose only marital option within the Christian community were to men of far inferior rank ... [H]igh born women would have lost many legal privileges and [the] control of their wealth." Wanting to provide a means for this growing inventory of women to secure the personal benefits of believing marriage, without imposing the legal obligations of marriage that would reduce their standing, the bishop opted for another arrangement. Irrespective of what one thinks of his position—or the women—clear is the fact that a Torah-based culture was gaining headway in a bankrupt world.

Dr. Stephen Spence posited "Jewish features underlie a large part of the Roman [Gentile] Church." This, according to him, is "explained by its proximity and familiarity with Jewish traditions, which lead some to believe that Christianity in Rome began within the well-established Roman Jewish community."

Though the notion that Roman Christianity evolved from a Jewish matrix may appear novel at first blush (especially for those inclined to think of a Roman Catholic Church as the original), a careful consideration of the sources supports the thesis that ancient Roman Christianity came by way of Judaism and Messianic Judaism, given the appeal of the egalitarian and redemptive natures of the respective Jewish movements. Jewish culture was virtue-rich; pagan culture operated with a virtue deficit. Greco-Roman utilitarianism humbled and dehumanized human beings—even the citizens of the empire.

Reducing non-citizens of lesser race, class and gender, to less-than-hoped-for lives, the doomed unfortunates were socialized into accepting their unfortunate lot. Many knew they were little more than utilities to be used and abused in the gladiatorial games, to be harvested as slave-stock for the mines, and used as human chattel to serve the various needs and interests of oppressive overlords, as agricultural slaves, as sex-slaves of both sexes, of both, or whatever. . . . Though this ubiquitous dehumanization tended to prevail in the larger culture, and on quite a grand scale, the Torah-based sub-culture within the regnant culture cast a loftier moral vision, where all people—irrespective of their race, class, or gender—had inalienable, God-given dignity and rights. This made Judaism and Messianic Judaism (or what some call early "Christianity") attractive to Gentiles.

In his "The Jews in Late Ancient Rome: Evidence of Cultural Interaction in the Roman Diaspora," Professor Leonard Victor Rutgers concludes that Jews and Christians shared much in common. A careful assessment of archeological findings in ancient Rome and Venosa similarly prompted Professor Eric Meyers to note in his "Report on the Excavations at the Venosa Catacombs" that: "Jewish and Christian burials reflect an interdependence and [a] closely related community of Jews and Christians in which clear marks of demarcation were blurred until the third and fourth centuries, CE." With this in mind, Dr. Rodney Stark goes on to parrot Dr. Meyers again, with: it was "only when a triumphant Christianity began, late in the fourth century, to pour money into Palestine [sic] for church building and shrines, was there any serious rupture with Jews."

Jewish and Gentile Interaction in the North African Cities of Carthage and Cyrene

Jewish experience in North Africa is lost to moderns—as is ancient Messianic Jewish experience, on the whole. Difficulties with reconstruction notwithstanding, herein, we will call upon extant sources and briefly consider Jewish peoples and communities in North Africa, and see what we can learn about Jewish and Gentile believers' experience.

Jews, Messianic Jews and Gentile Christians in Carthage

Dr. Stephanie Binder, of the Department of Classical Studies at Bar-Ilan University, Israel, brings strong Jewish connections to bear on ancient

B'Rit Hadashah (The New Covenant)

North African Christian experience. In her post-Trajan, post-war "Jewish-Christian. Contacts in the Second and Third Centuries, CE?," Professor Binder took up the matter of Jewish and so-called "Christian" interactions in African antiquity. She was particularly concerned with whether ancient Christians and Jews were "either different and isolated from each other or similar and intermingled, in the late second and early third centuries CE," in Carthage and elsewhere. Her assessment of both the principal sources and the scholarly discussions on those sources yield an affirmative "yes"—that indeed the Jewish and so-called "Christian" communities were much more connected than disconnected.

After referencing Dr. Timothy Barnes who says: "no one really knows how Christianity came to North Africa," Dr. Binder notes others, like Dr. Rene Braun, who suspects that Christianity came to North Africa through the Jewish community. After observing through Dr. J.C. Fredouille that the "African church seems closer to the East than the Occident" (i.e., the "West"), and Dr. J. B. Rives who says "African liturgy is more like that of the East than that of Rome" and Dr. W.H.C. Frend who notes that, "Christianity surely arrived through the Jewish community and from Eastern influences," she then offers her reasons for reasonable connections, based on how the North African church leader Tertullian's thought processes follows Judaism's *Mishnah Avodah Zarah*, on matters of festivals (pp. 197–202), immorality and idolatry (pp. 202–203), baths (pp. 203–204), games (pp. 204–206), garments (p. 206), saying the names of pagan gods (pp. 206–208), schoolmasters and teachers (pp. 209–210), swearing by the names of pagan gods (pp. 210–212), outsmarting the law (pp. 212–216), and then dealing with things dedicated to idolatry (pp. 216–217). After comparing and contrasting similarities between the *Mishnah*'s responses to these matters alongside Tertullian's decisions on them, Dr. Binder argued that the great church leader "Tertullian lived in close proximity to a Jewish community, founded his arguments on sources that he shared with this community, in the same cultural environment, and reached very similar conclusions." Those interested in her sweep of the aforementioned issues can refer to her monograph. Believing that one illustration will suffice, we will now pick up on a theme noted previously, and consider how both the rabbis and the African church leader Tertullian looked at festivals and sacred space.

The *Mishnah* says: "And these are the festivals of the idolatrous: the *Calends* and the *Saturnalia* and the *Kratesis*" (Avodah Zarah 1.3). Archaic as these expressions are, an explanation is warranted at the outset. "Calends" was used in antiquity to note the first day of a month—and seems to have particularly been used to denote the 1st of January, or the beginning of the Greco-Roman year. "Saturnalia," for its part, was an extremely popular Roman holiday, as well, one held in honor of Saturn (or Cronos), the youngest of the Titans and the father of the major gods celebrated by the Greeks and Romans. Foremost among Saturn's sons was the famous Zeus. "Saturnalia," the holiday in his honor, was inaugurated to lift spirits in the wake of a Carthaginian defeat in mid-December. Popular, it grew into a weeklong celebration, one accentuated by special foods, clothing and benefits—with special benefits even extending to slaves. Much as Santa is said to go "Ho, Ho, Ho," the greeting for the mid-to late-December Saturnalia holiday was "*Io, Saturnalia,*" or "e-o," with "e-o" being a Latin expression similar to Santa's "ho." Lastly, according to Dr. Peter Schafer in The Talmud Yerushalami and Graeco-Roman Culture, III: Texts and Studies in Ancient Judaism, the term *Kratesis* was presumed from the rabbinic point of view to hark to the founding and beginning of Rome, with Romulus and Remus, and the subsequent ascensions of the ruling emperors. *Kratesis* thus commemorates the beginning of civilization (*natalis urbis*) and in some sense, to the regnant culture's majestic, mythic, and seemingly mystical power. In sum, the aforementioned holidays hark to legendary triumphs in Greco-Roman mythology and history.

Avodah Zarah 1.3 put it succinctly and with a warning: "these are the festivals of the idolatrous: the *Calends* and the *Saturnalia* and the *Kratesis.*" So much for the Jews. In his *De Idololatria* 14.4, the church leader Tertullian similarly exhorts North African Christians to avoid "*Saturnalia et calends Ianurias*"—i.e., the mid-December feast to Saturn and the new year's celebration which comes on its heels.

Associated gift giving was to be shunned by both the Jewish and Christian communities. Tertullian wanted Christians to avoid receiving gifts, as per *De Idololatria* 14.6, much as the Jewish sage Resh Laqish wanted Yehuda the Prince to dispose of a gift received from a *min* (heretic—used at times to refer to Jewish believers in Yeshua/Jesus) as a New Year's gift, in the Babylonian Talmud *Avodah Zarah* 6B. How ought one to account for the similarity in thinking, here as elsewhere?

Tertullian's familiarity with Judaism may well be attributed to his having himself once come "near to conversion to Judaism," as some allege. This is no forgone conclusion, however. Dr. Michael Rydelnik, professor of Jewish Studies at the Moody Bible Institute, accepts the idea that Tertullian had not had

B'Rit Hadashah (The New Covenant)

"any personal knowledge of his opponents and their religion," i.e., Judaism, an idea he parroted from Williams in *Adversus Judaeos*. (I prefer the notion that he did have personal knowledge.) This discussion aside, that Tertullian's Carthaginian Christians were "found in synagogues" and that they had to be "encouraged to preach to Gentiles too," in De Fuga 6.2–3, speaks of common ground, natural degrees of familiarity, and mixed associations—something the churchman wanted to weaken and/or break up outright.

Though Tertullian takes on Jews in his *Adversus Iudaeos*, this is but a "stereotyped invention" of Jews—not the real-world Jews of his day. That "he does not attack or evenly openly refer to his Jewish neighbors" in Carthage leads Dr. Binder to argue that he wrote his strident opposition to "prepare Christians encounters with Jews of the city and wants them to have proper arguments in hand." Spirited disputation is thus not to be construed as being tantamount to disdain. She postulates: "Tertullian [actually] benefited from Jewish associations and inspiration while writing his treatise"—i.e, *De Idolotatria*.

How Tertullian came upon and applied Jewish notions is a matter of conjecture. Did he get them from Jewish believers in Yeshua/Jesus? Did he get them from his own Jewish associations? We do not know. We do know, though, that Jewish presence and influence is evidenced in Carthage, North Africa. Dr. Binder's best argument to this effect is that "social, ethnic and religious cosmopolitanism in Carthage [would have] prevented total separation between Jews and Christians;" and, not only that, but the communities could have been so close that, "there might [even] have been uncertainty about what makes a Christian different from a Jew." "The only definitive conclusion that can be inferred from the study," according to Dr. Binder, "is that when Jewish and Christian communities co-existed in the same place—even though their respective leaders worked hard to maintain a clear theological boundary—on the interpersonal, individual, and social levels, they were still intertwined and shared their ideas and religious experience."

Gentiles were attracted to Judaism and Messianic Judaism, and were received in the ranks of both communities. Impressed by this fact, I believe modern Jews and Messianic Jews would do well to make room in their hearts and minds for Gentiles today.

IN WHAT WAYS DID JESUS LIVE AS A JEW?[5]

by David Sedaca

We can assess the Jewishness of Jesus by his relationship to the people of his day, by his relationship to the Jewish religion, and by his relationship with his followers.

His own Jewishness stands out when we consider the audience of most of his teachings. He spoke to the common folk: fishermen, farmers, tax collectors, housewives, inquisitive rabbis, and learned teachers of the Torah. What do these people all have in common? They made up the fabric of the Jewish community at the time of Jesus. They are all Jewish, and they all connected to his message—or even reacted negatively—because they understood what Jesus was saying.

In addition, we see Jesus' Jewishness by the way he practiced the Jewish religion of his day. Although he did say "You have heard what it was said to the people long ago . . . but I tell you . . . " (Matt 5:21–22), he does not deny the validity of what was said before, the instruction (torah) that was handed down from Mount Sinai and constituted the core of the Judaism of Jesus' day. Rather, he provides a new understanding of this instruction.

Jesus went to synagogue, he went to the Temple, and he upheld the Law and the commandments. He affirmed the value of Scripture; what's more, he condemned any intent to modify what was written (Matt 5:18–19).

What Jesus did condemn was the hypocrisy of some religious leaders—those who took such a strong stand on the letter of the law but were leaving behind the spirit of the law. There is a misconception that Jesus utterly rejects the Pharisees and the Teachers of the Law. But although Jesus does condemn their sternness and hypocrisy, he rejects neither their function nor their teaching. This is clearly seen when Jesus says, "The teachers of the law and the Pharisees sit in Moses' seat. So you must obey them and do everything they tell you. But do not do what they do, for they do not practice what they preach." (Matt 23:2–3)

Nowhere do we find that Jesus came to start a new religion that would be different from what God had revealed to the Jewish people. Jesus' teaching was about the Kingdom of God having arrived in the midst of the people of Israel; not a new people, not a new religion. His was a message of repentance and new birth.

5. Sedaca, "In what ways did Jesus live as a Jew?"

years, Jewish believers—who were mostly in and around Jerusalem—continued in their Messianic faith. Gentiles, on the other hand, without taking on Jewish tradition, accepted *Iesous* (the Greek spelling of Jesus) as Lord and Savior, and continued to follow their Greek culture.

Then came the destruction of Jerusalem in AD 70. And the times of the Gentiles, which actually began with the death of Yeshua, emerged in its fullness after forty years. The times of the Jews, which actually began to ebb with the captivities, heard its death knell with the crucifixion of Yeshua. It finally came to a total halt with the destruction of Jerusalem.

Thereafter, Jews were scattered throughout the world. Any Jew who accepted Yeshua almost invariably became a Gentile; that is, his children were raised as Gentiles, and his grandchildren no longer thought of themselves as Jews. It was an exact reverse of the times of the Jews when Ruth, Rahab, and many others joined themselves to the Jews in order to serve God. Speaking as God's mouthpiece, Moses hinted at the phenomenon of the Gentiles:

They have made me jealous with what is not God; They have provoked me to anger with their idols. So I will make them jealous with those who are not a people; I will provoke them to anger with a foolish nation (Deut 32:21).

If God's Word is to be taken literally, the times of the Gentiles can be said to have ended in 1967 with the Jewish recapture of the Old City of Jerusalem. However, since God's times always gradually fade (instead of cutting off at a second's notice), we may be assured that God will continue to deal with the Gentiles a short time longer—just as he did with the Jews for forty years after the death of the Messiah. The move of God's grace began to deal in ever more powerful waves with the Gentiles as Gentiles after AD 30. Likewise, God has begun to bring Jews into repentance and faith as Jews. Why? Because the times of the Jews are once more upon us, and will continue to expand until his coming. And just as God has faithfully fulfilled his revealed will until now, so will he continue to fulfill it.

As far as I know, almost every Jew who accepted Yeshua into his life before the recapture of Jerusalem also claimed allegiance to the Gentile peoples. After June, 1967, a constantly increasing number of Jews have been redeemed by the blood of Yeshua, the Jewish Messiah, as members of the Jewish faith.

Beit Tefilah: A House of Prayer

MESSIANIC JUDAISM GAINING MOMENTUM IN ISRAEL[7]

by Rabbi Barry Rubin

In recent decades, Messianic Judaism, a movement of Jewish people who have accepted Yeshua (Jesus) as Messiah and continued to embrace their Jewishness, has been steadily growing—especially in the United States.

Jews have been coming to faith in Yeshua for centuries, increasingly so after Israel became a reality again in the late 1800s with the Zionist movement. After the Holocaust, when Israel became a nation again in 1948, the number of Jewish believers in Yeshua has been increasing worldwide, almost in lock step with Jewish immigration to Israel.

But what is the state of Messianic Judaism in Israel itself?

Because Israel is in an extremely dangerous area of the world, surrounded by Arab countries that have threatened its extermination, Jews there live with a certain amount of anxiety. When would the next Intifada take place? Which country would declare its desire to push Israel into the sea? When would Hamas rockets fly again?

Living with those concerns, the people have become cautious about "outsiders," especially after nearly two millennia of "Christian" anti-Semitism. Thus, Christian missions to the Jews of Israel often have been met with suspicion. Yet some have been successful, especially if they are sensitive to and supportive of Messianic Judaism.

There are historic Anglican Jewish missions from the United Kingdom. King of Kings (kkcj.org) is a congregational ministry of the Pentecostal Assemblies of Canada. The Caspari Center (caspari.com) is a Scandinavian Lutheran mission to the Jews. Christian Witness to Israel (cwi.org.uk) sponsors Grace and Truth congregation in Rishon L'Tzion. They also publish books, as does Keren Yeshua.

Modern Jewish missions are also active in Israel. Jews for Jesus (jewsforjesus.org) has a new center in Tel Aviv. The Christian Jew Foundation (cjfm.org), not only does missionary work, it also supports a number of national pastors. Chosen People Ministries (chosenpeople.com) has centers in Jerusalem and Tel Aviv and congregations in Jerusalem, Tel Aviv, Ashkelon, Ashdod, and Ariel. Maoz (maozisrael.org) is an Israeli organization that publishes books in Hebrew and supports Israel while helping Jewish people meet their Messiah. There are others as well, but, as with most

---

7. Rubin, "Messianic Judaism Gaining Momentum."

overseas missions, indigenous works have had the most success. Nowhere is this truer than in Israel.

The primary evangelistic work in Israel is not through missions. It is being done through local Messianic congregations. The larger ones are in Tiberias, K'far Saba, Netanya, Jerusalem, and Joffa. There are 150-plus congregations in Israel with as many as 15,000 Messianic Jewish believers, of whom about 60 percent speak Russian as their first language.

The growth in the number of congregations has increased over the last twenty years, just as it has in the United States and other countries. Nearly every year, another indigenous congregation or two springs up, and as more and more Jews from around the world return home, this will only increase.

Israel is a small country—about the size of New Jersey—so these congregations are easily noticed by their fellow Israelis. More and more, Israel is increasingly aware that there are Jews who trust Yeshua as the Messiah and savior, much as it was in the New Testament era.

These Messianic Jewish congregations are now led by Israelis, even though they may have a mix of Jews and Gentiles. Most services are in Hebrew (sometimes Russian, Amharic, French, or Spanish). The music too is indigenous, as is the style of worship—very Israeli. The melodies have a distinctly Middle Eastern tone to them. Most meet on Saturday when Jews generally hold worship services. These congregations of Yeshua-followers are clearly Jewish.

Messianic Jews are gaining more acceptance in Israel. Instead of being perceived as threats to the Israelis, due to prejudices going back 2,000 years, they are recognized as friends, fellow citizens, and an active part of Israeli society. In part, the groundwork for this was laid by the benevolence work of groups such as Chosen People Ministries (chosenpeople.com), The Joseph Storehouse (www.visionforisrael.com), the Messianic Jewish Alliance of America's Joseph Project (mjaa.org), and other similar works.

Israelis, who have been especially challenged during the wars with Lebanon, Hamas, and the high taxes used to pay for defense, are grateful to Messianic Jews, sometimes in spite of themselves, for food, clothes, medicine, and other supplies. They need our help. This is a very tangible expression of the love of Messiah. Messianic Jews are being trusted enough to allow them to materially assist Israel during her most difficult times.

It is known that there are many Messianic Jews serving in the army—mostly the children of immigrants from the United States and Europe—who were raised in Israel. This shows unity with the people, so much so that the funeral of one Messianic Jewish soldier killed in the last war was well attended by Israel's leaders. The newspapers noted that he was a Messianic Jew, part of a congregation in the Haifa area.

A television special featuring interviews of members of the Christian *Moshav, Yad Hashmonah*, was widely watched. It included a Messianic Jewish family celebrating Shabbat, etc., giving a very good impression of Messianic Jews in Israel. No longer are followers of Yeshua seen as people to stay away from. Now, they are embraced as fellow strugglers in Israeli life.

Over the past centuries, because of all the atrocities done to Jews in the name of Jesus, Jewish people have avoided having anything to do with him, his followers, or his teachings. It was too costly, too risky. And in Israel, where people are more vulnerable to attacks, this is acutely so. But Messianic Judaism is changing things. Now, Israelis are more open to talking about Yeshua and considering his claims to Messiahship.

The congregational leaders in Israel need connections with pastors in the West. Many would appreciate prayer, fellowship, and sometimes even financial support for special projects. Western pastors have a lot to give to Israel's Messianic leaders by way of training and guidance, as well as prayer. Most Israeli pastors do not have much formal training and would benefit from partnering with non-Israeli pastors. Most Israeli pastors are pioneers and need more seasoned spiritual mentors to guide them.

Encouragingly, the perception of Messianic Jews is undergoing a steady transformation in Israel these days—from one of mistrust and outright loathing to recognition and acceptance. Knowing the love of Yeshua in the Messianics' hearts, the bridge between them and Orthodox Jews is getting shorter all the time. Doors to hearts once closed are beginning to open wide.

B'Rit Hadashah (The New Covenant)

UNDERSTANDING MESSIANIC JUDAISM[8]

by Rabbi Stephen Luft

Throughout history certain dates and times are forever etched in our memories. For many, dates such as December 7, 1941 is a day that lives in infamy. That date is remembered as America's entry into World War II with the Japanese bombing of Pearl Harbor. Likewise, November 22, 1963 is equally as memorable to those who lived during that time. Many remembered exactly what they were doing or where they were when they heard the news that President Kennedy had been assassinated in Dallas.

A more recent date is September 11, 2001, otherwise known as 9/11. A date etched into many minds when our life as a nation would change. Never before had there been an attack on American soil in such magnitude by a predominantly stealth enemy. Radical Islam revealed itself in such a way that ultimately attacked our way of life.

However, of all the dates that need to be remembered of the last one-hundred years, there are two, that may appear to be insignificant to many, are extremely important and central to Adonai's redemptive timeline. The first is May 14, 1948, when after nearly 2,000 years of dispersion among the nations, the Jewish people supernaturally reclaimed their ancestral homeland. The second date is June 7, 1967, which commemorates the liberation of Jerusalem from the Jordanians. This date recognizes for the first time since Babylonian captivity that Jerusalem was in Jewish control. Not even in the first century was Jerusalem controlled by the Jewish people. In this case it was under Roman control.

These two modern events prove conclusively and without doubt that Adonai is restoring Israel. He is demonstrating too, that he governs all history. He alone determines the rise and fall of empires, and the course of all nations. Israel's reestablishment is no accident, but rather proof to the nations that the God of Abraham, Isaac and Jacob is true to his own Word. His Word is accurate, reliable, and relevant. This restoration not only transcends a physical Jewish return to Eretz Yisrael (the land of Israel), but also signifies a spiritual restoration to the God of Abraham, Isaac, and Jacob.

Messianic Judaism is an outward evidence of this great end-time restoration. Today, more than at any time since the first century, Jewish people are once again embracing the Messiahship of Yeshua. Today, Jewish

---

8. Luft, "Understanding."

believers are not abandoning their ancestral heritage, calling, and lifestyle, but embracing it. Like the Jewish believers of the first century they are zealous for Torah.

To some, the idea of a person who is Jewish and believes in Yeshua is a contradiction. The thought process goes like this . . . You can't be Jewish and believe in Yeshua (Jesus), you're either a Christian or a Jew, you can't be both.

This way of thinking is primarily a product of the way we have been taught and trained over the centuries. Church history has greatly influenced this mindset. Although the climate is improving, the influence of "you can't be both" still remains.

History and Scripture record that faith in Yeshua is inherently Jewish. Yeshua was a Jew. He ministered in a Jewish land and among Jewish people. He was the most prolific Torah teacher ever to walk the face of the earth.

The very first followers of Yeshua were all Jewish, including his twelve talmadim. The anticipation of the coming of Messiah was not borne out of the Gentile nations, but from the pages of the Hebrew scriptures. The first century Messianic Jew saw in Yeshua the fulfillment of those things spoken of by the Prophets.

"For among the first things I passed on to you was what I also received, namely this: the Messiah died for our sins, in accordance with what the Tanakh says; and he was buried; and he was raised on the third day, in accordance with what the Tanakh says; and he was seen by Kefa, then by the Twelve; and afterwards he was seen by more than five hundred brothers at one time, the majority of whom are still alive, though some have died" (1Cor15:3–6).

Being Jewish and believing in Yeshua wasn't the issue then. It couldn't be anything else but that. The most pressing issue of debate during the first century centered around the inclusion of Gentiles. Was Yeshua the Messiah for the Gentiles also? Must a Gentile be circumcised? Must a Gentile believer first undergo ritual conversion? Adonai has miraculously shown the Messianic Jewish community that Yeshua was the Messiah for both the Jew and Gentile:

Therefore, we hold the view that a person comes to be considered righteous by God on the ground of trusting, which has nothing to do with legalistic observance of Torah commands. Or is God the God of the Jews only? Isn't he also the God of the Gentiles? Yes, he is indeed the God of the Gentiles; because, as you will admit, God is one. Therefore, he will consider righteous the circumcised on the ground of trusting and the uncircumcised through that same trusting. Does it follow that we abolish Torah by this trusting? Heaven forbid! On the contrary, we confirm Torah (Rom 3:28–31).

Today, we are faced with one of the greatest paradoxes in history, whereby it is now a foreign concept for a Jewish person to believe in Yeshua as the Messiah of Israel. However, this end time revival, known as Messianic Judaism, is restoring what appeared to be lost. Many Jewish believers readily affirm that through their belief and profession of Yeshua as Messiah has encouraged a greater appreciation for Adonai, Torah, Israel, and their Jewish heritage. In the past, such a profession would warrant being ostracized by the Jewish community or forced assimilation into a non-Jewish culture.

Through Messianic congregations, Jewish believers are able to maintain their Jewishness, enabling them to convey their beliefs and values to their children. Likewise, non-Jews who profess faith in Yeshua as the Messiah of Israel become part of a Messianic congregation. They gain a deeper understanding and appreciation for their spiritual roots.

Our intention with this article isn't simply to define the term Messianic Judaism. If that were the case, we could accomplish that in one paragraph and save a lot of time. The purpose of this article is to provide you, our reader with a comprehensive understanding of Messianic Judaism as it continues to develop today. We will include several definitions, historical perspective (past and present) and scriptural support of this movement.

Definition 1:

A biblically based movement of people who as committed Jews believe in Yeshua as the Jewish Messiah of Israel, for whom the Tenach spoke. This first definition describes a movement of people. The Jewish nation is comprised of people in a general sense and a family in an expanded sense . . . a community, thus leading us to our next definition.

Definition 2:

A movement of Jewish congregations, committed to Yeshua the Messiah, that embraces the covenantal responsibility of a Jewish lifestyle and identity rooted in Torah, expressed in tradition, renewed and applied in the context of the New Covenant.

It was Yeshua himself who said: "Don't think that I have come to abolish the Torah or the Prophets. I have come not to abolish but to complete" (Matt 5:17).

Jewish identity is rooted in Torah. Yes there have been other influences, such as the Talmud and Hellenism that have influenced the Jewish identity, but it is Torah that truly makes the Jewish identity real. Furthermore, it is Yeshua who conveyed and taught Torah from its intended purpose. These other influences mentioned previously, have added more layers of observance than were originally intended. One need look no further than Shabbat for which we wrote an extensive article.

The next logical progression of this movement is within a congregational setting. The Jewish nation first began as a family when they entered the land of Egypt, however, when they left some 430 years later, they left as a nation of more than two million people. When Adonai conveys his message to the Jewish nation, it is as a congregation. The promises, the responsibilities, the covenants are to a people as a nation, not individually.

"I am speaking the truth as one who belongs to the Messiah, I do not lie; and also bearing witness is my conscience, governed by the Ruach Ha-Kodesh, my grief is so great, the pain in my heart so constant, that I could wish myself actually under God's curse and separated from the Messiah, if it would help my brothers, my own flesh and blood, the people of Isra'el! They were made God's children, the Sh'khinah has been with them, the covenants are theirs, likewise the giving of the Torah, the Temple service and the promises; the Patriarchs are theirs; and from them, as far as his physical descent is concerned, came the Messiah, who is over all. Praised be Adonai for ever! Amen" (Rom 9:1–5). Sha'ul writes to the congregation in Rome, regarding the position of his fellow Israelites . . . his brothers, regarding what has been entrusted to us, yet do not recognize Yeshua as Messiah, the Son of God. All that is mentioned above, is given to Israel as a nation, for the express purpose of being a light to the nations:

"He said to me, 'You are my servant, Isra'el, through whom I will show my glory.' But I said, 'I have toiled in vain, spent my strength for nothing, futility.' Yet my cause is with Adonai, my reward is with my God. So now Adonai says he formed me in the womb to be his servant, to bring Ya`akov back to him, to have Isra'el gathered to him, so that I will be honored in the sight of Adonai, my God having become my strength he has said, 'It is not enough that you are merely my servant to raise up the tribes of Ya`akov and restore the offspring of Isra'el. I will also make you a light to the nations, so my salvation can spread to the ends of the earth'" (Isa 49:3–6).

Adonai chose Israel, through his covenant with Abraham, to convey his message of Messiah for the reconciliation of Israel and the nations to himself. No other nation or religion can make this claim. No other nation has been given such a responsibility. Yet, when people think of one who is chosen, they equate it with privilege. A first born son is chosen to be the leader of the family as part of a succession plan. What does this do to the other siblings. Usually, feelings of envy, jealousy, or anger will become present, in that those who are not chosen feel slighted or rejected.

Those not chosen are viewing this selection as one who is favored over the others. Yet, on the other hand, the one who has been chosen may convey a feeling of pride toward the others, but may also look at their selection as one of great responsibility. The chosen one may consider their selection to be of burden, in that they are now responsible for everyone, while prior to succession, they lived their own life and were content.

The responsibility that Adonai has placed on Ya'akov is no different than the succession plan provided above. The nation of Israel was chosen to be a servant for Adonai and convey His salvation to the nations. Sha'ul is aware of this calling and the order in which it was intended:

"For I am not ashamed of the Good News, since it is God's powerful means of bringing salvation to everyone who keeps on trusting, to the Jew especially, but equally to the Gentile." For in it is revealed how God makes people righteous in his sight; and from beginning to end it is through trust as the Tanakh puts it, "But the person who is righteous will live his life by trust" (Rom 1:16–17).

Definition 3:

A term used to define Jewish people in Yeshua. Maintaining a lifestyle and form of worship that identifies Jewish customs and traditions while believing Yeshua is the promised Messiah of scriptures. Part of the universal body of Messiah that expresses itself in relation to a Jewish heritage.

There is an enormous divide within the Messianic community (Church and Messianic Judaism), founded primarily on misunderstanding that is lacking in context of scripture. Separation of a Jewish identity from the Messianic Community is an entire article for another day. For the purpose of this article Messianic Judaism recognizes a heritage that is biblically based and thus continues to follow these principles and traditions, not only as one who is Jewish, but also as one who believers in Yeshua. Separating one from the other is impossible. To be Jewish is not just a "religion" but is also a birthright. To deny a Jewish person their identity when them come to believe in Yeshua is denying who they are. It would be similar to say that now you are a believer in Yeshua, you are no longer an American citizen. When put in a context that is relevant to others, outside of the Jewish community, it is easier to understand the false premise that has been taught for hundreds of years.

Definition 4:

Not a new movement, but a resurgence/rebirth of an old movement. The first movement was of the apostles/talmadim and comprised a community of Jewish and non-Jewish believers during the first three centuries of this age, after Yeshua's resurrection. The latest stage of the development of authentic biblical Judaism is the same biblical Judaism that was followed by Moses, David, the Prophets, and brought to fulfillment by Yeshua.

To summarize the above definitions: A congregation comprised of both Jewish and non-Jewish believers with an emphasis on Jewish ministry. It is of, for, to, and by Jewish believers, yet includes the non-Jewish believer who has decided to come alongside Israel, is grafted into the olive tree of Israel and fully participates in the ministry. This movement is not to the exclusion of the non-Jewish believer, but to their inclusion in that they have embraced the vision of what Messianic Judaism is . . . a movement where you can be Jewish and believe that Yeshua is the promised Messiah of Israel, and yet, not have to give up your Jewish identity. You don't have to assimilate into a church.

Is Messianic Judaism Biblical?

You will probably receive different answers, depending on who you ask. From the definitions provided above we have expressed that a Messianic Jew is a person who has come to believe and accepted that Yeshua is the Messiah spoken of in the Tenach. Unfortunately, this view is not accepted throughout the Messianic community. There are many views regarding the

B'Rit Hadashah (The New Covenant)

Jewish person in relation to their decision regarding Yeshua. These views include:

In becoming a believer in Yeshua, you are now a Christian and are part of the Church. This view draws its foundation from the premise of "Replacement Theology" that teaches the Church has replaced Israel. It minimizes the Jewish identity of the believer and emphasizes the new creation of the Church as being central. In essence there is no Jewish identity. Everything Jewish has been done away with . . . it is "old testament"—we are now living under the "new testament." To deny the Jewishness of Adonai's redemption is in essence denying Yeshua, a Jew, from the tribe of Judah. Separation of the two is impossible. One need only take a journey through the book of Acts as evidence of the Jewishness of this movement.

At the beginning of the book of Acts, we see Yeshua teaching his talmadim of things pertaining to the Kingdom of God. (Acts 1:3–8) In Luke's account, 24:44, he provides the source of the material for the teaching that is taking place. Yeshua said to them, "This is what I meant when I was still with you and told you that everything written about me in the Torah of Moshe, the Prophets and the Psalms had to be fulfilled."

Acts 2. As instructed, the talmadim are waiting for Shavuot, a Jewish feast, where they would be receiving the Ruach Ha Kodesh (Holy Spirit), empowering them to convey the truth and New Covenant through Yeshua.

We witness Sha'ul's pattern when traveling to a city. He first would go to the synagogue and speak with regards to Yeshua as Messiah. He would use the same Jewish scripture that Yeshua used to convey this truth (Acts 13:14–15; 14:1; 17:1–2; 18:4; 19:8–9).

The main issue at the council held in Jerusalem in Acts 15 dealt with the issue of gentiles coming to faith in the Jewish Messiah. Should they be circumcised and become Jewish was the question at hand. This was a very Jewish problem of the day.

In order to truly understand what is happening in Acts, one must view and understand through a Jewish mindset, in that the context is Jewish. Unlike today, the issues have changed 180 degrees. Today, it is the Jewish person who becomes a believer in Messiah that must be "assimilated" into the church, in contrast with 2,000 years ago whereby the challenge was bringing the non-Jewish believer coming to believe in Messiah into the community.

Other positions include:

"Covenant Theology" is built upon Calvinism and states:

- Israel and the church are one and the same throughout history
- A covenant of grace has been partially revealed in all the covenants that Adonai has made
- Since its birth, the church is the only covenant people, because all covenants, prophecies and promises are fulfilled in the New Covenant.
- Jewish people are grafted into the church
- Jewish people, individually and as a nation have neither purpose or significance regarding the plans of Adonai.

"Dispensational Theology" is based on the following:

- The Jewish people through Israel and the church are separate and distinct from each other. Their promises and destinies are also separate and distinct.
- Israel as a people and nation have been set aside by Adonai during the "church age" and therefore not part of the picture. Adonai will deal with them again after the church age is complete and the rapture has removed the church from the tribulation.
- As a nation and a people the kingdom of David will be restored during the Millennium.
- Jewish people who come to believe in Messiah during the church age become part of the church and no longer receive the promises of national Israel.

"Dual Covenant Theology" is based on the following:

- Salvation for the Jewish people is found through Adonai's covenant with Abraham.
- Salvation for gentile people is found through the New Covenant and Jesus.
- The two remain separate from each other.

Whether prominent or subtle, the influence of these theologies can still be felt within the church today. There are so many errors in these views.

B'Rit Hadashah (The New Covenant)

You may also notice an overlapping of ideas between these theologies mentioned above. The primary theme between them is the diminished position of the Jewish people in contrast to an elevated position of the church. The primary origin of this position comes from the council of Nicea in 325 CE, where Constantine instigates Christianity as the official state religion of the Roman Empire. This view was not his own but is attributed to Origen and promoted by Eusebius.

Rather than expand upon these theologies, I encourage people to obtain a copy of "The Church and the Jews" by Dan Gruber. His book will provide you with a comprehensive understanding of these false teachings. Without doubt, to be a believer in Yeshua and maintain your Jewish identity is fully supported by scriptures. What does Sha'ul say:

"I say then, Hath God cast away his people? God forbid. For I also am an Israelite, of the seed of Abraham, the tribe of Benjamin" (Rom 11:1).

As a believer, Sha'ul continues to identify himself as an Israelite. Just because he is now a believer, doesn't change the fact that he is still Jewish. If he still considers himself to be an Israelite, why is it that others continue not to recognize this truth? (a rhetorical question).

4

Rosh Hodesh (Head of the Month)

Every month on Rosh-Hodesh and every week on Shabbat, everyone living will come to worship in my presence," says Adonai.

(Isa 66:23)

In Genesis, God fixed lights in the sky to divide day from night and to be timekeepers for seasons and years. The phases of the moon reflect the continuous cycle of spring to winter, from youth to age. From the appearance of its first crescent bringing light out of the dark, waxing into fullness, it tells of new beginnings.

The ancient text from the first century, chapters of Rabbi Eliezer,[1] unfolds the time when heaven and tens of thousands of angels glorifying God were open over Adam and Eve. "Months and days and nights and solstices and equinoxes and seasons were before God, and God taught them to Adam in the garden of Eden, as it is written—This is the book of the generations of Adam . . . And Eve taught them to Enoch, and he entered into every limb of the year . . . 'There will never cease from the earth planting (*zera*) and harvest (*katzir*), heat (*chom*) and cold (*kor*), summer (*kayitz*) and winter (*choref*).' Seedtime is the equinox of Tishrei. Harvest is the equinox of Nisan. Cold is the solstice of Tevet, and heat is the solstice of Tammuz. Summer in its time and winter in its time."

---

1. Eliezer, "The Course of the Moon."

Rosh Hodesh (Head of the Month)

"Therefore keep watch!" Jesus said. Keep focus on the heavenly cycles appointed to tell man of God's plan resonating in the cycle of annual feasts. Jesus held Israel accountable for not knowing the time of her visitation.

The cycle of the sky was so central to the continuity of Israel that the first commandment given to the nation when they left Egypt was to look to the light in the sky for their new way of living. God said to Moses, "You are to begin your calendar with this month; it will be the first month of the year for you" (Exod 12:2). The waxing moon is acknowledged with the *Kiddush Levanah,* the blessing over the moon, spoken when the moon sails into view. Across time and generations the light has united the Jewish people to recognize that God is the creator acting on their behalf, connecting them to their ancestors and binding to their future generations.

The calendar given by God defines their freedom, following the rotation of the earth around its axis from sunset to sunset, the moon circling the earth every 29.5 days, and the earth revolving around the sun every 12.4 months. The lunar month begins when the moon is completely invisible as it lines up with the sun and earth. The moment, the *molad,* is the birth of the new moon. When the first waxing crescent appeared over Jerusalem at least two witnesses reported it to the Sanhedrin (the Council). The Sanhedrin would send messengers to tell the people and the shofar would sound at the Temple announcing a Rosh Hodesh, festival of thanksgiving. The Sanhedrin lit fires on mountains to let everyone know it was the new month. In surrounding towns, the people would see the fire and would light a fire on their mountaintops to spread the word.

Rosh Hodesh is called *z'man kapara,* a time of atonement. The renewed cycle of the moon finding the sun's rays again brings a sense of God's faithfulness to emerge us out of darkness into light.

On the last Shabbat before Rosh Hodesh, the people gather for the *birkat ha-chodesh,* blessing of the new month, and ask God to bless the new month, fulfill wishes, and for announcing the time of the new month. The prayer praises God for his intervention for their people through history and asks for health and sustenance. Rosh Hodesh is a joyous day honoring the new beginning with *Kiddush Levana,* the sanctification of the new moon. The people go outside to stand in the light of the moon. Selections from the Psalms are read. Rabbis speak the blessings in the Talmud. Verses from Isaiah and 1 Samuel are read.

"Heaven is my throne," says ADONAI, "and the earth is my footstool. What kind of house could you build for me? What sort of place could you devise for my rest? Didn't I myself make all these things? This is how they all came to be," says Adonai (Isa 66:1–2).

Moving in rhythm with the cycles of creation, the seventh day Shabbat synchronized Israel with the cycles of God. Shabbat was given as a day of rest, beginning at sunset because Genesis 1 states that there was evening and there was morning, one day. It is the day God rested from laboring and calls his people from overwhelming stress to give them a time to cease from work and to rest.

The Shabbat day foreshadows a complete rest in Jesus who made the day holy. In him is our Sabbath rest relieving us from the struggles of a sin-fallen world by empowering with his promise. It was an honored day to the early believers but they did not just meet on Saturdays. They met every day in the temple courts and broke bread in each other's homes (Acts 2:46). Worshipping was a way of life offered to God every day, but the Shabbat belongs to a portion called *eidut*, meaning "testimony." The Shabbat became a day to gather because it is appointed as a sign between God and his people.

Time continues to circle, returning to recite the stories of what God has done to faithfully deliver the people from persecutions. During the 1,700 years between 250 CE and 1948 CE, Jews were forced to leave more than eighty countries in Europe, including Moravia, Bohemia, England, France, Portugal, Spain, Lithuania, Germany, Austria, and seventy-one other countries. This averages to experiencing the trauma of expulsion every twenty-one years.

Yet they have retained their identity as a distinct people who have carried the celebration of God's deliverance into every generation. The moon comes glowing everywhere around earth where the people have been scattered, its light high above, unchangeable by man, reminding of God's covenant. When it reaches its fullness for Pesach it brings the people together again in sacred assemblies. It's a collective memory of God's redemption of national Israel that continues through history and a personal relationship with the living God. Exodus 13:8 instructs the people to know that they were each present with their ancestors by commanding them to tell every generation about their inheritance of a covenant made with them and their progeny forever.

Also the foreigner who does not belong to your people Isra'el—when he comes from a distant country because of your reputation (for they will hear of your great reputation, your mighty hand and your outstretched arm), when he comes and prays toward this house (1 Kgs 8:41–42).

Rosh Hodesh (Head of the Month)

WHAT I BELIEVE AND WHAT I REJECT[2]

by Rabbi Loren Jacobs

Gentile believers are not the same as the gentile foreigners who lived in the nation of Israel under the Old Covenant. They are fully co-heirs of the Kingdom with the Jewish saints.

There is one Lord, one faith, one baptism, one spirit that lives in all believers in one hope. The instructions of the Torah formed Israel's constitution. In the book of Acts the apostles gave gentile believers only four necessary practices: abstaining from food dirtied by idolatry, from sexual immorality, from eating blood, and from the meat of animals that have been strangled, along with the moral laws in the ten commandments.

If someone wants to observe a biblical holiday or custom, there is freedom but no obligation to do so. Gentile Christians have the freedom to celebrate the Sabbath and the Jewish holidays or not observe them. If someone says, "Messiah is my Passover, and I don't need to celebrate a Passover Seder," that's fine. If someone says, "Messiah is my Sabbath, and I'm resting in him; and, therefore, I don't need to rest on the Sabbath," that's ok. If someone wants to observe the first day of the week as a day of rest and worship, he or she has every right to do so. If someone says, "I want to observe the Sabbath and celebrate the Passover to help me better remember and appreciate Messiah my Passover Lamb," that's fine, too.

The Torah explains the principles for salvation, atonement, and ordained ways of worship. The prophecies of Messiah, history of the creation, dispersing of nations and languages, and the covenants are here. Every Christian should be well-versed in the Torah.

Was a man already circumcised when he was called? He should not become uncircumcised. Was a man uncircumcised when he was called? He should not be circumcised. Circumcision is nothing and uncircumcision is nothing. Keeping God's commands is what counts. Each person should remain in the situation they were in when God called them (1 Cor 7:18–20).

Messiah came to unite Jews and Gentiles, not by turning Gentiles into Jews or Jews into Gentiles. This would bring dissatisfaction with who God made each person to be and not align with God's creation of diversity in the holy church of people from every nation, people, and language group. All share the Spirit of Holiness that writes the law on each heart. Interest in

---

2. Jacobs, "What I Believe and What I Reject."

the Jewish roots of the faith is to be encouraged but the focus is to be held on the Savior.

In this age, as the Gospel returns to the Jewish people from whom it first went forward, we need to remember that Christianity is meant to be trans-cultural.

Rosh Hodesh (Head of the Month)

EXPOSING THE ELITIST, SECTARIAN SPIRIT[3]

by Tom Martincic

There are some people, when they get this truth they are like, "Well, that really makes me special. That makes me above everybody else. And so, who will be the greatest? I guess I will be one of those who will be among the greatest." The disciples argued over who would be the greatest. Yahushua said, "Oh, it is the one who knows the most?" No, he said the one who serves, who puts himself underneath others—not exalts himself above others.

This happened in church history. There were Adventists, there were Jehovah Witnesses, there were different groups who found a little bit of something. Jehovah Witnesses found, okay, Christmas is not right. The Adventists found out, "Oh, the Sabbath. We need to keep the Sabbath."

And they have that little bit of truth, and they are like, "Okay, we have arrived. Here we are. Come to us. We know the truth. We have it." And there is the same spirit that can operate even in the home fellowship group where there is no denomination at all. The same thing can happen. Not all of them in churches are brethren. Some of them might be, might be sincere, walking according to the understanding they have. But when you share with them, they would receive it gladly, in Yahweh's timing, because they love truth. There are brothers there.

There are brothers here among us, also, who understand Sabbath, who understand the blessing of the Hebrew roots. And there are unbelievers out there in the churches, in the church world.

Our path is like the shining sun that shines ever brighter unto the perfect day. And so, we have not yet arrived to that perfect day, but that is the path of the just. That is the way that we are seeking to walk. That is what we are about right there—seeking that ever brighter path that we might shine ever brighter as a light unto the world. Now, there is no way we could possibly become that, there is no way we could arrive there unless we follow the One who was of the Way, who is the Way.

And sectarianism has a way of becoming an alternative identity. "Oh, I am this." "I am a Mennonite." "I am a Baptist." "I am a Methodist." "I am a Jehovah Witness." "I am an Adventist." "I am this." "I am that." That becomes an identity, and whatever we identify ourselves with, we have a tendency to just walk that out.

---

3. Martincic, "Exposing the Elitist."

Beit Tefilah: A House of Prayer

I say let our identity be one who is a follower of The Way, which will inevitably shine ever brighter, who will receive Messiah and shine ever brighter, but will never claim, "I've arrived. Come to me. Do like me. My group is the true one and nobody else is. We are the only ones." We cannot go there. We can't.

But there are little hints of this kind of spirit operating even in groups that have no denominational affiliation. There will be false teachers among you (2 Pet 2:1).

Now, if the Law is abolished, what are they arguing about? No, strivings about how to interpret different verses in the Law. It says they are unprofitable, and they are useless. Reject a divisive man after the first and second admonition, knowing that such a person is warped and sinning, being self-condemned (Titus 3:10).

The word translated "divisive" here is Greek Lexicon *hairetikos* (A heretic.) Meaning: 1) fitted or able to take or choose a thing (What is this thing about choice?) 2) schismatic, factious, a follower of a false doctrine.

It has to do with making a choice. They make the choice to say, "We are it. We are the ones. You must only go with us." They make division where there should be no division. Maybe they won't say, "We are saved and they are unsaved," but they will act in such a spirit as though they believe in their heart they are superior to others around them. And it has to do with pride. Paul talks about this. Prior to Passover, he says: Now in giving these instructions I do not praise [you], since you come together not for the better but for the worse. For first of all, when you come together as a church, I hear that there are divisions among you, and in part I believe it (1 Cor 11:17–18).

For there must also be factions among you, that those who are approved may be recognized among you. It is going to happen. It will be there. You cannot stop it completely, but it is going to happen (1 Cor 11:19).

We have the same thing today. We have the same thing because one says "I am of Luther" (the Lutherans). "I am a Mennonite" (men of Simons). "John Wesley . . ." Do you get this? There are certain men, and maybe they won't be named after their particular group, but there will be some influential man who started a line of thinking that developed into a denomination, and now they associate themselves with that particular man. The exact same thing that Paul said not to do.

Is Messiah divided? No, he is not. And so, at some point we do have to make some kind of distinction between who is a believer and who is not a believer. I mean, do you just let everybody come on in and have this real big ecumenical kind of a spirit and it doesn't matter what you think or do, or whatever?

It is not bad to be chosen. "Behold! My Servant whom I have chosen" (Matt 12:18). "My elect." There is an elect. "My Beloved in whom My soul is well pleased!" There is a people who belong to the chosen people. There are certain ones who are chosen. I am not against saying there are certain chosen ones, but we have to be really careful about that, where we draw a line.

I believe we can see a clear, very good example of a sectarian spirit infiltrating the first century congregation in the book of Acts, and we see how they dealt with it.

And certain [men] came down from Judea and taught the brethren, "Unless you are circumcised according to the custom of Moses, you cannot be saved" (Acts 15:1). Unless you "this," you cannot be saved. So, there is no salvation until you come under the knife. That is their declaration (these men from Judea). Who are these men who came down from Judea? It says: Therefore, when Paul and Barnabas had no small dissension and dispute with them, they determined that Paul and Barnabas and certain others of them should go up to Jerusalem, to the apostles and elders, about this question (Acts 15:2). What question? Is there salvation prior to circumcision?

So, being sent on their way by the church, they passed through Phoenicia and Samaria, describing the conversion of the Gentiles; and they caused great joy to all the brethren. And when they had come to Jerusalem, they were received by the church and the apostles and the elders; and they reported all things that Elohim had done with them (Acts 15:3-4).

I like that right there. Not "that they had done," but "that Elohim had done with them." And their ultimate ruling in Acts was, "Now, give them some necessary things. They cannot be worshiping idols, committing harlotry and drinking blood, but the rest they can learn in the synagogues every Sabbath."

And so, their decision in Acts 15 was: Let the Spirit lead them, not sectarian men. That was their decision. And that is a decision we need to make today individually. Their attitude is, "Look what I have learned here. This is amazing stuff I have learned. Would you like to hear?" And the person may not see it, may not accept it. Okay, but that is Yahweh's Spirit, it is Yahweh's responsibility to convict. I plant the Word. He makes it grow, not me. Bondage is in being a sectarianistic, "you are not saved until" mindset.

To whom we did not yield submission even for an hour, that the truth of the gospel might continue with you (Gal 2:5).

For they bind heavy burdens, hard to bear, and lay [them] on men's shoulders; but they [themselves] will not move them with one of their fingers. But all their works they do to be seen by men (Matt 23:4–5).

For not even those who are circumcised keep the law, but they desire to have you circumcised that they may boast in your flesh (Gal 6:13).

In denominationalism, you must subscribe to certain beliefs before being accepted as a "church member." In other words, there are groups, and not all groups are like this, not all denominations are even like this, but some have this thing where, "Well, when you come to our church, you need to get re-baptized into our church."

Wait a minute, were they baptized in the name of the church or in the name of the Messiah? But you have to be re-baptized, and you have to subscribe to this list of understandings, these different things you have to believe and do.

And there is even one group that has a four-page long letter you have to read through and check off, and say, "Yeah, I believe all these things," before you can become a baptized believer in that congregation.

"Ah, well, they need to learn some things first. You are not a full-fledged member of our group until we train you. We have to teach you some things above and beyond repentance and faith in Messiah. You have to learn this, this, this, this, this."

Yahweh is in heaven. He is looking down upon all the people of the earth. He is not looking down, and saying, "Hmm, that denomination is saved. That one is not saved. That denomination is saved. That group over there, they are among the saved." He does not look at the world in terms of denominations like man does. No, Yahweh looks at the heart.

Your glorying [is] not good. Do you not know that a little leaven leavens the whole lump? (1 Cor 5:6). We are talking about the Feast of Unleavened Bread here. We have to get the leavening out. This is a time, my brothers and sisters, yes, we do have to make a division. Sometimes we do have to cut away the old leaven, but it has to be in clear cut, obvious sin like what was going on in the first century.

We can make a distinction here. One who is a divisive man, a sectarian. One who says, "I am in. I am among the chosen. You come up higher where I sit, and you will be with us." We need to have no part with that. We need to reject them after the first and second admonition. But you have to offer the admonition. Don't just reject them. Offer the admonition before you reject them. And they have to be dealt with in any congregation.

We have to have a repentant attitude. We have to have a heart that desires and pursues that path, that way—the Way, the Truth, and the Life. If we do not seek that way, if we do not have the way in the sense of Messiah dwelling in us, he is the one who saves us, not how much Law we have kept, not how many Sabbaths we have kept, not how many church meetings we have attended. Not how many Feasts we have gone to, not how long we have been in it, but that our heart would be completely yielded to the Father's will. We may not fully understand what the Father's will is for our life, but our heart is yielded. If we have that mentality, we are believers.

He looks down upon us. He has mercy on us. He knows that we do not understand his will completely, yet. But he meets us right where we are.

And so, the issue here is an issue of repentance. That is the real issue.

COVENANT OF SALT: YOU GOTTA SERVE SOMEBODY[4]

by Chris Suitt

As a believer in Yeshua, if you don't serve Jesus, your life will not only be unsatisfying, but it will also lose its meaning and purpose. You'll become what Jesus said happens to salt that is no longer salty, "Trampled by men." Why would anyone want to listen to you? We are to be salty, which in turn leads to being a light.

The first time this phrase is found is in Leviticus 2:13 where the order of the words is "salt of the covenant." The context of this passage is the grain offering, which was to have salt added to it. But the Spirit didn't stop with just the grain offerings. He had Moses write in the same verse that the Israelites were to "add salt to all your offerings."

The second usage, found in Numbers 18:19, is also in the context of offerings. This time, however, the word order has been changed to "covenant of salt." In Numbers 18, the L-RD tells Moses to instruct Aaron and the Levites that it is their responsibility to take care of the Tabernacle. Moses was also to let them know that "all the holy offerings the Israelites give Me I give to you and your sons as your portion and regular share." G-d was letting them know that he himself was going to provide for them through the offerings given by the people. "Whatever is set aside from the holy offerings the Israelites present to the L-RD I (G-d) give to you . . . It is an everlasting covenant of salt before the L-RD." The Kohenim were to serve G-d and trust him for their livelihoods.

The last time the phrase is found is in 2 Chronicles 13:5. In this particular passage the L-RD gave the kingship of Israel to David and his descendants forever through a "covenant of salt." Although the previous two usages are found in the context of offerings, this one is clearly devoid of them. Since the bible itself never directly defines the phrase in any of these passages, how does one discover what G-d is trying to tell us through them? Equally important, what does it mean to the believer in Yeshua today?

One scholar noted that, "salt had an enduring quality and therefore in the Middle East salt was used in ceremonies to seal an agreement. Hence, the idea may simply be that G-d's call upon the Kohenim and their service should endure, i.e., overcome all things." I believe this definition is heading in the right direction, but it doesn't go far enough as it is used in connection

4. Suitt, "Covenant of Salt."

with the House of David and the Israelites who presented the offerings. Could it be that the "covenant of salt" was all about a relationship with G-d based upon trust?

The people were to trust G-d by giving the salt that was put into their offering. Their G-d would provide for them and they were to give back out of love and obedience. The priests and Levites were to trust G-d by serving him without a land inheritance like their brothers. David and his sons were to trust G-d as the King and serve him, believing he would keep the throne moving through David's line long after David and his sons departed the scene.

When we break down the phrase into its component words and put them back together again, this is the truth I believe the L-RD is trying to convey in the phrase "covenant of salt:" He desires a relationship with his people based upon trust that is seen in their actions and, eventually, through a changed life.

The first word in the phrase, "covenant," is the Hebrew word "*běriyth*" (ברית). This word basically means an agreement or alliance between two parties where each party makes a pledge to keep their end of the bargain. The first time this word is found is in Genesis 6:18. Noah was to build the Ark and gather the animals. If Noah would fulfill his end of the bargain, G-d would get them safely through the coming storm. This took trust. If Noah did his part, would he trust G-d to do His part? The answer is given right after G-d writes up the contract. Noah "did everything just as G-d commanded him." Noah showed his trust in G-d through his actions of living out the words of the contract, or covenant.

Now, sometimes these agreements are applied to both parties, as previously mentioned; at other times it was totally conditional upon one party. This is seen in Genesis 9:9 when G-d made a deal with Noah to never destroy the earth again by water. The passage never says Noah had to do anything but trust his G-d to fulfill his word. Noah had just gotten off the wildest ride of his life! I believe G-d was calming Noah's nerves a little here. When Noah stepped off the boat he could have been thinking, "I sure hope I never have to go through that again." And G-d comes to Noah's rescue, "Relax Noah, it's over. Neither you nor your descendents will ever have to repeat this heart-racing experience." Still, what would it take? Trusting in G-d's word. Every time the skies started clouding up, Noah would need to remember G-d's word—no more floods. As he trusted G-d's word, peace would replace the anxiety. But first Noah had to trust.

Now let's consider the idea behind the Hebrew word for salt, "melach" (מלח), a noun that comes from the root word "malach" (מלח) which means to rub to pieces or pulverize, to disappear as dust, or to season or rub with salt.

Melach is primarily used for the Salt/Dead Sea (Gen 14:3; Num 34:3,12; Deut 3:17; Josh 3:16), which will one day be made fresh again (Eze 47:11). Keep something in mind: this body of water was once salty or dead, but will one day be made fresh or alive again.

What I find interesting about *melach*, however, is the first time it is used in the Bible. In Genesis 19:26 Lot's wife is turned into salt for looking back. Though the word for covenant is not used in this story, the angel had an agreement with Lot. The angel would only destroy Sodom and Gomorrah after Lot and his family was out of town and had safely reached the city of Zoar. What did Lot's wife do? She did not keep her agreement to "not look back." It appears that she left her heart in Sodom with the accompanying lifestyle she left behind. In her heart, she didn't want to leave and thus was judged for it when she was turned into salt, or disappeared as dust.

This idea of pulverizing something in order to scatter it to the wind is also seen in Judges 9:45 when Abimelech destroyed the city of Shechem and poured salt over it. In this story, the people of Shechem rebel against their leaders, Gideon's sons. The citizens of Shechem made Abimelech king, after which Abimelech wipes out every single son of Gideon, save one Jotham.

In order to right this wrong, G-d moves the citizens to rebel or break their agreement with Abimelech, who in turn wipes them out. Again, it is the same as Lot's wife. Just as she rebelled and paid the consequence for it, so did the city of Shechem.

Melach is not only associated with death, destruction, and judgment. It is also associated with the sacrificial system (Lev 2:13). According to Hebrews 9:1, 10:18, sacrifices pointed to the one who would take the punishment or the negative consequences of all our sinful actions (death, destruction, and judgment)—Yeshua. In him we find forgiveness and restoration to a relationship that was broken because we refused to trust our G-d and his way of living.

Continuing on, Exodus 30:34–38 uses *melach* in the process of making the Temple incense. David wrote in Psalm 141:2, "May my prayer be set before You like incense; may the lifting up of my hands be like the evening sacrifice," both of which (incense and sacrifice) had salt added to them. Is it possible that salt aids our worship to G-d? Could every act of faith or trust/covenant (1 Cor 10:31) be an act of salting our worship?

Paul, as a Jewish Rabbi, would have known the above Tenach passages. In fact, Paul uses Temple and sacrifice images quite often in his writings. So when he penned the words in Romans 12:1–2 that we are to offer our "bodies as living sacrifices, holy and pleasing to God," could he have been thinking of the salt added to all the sacrifices? Paul goes on to say that once we offer ourselves to G-d, we are to let him change our lives through changing our thinking, which in turn changes our behavior, glorifying and thus worshiping the G-d we say we love.

It's interesting that Revelation 8:3 uses this same imagery—incense on the golden altar in front of the veil between the Holies of Holies and the Most Holy Place, where the coals from the outside bronze sacrificial altar were laid and incense was poured on top of the burning coals causing smoke. Do our lives smell (both the offerings and the incense) good to our G-d?

But there is more! Ezekiel 16:6 states that Israel was not born with a right to be G-d's child. When they were born their cord was not cut, they were not washed with water, rubbed with *salt,* or wrapped in clothes. No, G-d took them and made them his. The context here is that Israel was still living like her parents, the Hittites and the Amorites, in full idolatry mode. They were still tied by an umbilical cord to their mother. In other words, their behavior hadn't changed! And if her umbilical cord was not cut, she would die when the placenta started discharging from the womb after birth. Again we discover that salt carries the idea of worshiping the one true G-d, the G-d of Abraham, Isaac, and Jacob, through Israel trusting their G-d by cutting her ties to her idolatrous parents/past. Israel needed to make a covenant of salt with their G-d to follow him and worship him alone.

The next two places where salt is used are also very insightful. In 2 Kings 2:20–21 salt was used to heal a body of water so it could be drinkable. Now think about this for a second. When salt is added to water, one gets salt water, not fresh. You might use salt water to gargle, but certainly not to drink. Now imagine what was going through the minds of those watching Elisha throw salt into their putrid water hole.

"Elisha, hold on! You're going to make the situation even worse! Are you sure the L-RD said to do this? It doesn't make sense, Elisha. Why would you waste valuable salt by throwing it into an already bad source of water? You're just throwing it away!"

Why would Elisha do it? Trust. After Elisha threw the salt into the water, it "became wholesome." They would have to trust their G-d enough to dip their hand into the water and draw it to their lips. Pouring salt must have seemed like a crazy thing to do to them. But when it comes to walking with our G-d, isn't this what it takes—going against the way we think to do what he tells us to do? This is the same idea behind Job 6:6 when Job makes the point that salt is added to tasteless food to make it worth eating. Again, isn't this just like our G-d to make something tasty out of two things that don't belong together? The question is, "Will we trust him?"

Furthermore, didn't it take trust to give up the salt in the first place? Where did the salt for the sacrifices come from? The incense? The healing of the water? It came from the Israelites. Look at it from their point of view. Salt contained the very elements necessary for their survival.

During the Tenach times, Israel was primarily an agricultural society. They worked out in the sun for a living, which brought on a good sweat. Because of this, they would need to replenish their bodies with sodium and chloride, of which salt is a good source. These two elements, along with potassium, are involved in everything you do from nerve impulse conduction to muscle contraction. If these three elements get out of balance in your system, you're not going to have a good day.

Now, here comes your G-d telling you that you must give him some of your salt. Would you trust him? Would you give your precious salt to Elisha to throw in your bad spring? Would you trust your G-d and add salt to all your sacrifices? This is why I believe G-d put the last usage of "covenant of salt" with the House of David. It ties the two ideas of salt and covenant together.

The Talmud says, "The world can get along without pepper, but it cannot get along without salt." (Yerushalmi Hora'yot 3:5) This tractate is referring to the 2 Chronicles 13:5 passage where G-d gave, "the kingship of Israel to David and his descendants forever by a covenant of salt." Treaties were sealed in salt. Covenants were based upon trust. Giving someone your salt was a sign of that trust. And G-d was making a treaty with David to have his children sit on his throne forever, no matter how good or bad they were!

So when we put the words "covenant" and "salt" back together, it stands for the idea of two parties making and keeping an agreement with each other based upon trust. The word "salt" gives us the truth that we should trust our G-d enough to live with and for him in our everyday lives.

Rosh Hodesh (Head of the Month)

In the everyday decisions we encounter, we are to sacrifice our way of living and thinking and trust his Word. He can make life come out of the dead areas of your life. He can turn an unsatisfying life into a tasty one. Where we were once alone, we can now communicate with the G-d of the universe. Instead of fear and anxiety, we can have peace.

This covenant of salt is all about who you are going to serve: God or Satan? Serve Satan and be judged, eventually die, and spend your eternity with him. Serve God and be saved, and taste goodness both now and forever.

I believe we find this same meaning carried over into the New Testament. In order to help us see this, we must use the Septuagint, the Greek translation of the Tenach, to follow our words forward. According to the Septuagint, the Hebrew word for salt ("*melach*") in Leviticus 2:23 becomes the Greek word "halas" (ἅλας). "Halas," or salt, is used in Matthew 5:13 where Jesus states that we are "the salt of the earth." Most Christian commentaries talk about salt as a preserving agent. As believers live for Yeshua, they slow down the decay of this planet. When believers are finally taken off the planet, the decay happens rapidly. As Jesus said in Matthew 24:21–22, if G-d didn't shorten the days of Jacob's trouble no one would survive the tremendous evil being unleashed.

As I came to understand the Tenach concept of the Covenant of Salt, it made me re-examine this passage again. I discovered that the immediate context of Jesus' "salt of the earth" statement is being persecuted for righteousness. He just got done telling those listening to him on the mountainside they would be blessed over and over again if they followed him. One of those blessings was persecution! If one lives for Yeshua as "the salt of the earth," one should expect to be insulted, persecuted, and falsely accused.

He continues this line of thinking in Luke 14:34–35. In this passage, Yeshua also uses salt in the context of counting the cost of being his disciple. He tells those listening to him that they must love him more than their family and their very life itself. Then after talking about calculating the cost of building a tower and going to war, he states that once salt loses its saltiness, it's not good for anything, even for fertilizer. It has no value whatsoever, so he tells his listeners to listen up. Living for him will not be a walk in the park. It will cost them something; so think about it before they begin the journey.

In Mark 9:42–50, Yeshua moves past counting the cost to actually living for him. Salt is now used in the context of living in such a way as to not stumble other believers ("little ones who *believe in Me* to sin"). He goes on to emphasize his point by saying, "If your foot causes you to sin, cut it off." Notice Jesus changed the subject of the sentence from just anyone to you. Believers in Yeshua are to live in such a way that their lives will affect others in a positive manner.

After saying this, Yeshua then makes the statement "everyone will be salted with fire." Wow! Will you trust your G-d enough to live his way even during the trials of life? Jesus finishes his discourse in Mark 9 with this, "Have salt (ἅλας/melach) in yourselves, and be at peace with each other."

It's a sign a believer trusts and is living for Yeshua in their everyday lives. Jesus said there would be three distinguishing marks of those who call themselves his disciples. One, they would love each other (John 13:34–35). Two, they would bear the fruit of a changed life (John 15:1–8). And three, they would live in unity (John 17:20–23). We are to be salted so others will know he is G-d! We are to trust our G-d enough to live his way seven days a week. When we do, the world will know we are his.

And guess what happens then? It's the point of Jesus' next statement in Matthew 5:14, "you are the light of the world." A light doesn't necessarily draw attention to itself. Its real purpose is to shine on something else so it can be seen. As we live a salty life, one based upon trust, people will see Yeshua in us and hopefully want a relationship with him.

This is what the Spirit had written in Colossians 4:6, "Let your conversation be always full of grace, seasoned with *salt,* so you know how to give an answer to everyone." The context is sharing the gospel of Yeshua.

As we offer our bodies as living sacrifices (salt was added) you are dying to self and living for G-d. How is this seen? Trusting G-d's Word (basis of a covenant) and allowing him to change your life on a daily basis ("transformed by the renewing of your mind").

BEIT MIDRASH

A House of Study

Many peoples will go and say, "Come, let's go up to the mountain of Adonai, to the house of the God of Ya`akov! He will teach us about his ways, and we will walk in his paths." For out of Tziyon will go forth Torah, the word of Adonai from Yerushalayim.

(ISA 2:3)

5

Shavu'ot (Pentecost)

Salvation comes from the Jews

(JOHN 4:22)

Creation began with earth immersed in water. The next immersion to bring out a family from humanity was Noah's flood. Then a people were chosen and instructed to wash and separate themselves to be immersed in the Torah being given on Mount Sinai (Exod 19:10).

The giving of the Torah when God came down and showed his glory is celebrated seven weeks after Pesach in the festival of Shavu'ot (Pentecost). "This is a permanent regulation through all your generations, no matter where you live" (Lev 23:21). The Counting of the Omer, the counting of the days, connects Pesach that freed the people from physical bondage with the anticipation for Shavu'ot that redeemed the people spiritually. Shavu'ot is a holiday marking the end of spring and begins the summer of growth and the harvest. An offering of two loaves of bread, considered a presentation of firstfruits, was made at the temple.

Jesus took this journey, going to the plains of Jericho where he healed a blind man, and looking up to Jerusalem, coming not to offer a sacrifice but to be the sacrifice. Jerusalem was crowded with visitors when Jesus celebrated Shavu'ot to commemorate the fruits that were harvested and brought to the temple. He revered the Temple, calling it his Father's house.

From the time of Solomon to the time the Romans destroyed the second Temple in 70 AD, the Temple was the only place where sacrifices and certain rituals could be performed. Herod constructed the oldest layers of the western wall between 20 BC and 19 BC as the Second Temple was being rebuilt. The remains of the wall are 187-feet high and extend 1,600 feet at the hill where it was built, called the Kotel, or Wailing Wall. The wall is as near to the site of the original sanctuary as people can touch today, built with precision out of massive rocks of limestone, facing a large plaza where Jewish people have come on pilgrimages to pray daily. Many come on Tisha B'Av, the Fast of the Ninth of Av, a day of mourning to acknowledge the tragedies that the Jewish people have suffered. *Should I weep in the fifth month [Av], separating myself, as I have done these so many years?* (Zech 7:3). It is a time forced between the narrow straits when danger presses in on both sides (Lam 1:3).

Summer marks the times of the destruction of both the first and second temples. The first Crusade began on August 15, 1096, killing 10,000 Jews in its first month in France and the Rhineland. On July 18, 1290, Jews were forced to leave England, and forced to leave France on July 22, 1306. They were expelled from Spain on July 31, 1492. The Holocaust and upheaval in Europe began when Germany entered World War I on August 2, 1914.

Distress has fallen on Israel's history many times at this time of year, but the promise of God is a glorious future to keep in sight. Joseph reflected these times when he waited in a prison thinking of the vision he had been given in a dream. Though his feet were shackled, his neck clasped in iron, God had sent Joseph ahead of the famine.

Like Joseph, Israel was sent ahead of the nations to secure salvation for the world. Shavu'ot is the festival of the day of the Torah being given, coming at the waxing moon in a time of growth and blessing that would bless all peoples. It was during this holiday that the Ruach Hakodesh, the Spirit of Holiness, was given to the Jews gathered again in the upper room on a warm late spring day.

In that room 120 Jews celebrating the Shavu'ot after the Passover of Jesus' crucifixion suddenly heard a sound like a violent wind filling the entire house. The sound was breath coming from heaven. In John 20, Jesus had explained that he would ascend to his Father and then breathe out the spirit of truth on his talmidin to guide them and announce events of the future so they would have power to be his witnesses to the very ends of earth. When the apostles heard the sound of the wind, they would have recognized the meaning of wind that Jesus had told them about. In Genesis, Adam's body was formed, but he had no life in him until God breathed into him. In Acts 2 there was another body, the body of the church that was lifeless in that it wasn't able to impact the world. Jesus breathed his spirit into this body, filling them from heaven. They heard the wind and then they saw a pillar of fire that separated into tongues of flames that came to rest on each of them. It was a visible fire that does not burn, like the burning bush Moses saw in Exodus 3 when God revealed his presence.

Moses believed in God at the time he saw the fire on the bush. He had learned the faith, but was settled down in the desert without purpose in God. Then God came down with the fire and told Moses that he hears the cries of his people and anoints Moses for the mission. The church in Acts believed Jesus, but they were not yet advancing Jesus in the world. Fifteen-hundred years after Moses, the fire again appeared. The men and women who knew the life-giving spirit of God had come upon them became able to accomplish God's mission beyond their own limitations. Each one was anointed to participate so others could be freed to come and worship God through our wilderness time as we wait the return of Jesus.

The annointing brought back communication between the diversity of peoples. In Genesis 11 man's rebellions against God were escalating. They decided to build the tower of Babel to represent their own ambitions. God came down and broke the intent by introducing confusion into the human race by dividing their communities into language groups. In Acts 2, God came down and this time gathered the people from every nation as they heard the apostles speaking their own language. God entrusted his message to come into the world through the Hebrew language but now they spoke of God in other languages they had never learned as the Spirit enabled them.

At the feast of Shavu'at, Kefa (Peter) stood up, prophesied, and explained that Adonai had raised Yeshua from the dead and he was the Messiah. The crowd was stung in their hearts and asked, "What shall we do?" Kefa told them to be immersed into forgiveness through Yeshua and receive the gift of the Ruach HaKodesh. "For the promise is for you, for your children, and for those far away—as many as ADONAI our God may call!" (Acts 2:39). There were 3,000 believers coming to truth during the feast of Shavu'ot. Another 5,000 were added in chapter five. At Shavu'ot everything that divided them fades away.

The immersion of the Torah declared that God would dwell with the Jews. The immersion of the Holy Spirit now said that God will dwell in his people. Even when the Temple was again destroyed, God still had a dwelling place among the people. The Jews welcomed the non-Jews into the covenant of God and the name of Yeshua began to spread through the world. The Italians would pronounce his name as Gesù in their language. The Mandarin Chinese would say Yēsū. To the Albanian he is Jezusi and to the Fijians he is Jisu. Romanians called him Isus and the Irish and Scottish people called him Ìosa. Swahili pronounced his name Yesu. The Vietnamese say Giêsu and the Welsh spoke his name Iesu. A massive surge of indigenous identity honoring ancestors through preserving original language brought about renewed recognition of the name Jesus was born with in his own culture—Yeshua. A worldview that recognized that God intends for each community of people to have a sense of belonging unique to their heritages began changing the way missions identified with their work.

The day of Pentecost teaches that this is what Jesus is doing as the Spirit of God flows like a river through the generations. "I will pour out My Spirit in those days" (Joel 2:29) and gather in a people, not to homogenize them into one nation, but to be children from every nation.

Shavu'ot (Pentecost)

SHAVUOT, THE FEAST OF WEEKS[1]

by Rabbi Loren Jacobs

As many within Messianic Judaism seek to reclaim a biblically-based lifestyle, we are rediscovering the importance of the biblical holidays. The holidays bring order to our lives. Through them we pace ourselves; on a weekly basis, as on Shabbat we enter into God's perfect rest, and seasonally, as we mark our place during the year. God appointed these times to help us stay in touch with him, with our Jewish roots, with our ancestors, with our families, and with the eternal purposes that God has for his people.

During Passover we offered to God the firstfruits of the barley harvest. That was symbolic of Yeshua's resurrection. Fifty days later we returned to Jerusalem to offer the firstfruits of the wheat harvest. The harvest was extended from the barley to the wheat. Fifty days after Yeshua rose from death his first Jewish followers were gathered together in Jerusalem and the Spirit that raised him from the dead was poured out on his first disciples. The Messianic Community, the Body of Messiah, came into being. God's harvest was extended to more of humanity. That happened on the day of Shavuot, in fulfillment of Shavuot.

One name for Shavuot is "Atzeret shel Pesach," the completion of Passover. The coming of the Ruach HaKodesh (the Holy Spirit) completes the work of the Passover Lamb's death on the cross. The Spirit of God indwelling us gives us the power we need to overcome our tendency to evil and completes the work of salvation.

Though marvelous in its own right, God knew that the death of the Passover Lamb and the redemption from sin was not enough. Just as the cycle of the Spring festivals would be incomplete without Shavuot, the work of salvation is not complete until a man's sin nature has been dealt with and the power to overcome it has been granted. Therefore Shavuot is a time when we thank God for his gracious provisions in our life, both for his material provision, the firstfruits of the wheat harvest, and for his spiritual provision—the Holy Spirit which brought a rich harvest among those first Messianic Jews in Jerusalem.

The Megillah of Ruth is one of the texts that is read on this holiday. Megillat Ruth is about the harvest, but also included the message of gathering Gentiles into the commonwealth of Israel. Ruth, a Gentile, joins herself

1. Jacobs, "Shavuot, the Feast of Weeks."

to the Jewish people. Speaking to Naomi she says, "Your people will be my people, your God will be my God." Ruth later marries a Jewish man by the name of Boaz, and from that union, in the third generation, came King David, and through him, King Yeshua.

On Shavuot, the High Priest waved two loaves of wheat bread made with leaven. By waving the two loaves of wheat bread, Israel's High Priest was praying: "Lord, thank you for extending the harvest to the wheat. We offer up to you the first fruits, the beginning, the best of this crop, and Lord, we ask you to bring in the rest of the harvest throughout the year."

These two loaves of bread can be understood to be symbolic of the two peoples that make up the Messianic Community. In Romans 11, Rabbi Paul talks about the Olive Tree of salvation and blessing made up of the original branches, the Jewish people. Then wild olive branches, the Gentiles were grafted into the olive tree. It could be that the two loaves represent the original branches, the Jewish people, and the wild branches, the gentiles that we grafted into the Olive Tree. Each one is incomplete without the other. The Jewish loaf needs the Gentile loaf to be complete, and the Gentile loaf needs the Jewish branch to be complete.

At the time the Law was given (Exod 32:19–29), 3,000 Jewish men were put to death because their actions were now deemed "illegal." They were weak, and the giving of the Torah alone didn't strengthen them. But the Spirit gives us a new desire to fulfill God's Torah and the power to do so. The Spirit gives us power to live, power to witness, power to please God, and power to have victory over the world, the flesh and the devil. It is hardly coincidental that, on the day of Shavuot when the Spirit was given, 3,000 Jewish men were empowered to witness to Yeshua and his resurrection life.

The Spirit also baptizes us into the body of Messiah. He joins us, both to the Father and to one another. Believers in Yeshua all share the same Spirit. We have a new unity and oneness with each other. We are no longer alone, but are part of an eternal community. The Spirit assures us of eternal life and that we truly belong to God. "You have received a spirit of adoption as sons by which we cry out, "Abba! Father!" The Spirit himself bears witness that we are children of God" (Rom 8:15–16). Do you have that inner witness of the Spirit that God is your Father, and that you are truly one of his?

In one sense, Yeshua's ministry to the disciples was incomplete. There was more that he wanted to teach them, but they weren't able to understand it at that point. But the Spirit is like Yeshua, the Master Teacher, the chief

Shavu'ot (Pentecost)

Rabbi, the Guide, who illumines us and enables us to understand and apply Yeshua's teachings, his miracles, his unique birth, death, and resurrection to our lives.

The Spirit guides us, leads us, and teaches us all things. He brings to remembrance all the things that Yeshua taught, and guides us into all the truth. Further, he even transforms us into the image of Yeshua. He convicts us when we sin. He corrects us when we err. The Spirit also has a prophetic teaching ministry. He can and will reveal the future to God's people. He does this through the Scriptures and through New Testament prophets and revelation. The Holy Spirit is like clothing. "I am sending forth the promise of My Father upon you; you are to stay in the city until you are clothed with power from on high" (Luke 24:49). The Holy Spirit covers and protects us. He clothes us with God's divine power and wisdom from on high.

The Hebrew word for Spirit, Ruach, can be translated as wind (John 3:8, Acts 2:1–2). On the day of Shavuot the coming of the Spirit was accompanied by the sound of a violent rushing wind. Like wind his work may be not be visible, but the results certainly are. We can't see the Spirit, but we can easily see the effect of his transforming work in people's lives. And the Spirit's work is Sovereign. He touches whom he will and gives gifts as he sees fit. You can no more govern the moving of the Spirit than you can control the wind. Wind can be powerful, like a tornado or hurricane. It can carve exquisite structures out of solid rock. It will destroy those structures that oppose it, but not destroy those things that bend and yield to it. Allow the Spirit to have his way in your life, and he will make something beautiful of it. Wind can also be a cool, refreshing breeze. The Holy Spirit is like a cool breeze that comforts and refreshes; and just as the wind is from the heavens, so the new birth is from above. The Holy Spirit is like breath. Ruach is also translated breath. Without breath we die. God's Spirit, his "Breath" gives us life. We have life and tremendous intimacy with God due to his indwelling Spirit. Our breath is close to us. God's Ruach is as close to us as our own breath.

Shavuot is a time for feasting. We eat the festive loaves after the service, especially with milk dishes such as blintzes. One tradition states that after receiving the Torah, the Jewish people were too hungry to wait for meat to be cooked, so we simply made a dairy meal instead. According to another rabbinic interpretation, dairy foods are eaten at this time because the Bible compares the Torah to milk and honey. Other Shavuot customs include reading the Ten Commandments. This reminds us of the giving of the Law.

Beit Midrash: A House of Study

It is customary to decorate the home and synagogue with green plants and flowers. Grass grew on Mount Sinai, and the green plants remind us of the trimming used to adorn the people's baskets of first fruits that they gave to the Priests. It also reminds us that the Torah is a tree of life. As a tree provides fruit and nourishment, so does the Word of God.

Shavu'ot (Pentecost)

GENTILES IN THE MESSIANIC MOVEMENT[2]

by Dr. Bruce H. Stokes

Messianic Jews struggle with the question of religious expression. Are they Israelites? Do they identify with Israel by observance of the Torah covenant? How do they observe Torah? To what extent can the history of Rabbinic Judaism inform that observance? And how do primitive Gentile Christians and Messianic Gentiles participate in that process without confusing the issues? How can the five groups of Gentiles in the Messianic movement play a productive role? The Book of Ephesians declares that God has made Jews and Gentiles into one new man in the Messiah. This new man is neither Jew nor Gentile. This must be understood. The major error that must be avoided is to make Jews into Gentiles and Gentiles into Jews. Jews and Gentiles must remain authentic in their own identity or the unity of the body of the Messiah cannot be seen. The Body of the Messiah must show a unity-Jew and Gentile united by one Lord, one faith, one baptism.

The Gentile Role

Gentile believers have been grafted into the root of Israel. They are no longer strangers or aliens, but fellow citizens with the saints (Eph 2:19). But they are not Jews. Paul gives a clear and significant guideline when he tells those called in circumcision to "not seek to be uncircumcised, and those who were called in uncircumcision to not become circumcised" (1 Cor 7:18). The Gentiles in the movement have at least two Biblical roles to play in the Body of the Messiah. One is to identify with Israel. Another is to provoke unbelieving Israel to envy.

Identifying With Israel

The primary role of Gentiles in the Body of the Messiah is to identify with Israel. To identify with Israel is different from identifying as Israel. As Gentiles, our struggle must be to show that we have been brought into a relationship with the God of Abraham without being a replacement of Israel. But there is a danger here. If Gentiles lose their own identity and

---

2. Stokes, "Gentiles in the Messianic Movement."

become copy-cat Jews, or if the differences become hidden, the purpose for the body to be both Jew and Gentile in one new man will be lost.

Provoking Israel

A second, significant role for Gentiles is to provoke Israel to envy. Indeed, this role is used as an explanation for God's bringing Gentiles to salvation (Rom 11:11). This role involves an authenticity in obedience to the commands of God that makes unbelieving Israel envious that she is not participating in what is rightfully hers. Too often Christians and Messianic Gentiles provoke Israel to apathy (by not having significance in what we do) or to anger (by preaching replacement theology or acting like Jews). The role of the Gentile in the body must include an attractiveness in obedience that provokes unbelieving Jews to envy. Therefore, I believe that we can best fulfill this role by Torah observance that is consistent with the Torah commands but is distinctive with regard to Jews and Gentiles.

For example, the Jerusalem council in Acts 15 makes it clear that Gentiles are to abstain from blood. This command was not an option for Gentiles. It was an essential item. As a Gentile, when I observe this command in the presence of unbelieving Jews, or discuss my observance in their presence, I am often engaged in conversations regarding Judaism, Messiah, and other related topics. Another example is the Sabbath. In our home, we celebrate the Sabbath in a manner similar, but not identical, to the traditions of Judaism. All of the Torah's commands and elements of Judaism are present. But the form is distinct. Our Jewish neighbors who know of our observance sometimes express a desire to have what is rightfully theirs. They see an authenticity in what we do that reminds them of childhood Sabbaths at home. We are often asked why we observe the Sabbath. We respond with the text from Isaiah 56:6–8 which tells of the Gentiles who keep the Sabbath. Jewish and Gentile believers must work together to protect our separate identities while becoming one new man in the Body of the Messiah.

One Additional Role

One additional role is incumbent upon us because of the present lack of Messianic understanding within the historic church. Messianic Gentiles must make the movement understandable to Christians who have no idea of the Jewish roots of their faith. If Gentiles are absorbed into the movement and lose their Gentile distinctions, the historical church, like unbelieving Israel, will ignore us or become angered. There is a great need for authentic Gentile believers to identify with Messianic Jews and assist the remnant of Israel in being a light unto the Gentiles.

Getting Started

So what are we to do? I believe the first step is a recognition that Jews and Gentiles each have a role to play in the Body of the Messiah and the Messianic movement. The roles are distinct as we are distinct. We need authentic Jewish believers who observe the Torah in a manner that fulfills their role to identify as Israel and to be a light unto the Gentiles. We also need authentic Gentiles who understand their distinctive role to identify with Israel and to provoke unbelieving Israel to envy. We must also address the groups of Gentiles already participating in the movement who fall into the five categories of involvement described earlier. How do they grow from their present participation into the role as described here? The "wanna-be" problem must be addressed with sensitivity and candor. While it may be the smallest group, it is the one that has the most potential to cause serious damage. The problem is either a misunderstanding of what being Jewish means in the plan of God, or an identity conflict within the person. It is not a biblical doctrine that God calls some Gentiles to be Jewish believers. The group of Gentiles who enjoy the Jewish flavor of the Messianic worship style must be careful to not confuse ethnicity with Torah commandments. The Torah addresses the Jew as a light to the Gentiles. This is accomplished by observance of the Torah commands. There is nothing wrong with the Hebrew dancing and singing, but this is not the essence of what God is doing in reviving Judah. I would suggest a serious attempt to learn as much as possible about Jewish expression but make the focus of your study the Torah commands related to Gentiles.

To those who believe that the commands of God are identical to the Jew and the Gentile, the danger of Judaizing becomes a real concern. This group must find a way to establish a form of non-Jewish religiosity that embodies the essence of the Torah commands without simply copying everything that Jews do.

The Gentile married to a Messianic Jew is in a unique situation that must be addressed with great care. In the case of a Gentile man married to a Jewish woman, it is clear that maintaining the identity of the children is a significant goal. There is also a Biblical precedent for a woman married to a Jewish man to be absorbed into the community of Israel (Ruth). While conversion of these individuals is a possibility, and I am open on this question, it adds to the problem of acceptance by the larger Jewish community. Regardless of the disposition of the Gentile spouse, if the children are raised in an authentic observant manner, their identity will be questioned less by themselves and the larger Jewish community.

To those who, like myself, have been involved in the Messianic movement because of a desire to see an authentic Messianic Judaism that can be presented to the Jewish community with integrity, there is a need to be informed in the content and observance of Torah so that Messianic Judaism is encouraged to grow in authentic observance. We also need to maintain our obedience to Torah commands in a manner that is clearly Biblical-but-distinct from Jewish expression so that we identify with Israel but not as Israel.

In addition, we must reintroduce the Torah basis for the New Covenant among our Gentile brethren so that they will embrace observant Messianic Jews as their brethren and move toward the unity that God intended.

Shavu'ot (Pentecost)

WHY ALL CHRISTIANS SHOULD CELEBRATE PENTECOST[3]

by Pastor Ross Clark

It has been said that there are two kinds of responses made by people. Some people say why? Some people say why not?

I would like you to reconsider your preconceived attitudes about this day. Let's look at its relevance to us as Christian believers.

This day is the founding day of the church of Jesus/Yeshua (his Hebrew name).

The Holy Spirit came in a mighty way just as Jesus had predicted he would.

Some people might say that this belongs to the Old Testament past, but why then would God choose this special day to inaugurate his church? The bible says that the feast days are "The LORD's feasts"—they belong to God himself.

We have to be very careful to extradite ourselves from anti-Jewish bias that was unfortunately prevalent in the early Roman Church and in the days of the early church fathers.

The truth is that God made this day as the day associated with the final great harvest of the Jewish year. In a prophetic way it symbolizes the great final harvest of the world. And so it was that the world harvest of souls actually starts on this day!

Remember it was Jesus himself who told the disciples to wait in Jerusalem and not go out into the world to evangelize until they were endued with the Holy Spirit anointing that happened on the appointed day of Pentecost.

We are not trying to earn bonus points from God by celebrating this day, rather we are celebrating where the church comes from and its roots in God's plan going back thousands of years.

I can personally say that I have been blessed having celebrated Pentecost or Shavuot (the Feast of Weeks) for twelve years now. It is a time to rejoice at what God has done.

So my question again is, why not celebrate this event?

But you may say, this is not something that you are familiar with. Well it's time to move out of the familiar box, to something that is God given. Pentecost is not a man-made tradition, as are so many things that have been adopted by the church over the years. Instead it is biblical.

---

3. Clark, "Why All Christians."

Now we remember and celebrate God coming down gloriously to start something new on the earth. Jesus promises in John 14:18 where Jesus says "I will not leave you as orphans, but I will come to you." Later in John 14:26 Jesus promised, "But the counselor, the Holy Spirit, who the Father will send in my name, will teach you all things." It happened! Halleluyah.

How can we celebrate this day?

In our assembly we use the theme of Pentecost as the topic for the closest day of worship. The theme is seen in the scriptures in the Tanach (Old Testament). Leviticus 23 describes the seven yearly feasts with feast of Weeks/Shavuot as the 4th feast. The New Testament scripture describing the fulfillment of this feast is Acts 1:4 where Jesus told the disciples to wait in Jerusalem and Acts 2:1 where the day of Pentecost outpouring starts the church age. On this day we encourage the people to open their hearts afresh to God's Holy Spirit, to be revived, to take this opportunity to be renewed.

Afterwards we have a special feast of food brought by the members for fellowship together. There is no legalism in this for us, just a blessing. But we are not judging anyone who doesn't do it as Col 2:16 says, "Therefore do not let anyone judge you by what you eat or drink or with regard to a religious festival, a new moon celebration or a Sabbath day."

You should try it too. Make it your tradition, you won't be disappointed. This is part of recovering the good things from the Jewish roots of our faith. You will be blessed!

Shavu'ot (Pentecost)

INCONVENIENT TRUTHS: THE ONE NEW MAN[4]

by Rabbi Dr. Stuart Dauermann

In a day when Jews and Gentiles who believe in Yeshua are thinking new thoughts about their relationship to one another, one of the concepts often mentioned is the One New Man of Ephesians, Chapter Two. However this concept is often misunderstood and the label misapplied. This posting seeks to clarify the term's intended meaning and the range of acceptable applications, showing how and why it is an Inconvenient Truth.

By way of definition then:

The One New Man of Ephesians, Chapter Two, names a unity of two distinct communal realities living together not in uniformity, but rather in peace and mutual blessing. These two distinct realities are Yeshua believing Jews, living as Yeshua's people in Torah-based Jewish piety, and the Church from among the nations, serving him in their own contexts, apart from the requirements of Jewish piety.

When we speak of a unity, we do not mean a unanimity or a uniformity. While unanimity means everyone in agreement, and uniformity means everyone being the same, unity preserves diverse viewpoints and different styles as they live together in mutual respect and harmony. The miracle of the One New Man is that those who are and who remain essentially different are enabled to live together reconciled, in love and mutual blessing.

This was of course something new in the purposes of God. Formerly, if one wanted to become part of the people of God, one had to join with the Jewish community and accommodate to Jewish life, to convert and become a Jew. With the coming of Messiah, that is no longer necessary: Gentiles become part of the people of God through the Messiah who loved them and gave himself for them just he did for the people of Israel. Somehow, God wills that his people be diverse.

New Testament scholar Mark Nanos traces this to the Shema, "Hear Israel, the LORD our God is One LORD." The same God is Lord over all nations, not just the Jewish nation. If one had to become a Jew to become part of the people of God, then God would in effect be the Lord of only one nation—but this detracts from his glory. He is the Lord of all nations, and it is crucial that those of his people from other nations besides Israel honor him within the context of their own cultures, rather than imagining that

---

4. Dauermann, "Inconvenient Truths."

the Jewish culture is the only one he is prepared to bless and which may pay him due honor.

Paul insisted that Gentile Yeshua believers should not become circumcised and seek to keep the Law, not because the Law has been abolished, or because it is bad in some way, but because obedience to God's Torah is not God's call and will for Gentiles, who nevertheless become part of the people of God through Christ alone. This is also why James expected Paul to model Jewish piety, but said he required no such thing of the Gentiles who have believed (Acts 21:24–25), and this is why the Jerusalem Council disputed long ("much debate," Acts 15:6) before deciding that Gentiles did not need to be circumcised, and be required to keep the Torah. The dispute would never have happened if the Jewish Yeshua believers had themselves given up Torah observance, or if they viewed it merely as one option among many. No! The question motivating the dispute at the Jerusalem Council was this: "Do the Gentiles need to keep Torah the same way we do?" (see Acts 15:1–21).

Rather than superseding the Jewish people, the church from among the nations joins with them as part of the Commonwealth of Israel. Only in this way can the "dividing wall of hostility"—which supersessionism maintains—be removed. Gentiles are no longer categorically outsiders to the community of God's people, but neither do they supplant Israel. However if Gentiles were required to obey Torah and live as Jews, one would be perpetuating their categorical exclusion as Gentiles. And it is a major component of the good news as proclaimed by Paul that this former categorical exclusion is over and done with through the work of Messiah!

The balance of unity and diversity in the One New Man is further highlighted in Ephesians 3:6, where Paul says "Gentiles are fellow heirs and fellow members of the body, and fellow partakers of the promise in Christ Jesus through the gospel." The terms "fellow heirs, fellow members, and fellow partakers" require another communal reality with whom the Gentiles are joined, and that other partner is the community of Messianic Jews living in solidarity with wider Israel. It is only as Messianic Jews embrace this calling that their communities become the communal joining point whereby the Church from among the nations is joined to the Commonwealth of Israel.

Together, the Messianic Jewish Remnant, living in the context of Jewish community and covenant faithfulness, and the church from among the nations, constitute the One New Man. But this One New Man is created

Shavu'ot (Pentecost)

not through abolishing differences, but rather through transcending them, bringing unity (not uniformity) between two communities that yet remain, and must remain, essentially distinct.

Although many translations have trouble expressing this nuance, the Weymouth New Testament gets it right:

> His design was to unite the two sections of humanity in Himself so as to form one new man, thus effecting peace, and to reconcile Jews and Gentiles in one body to God, by means of His cross–slaying by it their mutual enmity. So He came and proclaimed good news of peace to you who were so far away, and peace to those who were near; because it is through Him that Jews and Gentiles alike have access through one Spirit to the Father.

Commentator Markus Barth helps us understand the flow of Paul's argument:

> The new man is "one . . . out of the two." . . . The new creation is not an annihilation or replacement of the first creation but the glorification of God's work . . . Ephesians alone calls God's covenant partner "one new man" and emphasizes that this man consists of two, that is, of Jews and Gentiles . . . The incorporation of the Gentiles into Israel and the formation of one people consisting of Jews and Gentiles certainly does not mean that the Gentiles must become Jews, or the Jews Gentiles! (Markus Barth, Ephesians 1–3).

We might add, and Barth goes on to explain, that Paul is not arguing for some sort of third race, as the late second century Epistle to Diognetus suggested, whereby in the One New Man Jews are no longer Jews nor Gentiles, but both constitute a third race. Precisely the opposite! The glory of God is that he enables those who are and who remain essentially distinct to live together as the people of God, reconciled not only to him but to each other, without either community sacrificing its intrinsic distinctiveness.

Why then is the One New Man an Inconvenient Truth?

The One New Man is an Inconvenient Truth because it reminds us that God intends that Jewish Yeshua believers live in the context of Jewish life and community, integrated with the Jewish world rather than being assimilated into the Gentile or Church worlds. Although in some cases due to factors such as intermarriage, this priority cannot and even should not be honored, nevertheless that would be an exception to the rule which affirms that those who call themselves Jews should be living communally Jewish

Torah observant lives. This comes as an inconvenience to most of us who have accommodated ourselves to secularism or to other ecclesial contexts.

The One New Man is an Inconvenient Truth because it states that God intends that Gentile Yeshua believers should normally live in the context of their own cultures, sanctifying these by offering them up for the honor of God in the power of the Spirit, through Yeshua the Messiah. However, aren't there many who needlessly abandon their contexts of origin imagining that the Messianic Jewish context alone is the place where God may be acceptably served?

The One New Man is an Inconvenient Truth because it exposes how inappropriate our imagining that the Church, from among the nations, is somehow inferior to the Messianic Jewish Movement or Jewish life. On the contrary, both communal entities are essential aspects of the One New Man, and neither the Messiah nor the Father are properly honored apart from this One New Man comprised both of Messianic Jews honoring Yeshua within Jewish life amidst other Jews, and Gentiles glorifying God by redeeming their own cultural contexts for the glory of God.

The One New Man is an Inconvenient Truth because it challenges both the Messianic Jewish component and the church component to confront their attitudes and behavior toward each another. The church from among the nations must not look down upon the Messianic Jewish context, nor the Messianic Jewish context look down upon the church. Much work remains to be done in this area!

The One New Man is an Inconvenient Truth because it calls us to examine whether our congregations are maintaining and advancing proper distinctives, or rather ignoring and obscuring them. This is a most Inconvenient Truth for the Messianic Jewish Movement to contemplate. Many will become enraged by the question. But eventually even such a bright flashlight, having first painfully blinded one, in the end illumines the way forward. It is not that the Messianic Jewish movement must be free of Gentiles! It is that the movement fails to serve its purpose when Jewish life is not seriously pursued on the one hand, and the distinctions between calling of the Seed of Jacob and that of others preserved. To the extent that the Messianic Jewish movement creates a *tertium quid* in its congregations or in its entirety, it fails to preserve and advance these One New Man distinctives, but instead works against them.

Finally, we must not imagine that the One New Man is a model for each congregation. The term is not meant to apply to the micro-context (each congregation being a manifestation of the One New Man), but rather to the macro-context (the people of God taken as a whole are the One New Man with these two varieties of congregations represented).

Although the community of God's people throughout the ages needs to be comprised of Jews living in covenantal community with other Jews and Gentiles glorifying God through the sanctification of their own cultures, this does not mean that every congregation must have some Jews as well as Gentiles to be legitimate. If that were the case, then every Lutheran congregation comprised entirely of Northern European Gentiles and every Korean Congregation comprised entirely of Koreans, with Torah observant Jews absent in both cases, would be substandard and out of compliance with the will of God! Obviously, this is not Paul's message.

6

Yeshua HaMashiach (Jesus the Messiah)

You were estranged from the national life of Israel. You were foreigners to the covenants embodying God's promise. You were in this world without hope and without God. But now, you who were once far off have been brought near through the shedding of the Messiah's blood

(Eph 2:12–13)

The last companion of Jesus, the thief on the cross, did nothing to earn his salvation. In the last heartbeats of his life, it was too late for that. All he had to give was recognition of the son of the father of lights and for that he was brought with him to heaven. "Therefore it is my judgment that we do not trouble those who are turning to God from among the Gentiles. For it seemed good to the Holy Spirit and to us to lay upon you no greater burden than that you abstain from things sacrificed to idols and from blood and from things strangled and from fornication. If you keep yourselves free from such things, you will do well" (Acts 15:11, 19, 28, 29).

After Israel was gathered to become a nation, the other nations continued living under the covenant God made with Noah. Humanity was prohibited from establishing idols. They were forbidden from immoral sexual relations (Gen 2:24), stealing (Gen 2:16–17), eating flesh from live animals (Gen 9:3–4), blasphemy (Gen 3:17, and murder in Gen 9:6). They would be held responsible if they took the life of another human. They would each establish legal systems to maintain justice (Gen 9:5).

Yeshua HaMashiach (Jesus the Messiah)

After the Tower of Babel, the people had scattered and became the beginnings of nations. They each followed the times of the moon in their own ways, giving thanks in their own languages in relationship with the lands, the water, and foods that sustained them. They lived in the cycle of seasons with times of planting and times of harvest, ways to mourn and gatherings to celebrate. The people of Noah's eldest son, Shem, would occupy the northwest of Lydia, parts of Assyria, Persia, and the Arabian peninsula with their own language. Noah also blessed his son Japheth, and through him the Gentiles are thought to have been peopled. Abraham would descend from Shem, and through him Israel would be chosen to be the messenger of light.

God chose Israel's tribe of Judah for the lineage of Messiah. Judah's mother, Leah, was a woman of unrelenting sorrow. Her husband Jacob loved her sister Rachel. Her father had manipulated her into a marriage Jacob did not want with her, yet it would be Leah revered as the matrilineal line of the Messiah.

After her first son, Reuben, was born, she said "surely now my husband will love me." Her second son, Simeon, was birthed and she said, "God heard that I am hated so he's given me this child too." The next son was Levi and she continued to wish, saying, "now my husband will join himself to me." Not until her fourth son, Judah, was born, did she go beyond her anguish and say, "This time I praise God." God, drawn to the lonely and the grief-stricken, heard Leah's heartbreak and transformed her voice to lift in praise.

Although the dysfunction all around her did not change for Leah, her heart had changed to give thanks to God even in the agony of her struggles. Generations later Paul and Silas would be beaten and imprisoned in a dark cold prison surrounded by the worst of people. But they decided to sing and to give thanks in all circumstance. Because of praise, the message of hope in God opened prison doors and the jailer was brought to repent with his entire family.

The message that a Jew had died for them was brought to the nations, born from a people of praise. God who had created everyone is the Yahveh Elohim Abba, the eternal God the Father drawing people from every language to worship in thirst for more of God's love. Paul answered the question of cultural differences saying we are to do nothing that would offend each other, but each people will answer to God for what they did right and what they did wrong.

Beit Midrash: A House of Study

WHY SHOULDN'T A CHRISTIAN TRAIN JEWISH PEOPLE TO SAY "JESUS CHRIST"?[1]

by Shira Sorko-Ram

The whole idea of Messiah, the Anointed One, is Jewish in origin. Yeshua said, " . . . Salvation is from the Jews" (John 4:22). No other people or religion has ever conceived of a son-redeemer sent by his father to save the world.

Furthermore, when Yeshua was born, the angel told Miriam (Mary) to call the child "Yeshua." As the boy grew, he answered to the name Yeshua—not the English equivalent of Jesus nor that of any other language. There was literally no other name except Yeshua!

So when the first Jewish believers went into non-Jewish regions, they had to bring these Jewish concepts and Hebrew names into a pagan world. One tool that greatly helped them was the Septuagint–the Greek translation of the Old Testament. The Septuagint was used by the Greek-speaking Jewish community scattered throughout the Hellenistic world.

The Septuagint translators sometimes encountered a word that, being rooted in a Jewish concept, had no Greek equivalent. For example, they "greekized" *Maschiach* (found in Daniel) in order to make it more familiar to the Greek-speaking Jews and easier to pronounce. They decided to literally translate the concept "Anointed One" into its Greek equivalent. The word that was created was *Christos*—a "native" Greek word that was understood by non-Hebrew speakers.

As Jewish believers like Paul began to spread the Good News to the pagan Greek world, they keenly felt the necessity to greekize many more Hebrew words which were based on Jewish concepts.

God is a universal God, they reasoned, and Yeshua is the Lamb of God who came to take away the sin of the world. Why then cause a stumbling block by preserving Hebrew-sounding names? Why not convert them to words which had meaning and were familiar to Greek people?

The same process obviously occurred with the Hebrew name "Yeshua." It certainly didn't sound Greek, didn't look Greek, and was probably difficult for Greek-speakers to pronounce. Certain disciples of Yeshua, who were crying out to God for the souls of the pagan men and women, felt it expedient to allow these people to easily and comfortably pronounce Yeshua's name. Result: "Iesous."

1. Ibid.

Yeshua HaMashiach (Jesus the Messiah)

In this greekized form, therefore, Iesous Christos was preached throughout the known world. The name of the Messiah was further adapted into various languages beyond the Greek-speaking communities. Jesus Christ in English, Jesu Christo in Spanish, and Jesus Christus in German, are but a few of the adaptations found in the western languages alone. Other examples of English adaptations include: Lord (Adonai), Passover (Pesach), Mosaic Law or Pentateuch (Torah), Sabbath, a day of rest (Shabbat).

Never in their wildest dreams, however, did early Jewish evangelists consider preaching to the Jews about Iesous Christos. This was against the principle and spirit by which they adapted Yeshua's name to the Gentile languages. The early believers understood that the truths of the Gospel are to be preached in the vernacular, the language and the understanding of the person being reached.

So also you, unless you utter by the tongue speech that is clear, how will it be known what is spoken? For you will be speaking into the air (1 Cor 14:9).

Even though the context of this Scripture is completely different, the principle of speaking to be understood applies to every situation.

Those who truly love the Jewish people will find a way to "speak clearly" so as not to speak into the air. They will find a way to communicate rather than expect the unsaved Jew to "understand" the real and original meaning of greekized words. Gentilized words may be precious to the one witnessing, but they are usually meaningless, or worse yet, may arouse negative associations within the Jewish heart.

If men have adapted the name of Yeshua HaMashiach to hundreds of languages, should not the Jewish people be free to use the original name of the King of the Jews? In being all things to all men, you will be following in the footsteps of Paul, the Jewish Apostle to the Gentiles, and other like-minded early ambassadors.

Beit Midrash: A House of Study

ANY OTHER NAME WOULD STILL BE A JEW[2]

by Patricia Pason

Why does it matter if Rabbi Sha'ul is known by his Hebrew name Sha'ul, if he is called exclusively by the name of Paul, or if we refer to him, as he is in some denominations, as St. Paul? Unfortunately there is a false belief common among many believers that associate this Pharisee, who was known as Saul, had a name change to Paul. It is thought by many to be indicative of his "conversion" from Judaism to Christianity. I would like to address the issue of this imagined name change to dispel the notion that Sha'ul adopted a new name in order to rid himself of his Jewish status.

Many will wholeheartedly refer to him as Paul, the one formerly known as Saul. Without a doubt, most English Biblical interpretations refer to this learned Jewish Pharisee who wrote a great amount of the Messianic Writings as Paul. There are many who will not hesitate to inform us that he was Saul (not even using the proper Hebraic transliteration of Sha'ul) who became Paul after he was knocked off his horse and became a Christian. Choosing not to dispute whether or not there was a horse present or that he remained fully Jewish after his encounter with the Jewish Messiah, I will investigate what his name really was. Was there a reason he would have had to change his name to follow Yeshua, or did he remain known as Sha'ul?

From Scripture we do know that Sha'ul was a Roman citizen. Acts 22:27–28 tells us:

> The commander came and said to him, "Tell me, are you a Roman?" And he said "Yes." The commander answered, "I acquired this citizenship with a large sum of money." And Sha'ul said, "But I was actually born a citizen."

Sha'ul was born in Tarsus, and he came from the tribe of Benjamin. He said of himself, "I am a Jew, born in Tarsus of Cilicia, but brought up in this city." (Acts 22:3a) He was a Jew and he was a Roman citizen.

During this time of the Roman Republic, a Roman citizen's name had to consist of three parts, and Rabbi Sha'ul's was no different. The first part of the name was the *praenomen*, or the person's given name. Sha'ul would have been his given Hebrew name. The *nomen* was what the second part of the name was called. This name would have been granted to the person of

---

2. Pason, "Rabbi Sha'ul by Any Other Name."

non-Italian descent, the privilege of taking to his own name, an emperor's name, or a Roman general's name. A name that might have reflected perhaps some service to a general or emperor would have been ideal and an honor. It was believed that Sha'ul's father may have served under General Paulus. Sha'ul's *nomen* was Paulus. This name would have been bestowed upon him at birth, not at a new birth experience or a conversion from Judaism to Christianity. The last part of the name was the *cognomen*, which would have been reflective of the person's place of birth, in this case Tarsus. Hence, we can know that this Jewish Rabbi had the names of Sha'ul Paulus of Tarsus.

Contrary to popular opinion, Sha'ul of Tarsus, did not "convert" to a new faith called Christianity, but remained fully Jewish; keeping the name that was bestowed upon him early in his life. There was no conversion or renaming for Sha'ul or for any of the other tens of thousands of Jewish followers of Yeshua in the first century.

A CHALLENGE TO BELIEVERS[3]

by Geoff Davenport

As believers we say that Messiah Yeshua has Lordship over our lives, but do we merely quote what he said or do we do what he did. There are three levels we can go to: 1) We accept him as Saviour—a little bit like an insurance policy in case anything goes wrong, nice and reassuring to have but does it completely change your lifestyle, or behaviour? 2) We accept him as Lord, a deeper step involving obedience and doing things for him, even changing your lifestyle sometimes to great extremes, involving harsh treatment of your "Flesh" and travelling to far off places "In his name" or cutting ourselves off from "the world" or, 3) We accept God as our Abba, our Father and desire a daily relationship and doing things with him. Having two way conversations, rather than just delivering shopping lists. When he talks, we listen, then we obey and do what he says. We recognize his calm loving voice. We accept his non-critical advice and act on it with his help and guidance.

If we feel condemned it's not from Abba, because condemnation only produces shame and guilt. If we feel convicted then we know it's from him because conviction produces repentance, which produces forgiveness, which comes with the way and ability to change the behaviour.

Over and over again Yeshua told us to relate to The Father just as he did. In the Garden when Adam walked with him and talked to him, relationship was the key. Walking with the Father and one another, that's why Yeshua came, to restore the relationship personally. His time on Earth was totally devoted to living, eating, sharing, loving, and instructing those around him. He didn't live in a palace. He didn't start a franchise operation. He didn't establish a university or Bible College. He didn't raise an army. He simply stated only what he heard from the father and practiced what he preached! He didn't start a new religion. He simply confirmed what Yahveh has been saying from the beginning and told us how to put it into practice. He asked for followers not climbers (no hierarchy).

We Messianic believers (Jew and Gentile) need to get real. Yeshua said we would be known as his Talmidim (Disciples) by our love for one another. Yet I hear people constantly telling me that this is unworkable, that unconditional love is absolutely impossible. Well Yeshua proved by his

---

3. Davenport, "A Challenge to Believers."

actions that not only is it possible, but the unconditional aspect is what actually makes it possible. We are told in Yoch 15:8 that The Father is glorified in us bearing much fruit, that this is how we prove we are his Talmidim (Disciples).

How much fruit have you produced? What does it look and taste like? Yeshua said you will know them by their fruit! Many groups are claiming they are oranges but look and taste like lemons. If people say one thing but produce bad fruit, they are NOT grafted into Yeshua! Only his cultivated Vine can produce good fruit. Life in all its fullness produces growth and healthy changes. If they are not present then Yeshua is not part of it. If the fruit doesn't look like him, taste like him or sound like him then it is not from him. Yeshua said I AM the vine, Father is the Gardener, and we are the branches, and unless we are grafted into this vine and abiding in it we can produce nothing worthwhile.

Loving one another is not a nice suggestion, it is a COMMAND, and it means loving the not nice people as well as the nice people Yeshua chose us when we were still not nice! He didn't choose us because of our past, but in spite of it focusing only on our future in him. So it was for the first century Messianic believers and so it must be today. We need to back up our claims in the Messiah, in obedience to YHVH through the power of his Ruach Ha Kodesh (Holy Spirit), by allowing him to create reality in our lives that will show "The Way" not just imitate it.

The Body of Messiah is one new man, Jew and Gentile, united in him with neither able to say, "I have no need of you" but rather building ourselves up in love as servants fit for his service. We are the only bridge between two communities separated by 2,000 years of hate, mistrust, persecution, rejection, and lies. Healing can only come through a people absolutely surrendered to serving an unconditionally loving father, doing everything his way, wherever, whenever, and however he chooses. Total obedience! Yeshua Ha Maschiach said, "I AM-The Way-The Truth-The Life. No one comes to the Father but by Me!"

WHY JEWS DON'T LIKE EVANGELICALS[4]

by David Lazarus

The most popular religious group in America is the Jews. Jews, however, do not particularly care for their Evangelical admirers. That is the conclusion of a massive survey published this summer by the Pew Research Center. The study asked Americans of every race, religion, and political persuasion how they felt about a variety of religious groups. Of all the different groups, Jews ranked highest (63 degrees on the warm survey meter) and second were Catholics (62). Muslims finished dead last (a cold 40).

Of the people who like the Jews, Evangelicals warm the most to the tribe (a hot 69). Those warm fuzzy feelings, however, are not mutual. American Jews scored white Anglo-Saxon Evangelicals a frigid 34 degrees. Only atheists disliked the Evangelicals more than the Jews (29)! These chilly Jewish attitudes towards Evangelicals should be a wake up call for those trying so hard to win the Jews over with Christian love and support.

To begin with, Jews don't like to be evangelized, and Evangelicals are, well, Evangelical. Jews do not like missionaries either, especially when Christians try to tell them that their 4000-year-old Jewish religion is outdated. As the People of the Book who gave birth to Christianity, many Jews feel disrespected when Christians try to convert them without any sensitivity to their Jewish traditions. Modern Jews in general don't like being told how to live (who does?) and feel uneasy with excessive Evangelical proselytizing. In spite of all the good will and support, Evangelical Christians shower on Israel (and even that is waning), Jews remain suspicious.

One might assume that the strong support by Evangelicals towards Israel (that is waning as well) would impress Jews. But that is not always the case. Under Republican George Bush's administration there were thirteen Jewish Senators and twenty-seven Jewish Representatives. All of them were Democrats except for Joe Liberman (Independent Ct.), Bernard Sanders (Independent Vt.) and Eric Cantor (R-Va.). The current Congress has exactly the same number of Jewish Congressmen except for Joe Liberman who is no longer in Congress. So while some American Jews are turning to the Republican party which is strongly favored by Evangelicals, the overwhelming base of Jewish involvement in politics remains with the more liberal Democrats.

---

4. Lazarus, "Why Jews Don't Like Evangelicals."

Yeshua HaMashiach (Jesus the Messiah)

The most common argument is that Jewish people prefer a liberal agenda where the rights of minorities are protected. Many Jews still fear conservative Christian politics that could lead to Jewish and other minorities being excluded or even persecuted by a strong, white, Anglo-Saxon, Protestant majority—a phenomenon that occurred not that long ago in Europe. The strict adherence by Evangelicals to standardized theological doctrines also tends to intimidate Jews who have experienced Inquisition, Crusades, and Pogroms because of dogmatic Christian beliefs.

In some quarters Evangelical support for Messianic Jews contributes to the negative views Jews hold toward Evangelicals. While the return of a growing number of Jewish people to faith in Jesus the Messiah is challenging traditional Jewish beliefs, Evangelical support for Messianics is only a minor factor in determining negative Jewish attitudes towards Evangelicals. Some Evangelical groups try to avoid Messianics hoping to build closer relationships with Jews, but according to this important Pew survey, they are still being left out in the cold.

There is a lot of concern among local Christians that Evangelicals are turning against Israel and that is disturbing on many levels. But the fact that Jews do not like Evangelicals is even more critical for the preaching of the Gospel. That is why it is so important that all of us continue to work together to help show our people that Jesus is the Jewish Messiah for the Jewish people.

7

Talmidim (Disciples)

A<small>DONAI</small>-Tzva'ot says, When that time comes, ten men will take hold—speaking all the languages of the nations—will grab hold of the cloak of a Jew and say, "We want to go with you, because we have heard that God is with you."
(Z<small>ECH</small>. 8:23).

The world after the Messiah comes is often referred to in Jewish literature as Olam Ha-Ba, the World to Come, also known as the Messianic Age. The renewal of the world comes only with the renewal of Israel. The Jewish people will return from exile among the nations and come home to Israel (Isa 11:11–12; Jer 23:8, 30:3; Hos 3:4–5). They will again celebrate the Jubilee. In the Olam Ha-Ba, Adonai, the God of Israel, will be recognized by the entire world as the only true God. To a Jew, the world beyond Israel is referred to as "*galut*," dispersion, exile, or captivity.

The Messiah was anticipated to be a great political leader descended from King David (Jer 23:5) and well-versed in the law of Moses (Isa 11:2–5). An inspiring leader, he was prophesied to be "a priest forever, in the order of Melchizedek." (Heb 7:17). The name Melchizedek means "king of righteousness" and "king of salem (peace)." Abram had settled near the Dead Sea. His nephew, Lot, had gone south to Sodom. The king of Sodom had made an alliance with three other kings. The king of Elam had made an alliance with four other kings and after thrashing the king of Sodom and the others, Elam's alliance ran to the north. A messenger was sent to

Talmidim (Disciples)

tell Abram that Lot and all his possessions were being taken away. Abram called together 318 of his men and went after the kings. Catching up with them in Dan, they gave chase and brought back Lot, the other people, and the plunder.

When he returned the king of Sodom came out to meet him in the valley of Shevah, the king's valley. Then Melchizedek brought out bread and wine. Without beginning of days and no genealogy, he seems to have come out of eternity. The meeting of the three men in the valley is a defining moment of Abram's life. The king of Sodom represents darkness. The priest represents Jesus, one whose name indicates that righteousness is followed by peace.

For all of time the Father of Israel would tell Israel to return to righteousness and he would bring them back to peace. He will establish Israel's government and it will be the center of all government for both Jews and Gentiles (Isa 2:2–4; 11:10; 42:1). The redemption is dependent on the Messiah (Isa 11:11–12). Instead of instructing his talmidim to become masters who gather others to themselves, Jesus told them the son of God alone would be master to all who trusted him and in him they were all brothers.

The Hebrew word talmid means student. The plural is talmidim. In ancient times the sages all had their own talmidim who denied the pursuit of their own lives to commit to learning everything their revered teacher would teach. They would follow him everywhere, eat and celebrate the Shabbat with their rabbi, and pray and fast along with him. The talmid reflected his rabbi and passed down oral teachings so that the Torah would be preserved.

Before ascending to heaven, Jesus instructed his talmidim to make people from all nations into talmidim, immersing them in the Holy Spirit (Matt 18:19–20). They were appointed to be a kingdom of priests to the entire world.

Jesus wore a tallit, a prayer shawl, when he said blessings over the meals he shared with his disciples, during morning worship, the Shabbat, and reading the Torah. "Tal" means "dew," alluding to the morning dew that brought manna in the wilderness (Exod 16:13–4), the unity of brothers that is compared to dew (Ps 133:3), and the favor of God (Prov 19:12).

The tallit identifies the Jewish men as a distinct people set apart to serve God in a world surrounding them with pagan thinking. The tzitzits, fringes, on the tallit are a commandment of God, with a blue cord on each tassel to remember all the commands of God (Num 15:37). Tzitzits are sewn on the four corners of a garment. When David cut off the edge of Saul's robe, he was symbolically speaking of death. A fringe is cut off a man's tallit when his life and work are at an end. A woman was healed who reached out to the hem of Yeshua's garment and touched the tzitzit. Jesus would have wound the four threads on each of the corners thirty-nine times in tradition to correspond numerically with the words, "Adonai Echad," the Lord is One.

Talmidim (Disciples)

THE JEWISHNESS OF THE GOSPELS[1]

by Rabbi Frank Lowinger

Sadly, only a small minority truly understand the origins and context of authentic biblical faith. Sadder still is the majority's less than eager willingness to make inquiry. Thus, established norms remain, perpetuating the dissemination of tainted history and mythical theology.

And so we grapple with such dichotomies as grace and law, faith and works, Old Testament and New Testament. We are confronted with giving answer to issues of Replacement Theology, accusations that we are "under the law," anti-Semitism in the church, and the overall wanton rejection of anything perceived to be Jewish (i.e. the Sabbath and festivals). These represent a brief compilation of the collective problems resultant to forsaking and forgetting one's point of origin. There has been a noticeable shift from having a "debt of gratitude" to a hands-off attitude.

That this topic is even discussed is evidence of a major paradigm shift. How would first-century Messianic Judaism receive a topic like this? It would be laughable. In all likelihood they would ask, "Are you serious?" Of course the gospel is Jewish, what else can it be? Logically, what would the Gentile world know of a gospel? How could the Gentile world even relate to a personal God who dies for the sins of his people?

The New Covenant, or more appropriately, the Messianic Writings are not a foray into Gentile Christianity. Its subject matter, its content, concepts, and context are all richly rooted in Judaism. If there can be a Jewish practice that embraces Yeshua, then it must be demonstrated that Yeshua is not a Gentile. What better a place to start than Matthew 1:1, "The book of the genealogy of Yeshua HaMashiach, the son of David, the son of Abraham."

With fondness and awe, I treasure the memory of my first endeavor to read the New Covenant. In those early morning hours, in the winter of 1974, as I sat in a state of inebriation, God was setting me on course for a life changing experience.

Matt 1:1 was the "hook" that had drawn me in. Never before was I able to equate Yeshua (Jesus) to anything Jewish.

This opening text of the Messianic Writings establishes a very critical link. The Messianic Writings do not appear out of a vacuum, but are directly traced to the covenants of promise God has made with the Jewish people.

1. Lowinger, "The Jewishness of the Gospels."

Who is David? Who is Abraham? In the Greek world (except for Diaspora Jews) these would be names without content. In the Jewish world, the reference is specific and overflowing with meaning. Woven into this text are the Patriarchal covenants along with the promise of a Davidic Kingdom that would be without end.

While the Messianic Writings are written in Greek, the content, context, and concepts are not. Not a single word of Matthew 1:1 is independent of the prevailing, pre-existing, cultural, and spiritual heritage of Israel. This verse is a Hebrew phrase given in a Greek format.

Yeshua's name is an excellent case in point. His name is not Greek. "Iesous" is a transliteration of the Hebrew "Yeshua" or "Joshua" meaning "God is my salvation."(2) And "Christos" is not Jesus' surname, but a title; the "Anointed One." This too draws its meaning from the Hebrew Scriptures. Logically speaking, what would the Greek world know of a "Messiah?" Further, how could they relate to other Hebrew concepts such as "repentance," "atonement," or even the love of God? Yes, even (agape) love! If "agape" is truly of Greek origin, then to which god would it refer? Zeus? Bacchus? Artemis? Or Venus? Again, this was not a Greek concept.

The Jewishness of the Gospel is readily observed in the central role of Israel in God's redemptive purposes. The B'rit Hadashah (New Covenant) is made "with the house of Israel and with the house of Judah" (Jer 31:31). There is no prophetic record of God making a covenant with the church. The commonwealth of Israel forms the context of the redemption of all people. Yeshua died and will return as "THE KING OF THE JEWS." In his resurrection, at the end of the age, he will be seen as "the Lion from the tribe of Judah, the root of David" (Rev 5:5). His kingdom's reign will be from the earth's capital—Jerusalem. The Messiah's glorious return will be prompted by "all the nations coming against Jerusalem" (Zech 12:2-4, 14:2-4). In that day he will come against all who have raised their hand against his people. Why would he have an interest in such a small minority? Especially a minority who, (like the Messiah himself) is despised and rejected by men (Isa 53:3)? Simply because "the gifts and the calling of God are irrevocable" (Rom 11:29). The covenants of promise through Abraham and his seed are without contingency, they are unconditional.

After his resurrection, Yeshua appeared to the talmidim (disciples) and continued in teaching them from the Law, the Writings, and the Prophets. In these teachings he explained how all the Messianic prophecies were about him. There are many details worthy of consideration. First, Tanach

Talmidim (Disciples)

(Hebrew canon) was the exclusive teaching material for sound doctrine and authority. That being the case, any further revelation had to be measured and weighed in accordance with Tanach. If any writing or prophecy did not line up to Tanach, it was deemed false. Thus, the New Covenant canon had to be in alignment with the Hebrew Scriptures. The Hebrew Scriptures can stand on their own, not so the Messianic Writings. They had to be aligned with what had already been written.

Secondly, the talmidim ask Yeshua, "Lord, is it at this time You are restoring the Kingdom to Israel?" (Acts 1:6). Yeshua does not disavow the restoration of the kingdom to Israel. He confirms it. He says, "It is not for you to know times or epochs which the Father has fixed by His own authority." In other words, the Father has fixed a date for restoration but it is not for you to know. Logically, only something that has already been, can be restored. The Kehillah (assembly of new believers) was something new, born after Shavuot (Pentecost).

The Jewishness of the Gospel is not difficult to prove. Its main characters and authors, when viewed from their Jewish background, shed light not readily seen in the twenty-first century. Sha'ul (Paul) says it well when he asks: "Then what advantage has the Jew? Or what is the benefit of circumcision? Great in every respect. First of all, that they were entrusted with the oracles of God" (Rom 3:1–2). He expands on this by saying of his own kinsmen that they "are Israelites, to whom belongs the adoption as sons and the glory and the covenants and the giving of the Law and the temple service and the promises, whose are the fathers, and from whom is the Messiah."

David Stern observes: Even if one is to accept the false premise of Replacement Theology that the Jews are no longer God's people, this would not change the fact that Christianity is Jewish. To try to understand it differently can only distort God's message.

Lastly, the B'rit Hadashah presents the Gentile world being grafted into a Jewish olive tree. Thus, the admonition—"remember that it is not you who supports the root, but the root supports you" (Rom 11:19). Sha'ul would also adequately describe the condition of the Gentile world before and after Messiah:

"Therefore remember that formerly you, the Gentiles in the flesh; who are called 'Uncircumcision' by what is called the 'Circumcision' which is performed in the flesh by human hands—remember that at that time you were separate from Messiah, excluded from the commonwealth of Israel, and strangers to the covenants of promise, having no hope and without God in the world. But now in Messiah Yeshua you who once were far off have been brought near by the blood of Messiah" (Eph 2:11–13). In this we find fulfillment of the Abrahamic covenant. It is through Abraham that "all the families of the earth shall be blessed" (Gen 12:3).

The Gospel may be Jewish, but it is all inclusive. "But as many as received Him, to them He gave the right to become children of God, even to those who believe in His name" (John 1:12).

Conversion is an issue that periodically makes its way into Messianic Jewish dialogue. I am personally of the conviction that there is no need for conversions. Those who have joined themselves to the L-rd are "grafted into" the commonwealth of Israel. They are "no longer strangers and aliens," but are "fellow citizens." They have a heavenly citizenship, a dual-citizenship and have no need of a passport and visa.

It is my fervent prayer and desire to see all come to recognize and embrace the "Jewishness of the Gospel"—"to the Jew first" (Rom 1:16).

For everything that was written in the past was written to teach us, so that through endurance and the encouragement of the Scriptures we might have hope (Rom 15:4).

Talmidim (Disciples)

A CHALLENGE TO BELIEVERS[2]

by Geoff Davenport

Will the real Jewish and Gentile Messiah please stand up. The Egyptians worshipped numerous gods, the Greeks an unknown god, the Romans Zeus and many others, including Caesar himself, the Mesopotamians Sin or Nana the moon god. Many groups today worship thousands of gods. But only one is the creator of the universe, the creator of Man. Yahveh Elohim the God of Avraham, Yitz'chak and Ya'akov. Yud Hay Vav Hay, or Yesterday, Today, and Eternal.

So Yeshua's question was simple and direct; and the answer defined him and his role. "Who do men say that I am?" The right question is crucial if you want the right answer, but today many are asking the wrong questions and getting all the wrong answers. So what is the answer? Is he the Greek gentile baby "Iesous" celebrated at the Roman Mardi Gras on December 25th, or maybe the Roman crucified Italian Jesus still celebrated as hanging from their Pagan cross? Or is he the subordinate son of the Queen of heaven? Is he just another subservient prophet acknowledged in the Koran? A deluded troublesome Rabbi in whose name the Jews have been persecuted for 2,000 years and accused of deicide (Murdering God)?

Who do you say that he is? His own Talmidim answered his question by repeating rumours spread around the city, saying, some say you are Yochanan the immerser, and others Eliyahu, still others, one of the prophets. So he pinned Kefa down, asking him directly, but who do you say that I am? His Ruach inspired answer? Mashiach (Messiah).

Pontius Pilate declared him King of the Jews with a sign placed above his head on the stake. He declared himself to be the son of man. A voice from heaven declared that, "this is my beloved son." But what does Torah say? In Yesha'yahu and Mattiyahu he is the servant who will establish justice on the Earth, describing him as not well formed or especially handsome, despised and avoided, a man of sorrow acquainted with grief, wounded for our crimes, crushed for our sins, Immanu'el (God with us).

In Micah and Mattityahu he is the King, the hereditary ruler of Israel, the Cohen Ha Gadol (High Priest), the prophesied promised Messiah, a kinsman redeemer whose origins are far in the past, at the creation of the beginning of time. In Tehillim (Psalms) and Mattiyahu and Acts he is the

---

2. Davenport, "A Challenge to Believers."

redeemer of mankind, the rejected cornerstone. Throughout the Tanakh and the B'rit Hadashah he is the second Adam, our Advocate, the Living Vine, Heavens Bread, Mankind's Shepherd, our counselor, the first and last, Lord of Lords, King of Kings, Resurrection and life, restorer, The Way-The Truth-The Life, the gateway, Shepherd, Lamb, Rose of Sharron, Light, Living Torah/Word, Comforter, Master, Rabbi, Natzrati, Carpenters son, Bright morning star, Emmanuel, Messiah, Kinsmen Redeemer, Yeshua ben Yosef, Son of God, Teacher, Lord of Shabbat and so many other descriptions.

And yet we still come back to that direct personal question, who do you say that I am? Am I just an insurance policy tucked away for a rainy day? A handy ATM you can go to only when you want something?

Or is he that deceased skinny Italian guy portrayed on thousands of crosses hanging on walls and around countless people's necks? To most he is the tiny baby in the cow shed that started the whole Christ mass present industry, the "reason for the season" (unfortunately it's the wrong season at the wrong time of year).

Or perhaps he is who he says he is—Yeshua (My Redemption) Ha Maschiach, the only procreated son of Yahveh Elohim, a Jewish man born in Beit Lechem, (House of Bread), a direct descendant of King David, who sits on his throne to fulfill Yahveh's promise. Our kinsman redeemer who became the Pesach Lamb sacrificed on our behalf, interceding on for us before the throne. A bridegroom who is preparing a place for us in his Abba's Kingdom and will return for his betrothed, his future bride at the end of time. Then he will take his rightful place with us here on Earth in Jerusalem ruling the nations from the new temple in the New Jerusalem.

We are his body here on Earth, the grafted and re-grafted branches of his olive tree, his appointed ambassadors representing his Kingdom by portraying and living his lifestyle, his teaching, his principles, as we walk and talk with him minute by minute in a daily intimate relationship as we listen to his answers and carry them out.

Is he the one and only way to a restored relationship with a loving Abba? Is he the firstborn among many brothers? Our cornerstone, our firm foundation, our healer, the one who will wipe away every tear from our eyes? The one who opens the eyes of the blind, makes the lame walk, removes the burden of oppression and sets us free from lies and corruption? The Author and Editor of our trust, the beginning and the end of every question and answer? Someone who defines Unconditional love? How? Because he is love! (read 1 Cor 13:1–13).

Talmidim (Disciples)

In the beginning Abba walked in the garden with Adam but then sin came and corrupted the Earth. Since then Abba has had to find ways of interacting with us that wouldn't overwhelm or destroy us. He simply cannot come to us face to face while sin reigns. We wouldn't survive the encounter. But in Yeshua we have a solution. Yeshua isn't the loving one and Yahveh the distant, harsh judgmental one. They are one and the same, same nature, same forgiveness, same righteousness, same love. Yeshua said if you have seen me you have seen the Father (not physically, but spiritually because Yahveh is spirit).

So again Selah. Who do you say that he is? How do you interact with him? What kind of ongoing relationship do you have with him? Is he an occasional visitor? A frequent visitor? An invited resident? Or do you just visit him once a week at "His house?" Does he go to work or school or shopping with you? Do you invite him on trips and holidays? Have you introduced him to your family, friends, and neighbours? Do you share your most intimate thoughts and dreams and desires with each other?

Your answers to this will define who he really is to you, and will reflect him to others who know you. Of course some will reject him and say he is something different, a historical figure, and not agree with my definitions, but my answer to them is always the same, "You don't know him, really know him the way I do. You only know about him through myths and legends that are untrue." Then I introduce them to the real person, not some fictional character or so called celeb, maligned and misquoted like a story in some women's gossip magazine who because they don't know the truth have to make the story up as they go along.

So who and what do men say that he is? Whatever they have been taught and seen in the lives of those who say they are his followers and earthly representatives. Talmid, it's way overdue to set the record straight and introduce the real Jewish Messiah, Yeshua, to a confused, broken, desperate, and hurting world as he really is—Emanu'el, God with us, the promised Messiah, the provider of everlasting life and forgiveness from sin, who sets the prisoners, Jew and non-Jew. completely free from sin and slavery and straight into the arms of a patiently waiting, loving Abba.

WHAT IS THE ROLE OF THE CHURCH?[3]

Shalom Messianic Congregation Northern Ireland

Ephesians 2:11–14 indicates that Israel and the Jews (we) were chosen, but Gentiles (you) were also included. The church is related to Israel and partakers of the covenants, promises, and hopes, but we have not been called to replace them. Our relationship is as "grafted in" (Rom 11:17); "brought near" (Eph 2:13); "Abraham's offspring" (by faith) (Rom 4:16); "heirs" to Abraham's promise as adopted sons (Gal 3:29) and "partakers" (Rom 15:27). To the world, the church is called to . . . preach the Gospel to all nations and make disciples (Matt 28:19–20); to love the Lord our God with all our heart, soul, mind, and strength; and to love our neighbour as ourselves (Mark 12:30–31). To the Jewish people, we are called to show God's love "for the sake of the Patriarchs" (Rom 11:28), for without them we would not have had God's Word or our Saviour who was a Jew from Israel. We are to show God's mercy (Rom 11:31). We are to give our material gifts to help them (Rom 15:27). We are to pray for them and for Israel (Ps 122:6). We are to be watchman on the walls to protect them (Isa 62:6,7). We are to help with the aliyah (immigration) to Israel and the building up of Zion (Isa 60:9–11; Jer 16:14–16; Isa 49:22–23).

According to Romans 11, we are TWO DISTINCT GROUPS, both grafted into the same tree, which are the covenants and promises given to Israel; grounded in the same root, the Messiah; drinking of the same sap, God's Holy Spirit. We do not hold up the tree, but the tree us, and we are forbidden from boasting against or being arrogant to God's covenant people the Jews (Rom 11:17–18).

What Happens When the Church Replaces Israel?

1. The Church becomes arrogant and self-centred.
2. It boasts against the Jews and Israel.
3. It devalues the role of Israel or has no role for Israel at all. These attitudes result in anti-semitism in word and in deed.

---

3. Shalom Messianic Congregation, "What is the Role of the Church?"

4. Without a place for Israel and the Jewish people today, you cannot explain the Bible prophecies, especially the very specific ones being fulfilled today. Many New Testament passages do not make sense when the Jewish people are replaced by the church.

5. You can lose the significance of the Jewish Scriptures (the Tanach) for today. Many Christians boast of being a New Testament (NT) Christian or a NT church as in the Book of Acts. However, the early church was not the New Testament, which did not get codified until the fourth century, but rather the Hebrew Scriptures.

6. You can lose Hebraic/Judaic context of the New Testament, which teaches us more about Yeshua and how to become better disciples.

7. The church loses out on the opportunity to participate in God's plan and prophecy for the church, Israel, and the world today.

What Happens When the Church Relates to Israel?

1. The church takes its proper role in God's redemptive plan for the world, appreciating God's ongoing covenant relationship and love for Israel and the Jewish people.

2. We can see the consistency of God's redemptive plan from Genesis to Revelation as an ongoing complementary process, not as disconnected snapshots.

3. We show love and honour for God's covenant people, not contempt.

4. We value the Hebrew Scriptures and New Testament as equally inspired and significant for the church today.

5. Bible prophecy makes sense for today and offers opportunities for involvement in God's plan for Israel.

6. We become better disciples of Yeshua as we are able to appreciate the Hebraic/Judaic roots that fill in the definitions, concepts, words and events in the New Testament that are otherwise obscured. Why? Many were not explained by the Jewish writers of the New Testament, because they did not feel the need to fill in all the details that were already explained in the Tanach.

Had the church understood this very clear message from the beginning, then the sad legacy of anti-Semitic hatred from the church may have been avoided. The error of Replacement Theology is like a cancer in the church that has not only caused it to violate God's Word concerning the Jewish people and Israel, but it made us into instruments of hate, not love, in God's Name. Yet, it is not too late to change our ways and rightly relate to the Jewish people and Israel today. Not only do we need to learn and do for ourselves, but we need to teach others so as to counteract the historical error that has been fostered in the church for nearly 2,000 years. Thank God, he is a God of mercy, redemption and second chances.

Talmidim (Disciples)

LET US RECLAIM OUR FAMILY[4]

By Rev. Canon Brian Cox

The Toward Jerusalem Council II movement seeks reconciliation between Jews and Gentiles, drawing its vision from the first Council of Jerusalem. This global movement has offices in Austria, Germany, the Netherlands, and the United States. My experience with this movement began with two people, a laywoman in Germany and a rabbi in Texas, more than twenty years ago.

While participating in an ecumenical charismatic conference in 1991 I met Christa Behr, a Lutheran from Hamburg who organized services of repentance at former Nazi concentration camps in Germany and Poland. Christa invited me to participate in one such service at Sachsenhausen Camp near Berlin in 1994. Led by the Rev. Paul Toaspern from East Berlin and Rabbi Benjamin Berger from a messianic congregation that meets at Christ Church in Jerusalem, 300 older Germans confessed, wept, and asked God for forgiveness for taking loyalty oaths to Hitler, crying "Sieg Heil," and doing nothing when their Jewish neighbors were beaten or arrested by the Gestapo. While this was happening, the Holy Spirit drove me to soul-rending sobs. Finally, I turned to Peter Dippel, a West Berlin pastor sitting next to me, and said, "Peter, I don't understand what is happening to me!" He simply smiled and replied, "Brian, the Lord did the same thing to me when he gave me a supernatural love for the Jewish people."

In the weeks that followed I realized that something had changed inside my heart. Previously I had been indifferent toward my Jewish neighbors; not hostile, but indifferent. I found myself beginning to seek Jewish friends. I became friends with a rabbi and with two Holocaust survivors.

A few months later I received a short note from Barbara Bolte Smith, a parishioner at St. James, Newport Beach, where I had served as senior associate. Her note simply said that the Holy Spirit had guided her to write to me about the vision that the Holy Spirit had given Marty Waldman, the rabbi at Baruch HaShem Messianic Synagogue in Dallas. As I read the vision, which Rabbi Waldman called "Jerusalem Council II," my heart leapt with joy.

I spent two weeks praying about this vision. When he and I finally spoke, we quickly sensed the Holy Spirit's presence in our conversation. A

---

4. Cox, "Let Us Reclaim Our Family."

month later the rabbi invited me to attend an initial meeting of messianic Jewish and Gentile Christian leaders. This group evolved into the Executive Committee of Toward Jerusalem Council II, on which I serve.

What does our group hope to achieve? The first Jerusalem Council, as recounted in Acts 15, was called as a result of a crisis in the early messianic movement. We should remember that the first followers of Jesus were not Christians but messianic Jews. They retained their Jewish identity but recognized Jesus (Yeshua) as the Messiah. Once they began to share the Abrahamic blessing with the Gentiles it created a crisis. Some of these messianic Jews believed that the Gentiles must take on Jewish identity. There were good reasons for this; it would create less tension with mainline Jews who tolerated "messianic Jews" as another sect. Instead, the Jerusalem Council decided to honor Gentile identity, requiring converts to "abstain only from things polluted by idols and from fornication and from whatever has been strangled and from blood"—practices that would grieve observant Jews. God honored this decision and the gospel spread among Gentiles. Over time Gentiles began to outnumber Jewish believers, eventually to today's wildly disproportionate numbers. The Church was intended, theologically speaking, to be the missionary arm of Israel and, through the Messiah, to carry the Abrahamic blessing of faith-based reconciliation to the nations.

The Church was not raised up as a replacement for Israel, but as a branch to be grafted into the olive tree (Rom 9–11). As a result of Gentile arrogance the Church began to detach itself from its Jewish roots and the virus of anti-Semitism began to grow within our DNA. It became a widespread assumption that God had rejected Israel and the Jewish people for killing the Messiah and that the Church was "the replacement" which inherited all the blessings intended for Israel.

In AD 787 the second Council of Nicaea adopted Canon 8, which declared:

> Since some of those who come from the religion of the Hebrew mistakenly think to make a mockery of Christ who is God, pretending to become Christians, but denying Christ in private by both secretly continuing to observe the sabbath and maintaining other Jewish practices, we decree that they shall not be received to communion or at prayer or into the church, but rather let them openly be Hebrews according to their own religion; they should not baptize their children or buy, or enter into possession of, a slave. But if one of them makes his conversion with a sincere faith and heart, and pronounces his confession wholeheartedly,

Talmidim (Disciples)

disclosing their practices and objects in the hope that others may be refuted or corrected, such a person should be welcomed and baptized along with his children, and care should be taken that they abandon Hebrew practices. However if they are not of this sort, they should certainly not be welcomed.

The Church and Jewish leaders came to agree on one thing: you cannot follow Jesus and remain a Jew. That agreement prevailed for almost 1,200 years.

God seemed to have a different idea. Beginning in the late 19th century, Jewish belief in Jesus experienced resurrection in such places as Moldova, Bulgaria, Poland, and the United States. During the Jesus Movement of the late 1960s and early 1970s many Jewish hippies became followers of Jesus. For them it created a predicament: "I'm Jewish, but I believe that Jesus is my Messiah. What do I do now?"

Many were rejected by their families as having "gone over to the Nazis." But in 1967, as Israel was taking possession of the Old City of Jerusalem for the first time in 2,000 years, the messianic Jewish movement was born. It is a small but growing movement. In Israel there are more than 10,000 messianic Jews. There are more than 200 messianic congregations in the United States. There are also messianic congregations in Argentina, Brazil, Canada, Mexico, England, France, Germany, Ireland, Russia, and Ukraine.

Toward Jerusalem Council II is a movement of prayer, repentance, and relationship-building with an eye toward reconciliation of the Jewish and Gentile parts of the Body of Messiah (Christ). It is a targeted initiative that seeks to address the most ancient rupture in the Body of Messiah that preceded the rupture between East and West and the Protestant Reformation. Since the center's beginning in 1995 there have been prayer journeys to Israel, Poland, Rome, Spain, and Turkey. There have been diplomatic initiatives to Africa, Europe, Latin America, and the Middle East. Conferences have met in Addis Ababa, Buenos Aires, Chicago, Dallas, Gnadenthal, Jerusalem, and Nairobi.

Roman Catholic leaders have welcomed our work. In 1997 Christoph Cardinal Schönborn of Vienna, Austria, became our patron. In 1998 a small group of us met at the Vatican with Joseph Cardinal Ratzinger, who has since become Pope Benedict XVI. He welcomed the rise of the messianic Jewish movement as an important eschatological sign and, through papal theologian Georges Cardinal Cottier, began a dialogue with messianic Jewish leaders.

Archbishop Rowan Williams has met at Lambeth Palace for half a day with messianic Jewish leaders from Israel and England. Our vision has met the most enthusiastic reception among Anglicans in Africa and Latin America. A TJC II team spent two days with the West Africa House of Bishops. There are invitations to meet with the Houses of Bishops in Kenya, Uganda, and Tanzania. Many African Christians consider reconciliation with Israel a precursor to experiencing the fullness of God's blessings on Africa.

One year ago Rabbi Waldman and I convened a small summit, in Chicago, of Episcopal and messianic Jewish leaders. It is easy enough to recognize Jewish congregations in our neighborhoods and cities as our elder brothers and sisters in faith. I believe it is time for the Episcopal Church to join other provinces of the Anglican Communion in acknowledging the same of our messianic brothers and sisters.

8

Church and Israel

For he himself is our shalom—he has made us both one and has broken down the m'chitzah which divided us by destroying in his own body the enmity occasioned by the Torah, with its commands set forth in the form of ordinances.

(Eph 2:14–15)

Yeshua's death tore the veil that separated the Holy of Holies and Jews and Gentiles streamed into one flock with one shepherd, fulfilling God's plan for humanity. You will be known by how you love each other (John 13:35). Make every effort to attain unity through the bond of peace (Eph 4:3).

The New Covenant introduces the word *henoteis*, unity, made possible when Jesus is our peace. He announced the shalom to those near and those far off, bringing both into relationship with the Creator. When the apostles taught that they were no longer under the law, but under grace, they were saying the people no longer were under requirement to sacrifice animals for their sins. The sacrifice of Jesus was enough for all time. The commandments became a declarative empowered by the Spirit of Truth. You will worship the living God! You shall not lie! You won't steal! You will have Sabbath rest.

The problem that confronts each of us is that the old self was formed out of deception. The old self is corrupt spiritually and physically. Ephesians explains that the deception of the old self leads us to sin which leads to death. Giving reign to self through practices of self-realization, self-fulfillment, or self-expression bring no solution. This can slow the corruption but the old rebellion within remains. A rotten tree cannot produce good fruit. God's solution is execution of the old nature. Jesus says it's to be cut down and thrown into the fire (Matt 7:17–19). This is God's plan, explained in Romans 6 and 7 when Paul laments the predicament and cries, "who will free me from this deadly lower nature?" In gratitude he says, thank God it's been done in Jesus our Lord. For we know that our old self was crucified with him so that the body of sin would be rendered powerless.

The cross on Calvary had been fashioned for Barabbas. We are all Barabbas. The cross was made for us because of our enmity against God. It's where we would be but in a glorious moment an exchange was made and Jesus took the place of criminals. God did not reform, reprove, or send to a church to discuss problems or to a psychiatrist. God executed sin so that we would be free.

Israel being freed from Egyptian slavery was a redemption for the entire nation. Jesus said he came for the lost sheep of the house of Israel. They were to be the light of salvation for all the world by coming through the gate of the Son of God. The salvation went out to non-Jews being called individually, each by name. They were not called because of a covenant with their ancestors. They are each called because they are in the mind of God to share the work of holding up the light.

No longer strangers, the Gentiles became fellow citizens in God's kingdom, built from the foundation of the prophets and Jewish rabbis. The cross became the symbol of Jesus trusting in his father. God had not cut down the olive tree that brings the living waters to the branches. Both Jew and Gentile are dependent on the tree's roots.

They are to work together for truth (3 John 1:8). Together they are to further the cause of Jesus each walking according to how they are called without one becoming the other. But the Gentiles did not heed Paul's warning not to be arrogant against the natural branches (Rom 11:18–21).

After Emperor Constantine declared Christianity the legal religion in the fourth century, the leaders turned against the Jews in contempt. Augustine declared the church triumphing over the synagogue as an act of God. The archbishop of Constantinople, John Chrysostrom, preached scathing sermons that called the Jews "men possessed by the devil. I hate the Jews for they have the Law and they insult it." Six centuries later the Crusades mounted cruelty against the Jews and enlisted Christian people into their atrocities. Jews were burned alive in their homes or forced to convert and deny being Jewish. Mobs murdered several thousand Jews in Prague alone. The Crusades arrived in Israel in year 1,000 when there were 300,000 Jewish residents. Two centuries later only 1,000 Jewish families remained. Reformer Martin Luther advocated expelling Jews from Germany. He wrote, "First their synagogues should be set on fire and whatever is left be buried in the dirt so that no one may be able to see a stone or cinder from it . . . Jewish prayer books should be destroyed . . . then the Jewish people should be dealt with, their homes smashed and destroyed. Jews should be banned from the roads and markets, should be drafted into forced labor and made to earn their bread by the sweat of their noses." The Nazis built their plans using Luther's words and the writings of other anti-semitic theologians.

Born in New York City in 1849, Emma Lazarus responded when she heard of the Russian pogroms being carried out against her people in the 1880s. She became their advocate and helped establish the Hebrew Technical Institute to provide assistance for the thousands of homeless Jewish immigrants that came to the shores of North America.

In 1883 she penned "The New Colossus."

> Not like the brazen giant of Greek fame,
> With conquering limbs astride from land to land;
> Here at our sea-washed, sunset gates shall stand
> A mighty woman with a torch, whose flame
> Is the imprisoned lightning, and her name
> Mother of Exiles, From her beacon-hand
> Glows world-wide welcome, her mild eyes command
> The air-bridged harbor that twin cities frame
> "Keep, ancient lands, your storied pomp!" cries she
> With silent lips. "Give me your tired, your poor,
> Your huddled masses yearning to breathe free,
> The wretched refuse of your teeming shore.
> Send these, the homeless, tempest-tost to me,
> I lift my lamp beside the golden door!"

The last lines were inscribed on a bronze plaque placed on the Statue of Liberty in 1903. But the bias against Jews found a way into America. After World War I, Henry Ford bought The Dearborn Independent, a weekly newspaper, and published accusations against Jewish people for instigating the war for profit and blaming German-Jewish bankers. The Great

Depression fueled Father Coughlin, a Catholic priest, to create a weekly radio program with an audience of twelve million. His broadcasts accused Jewish bankers of causing both the Depression and the Russian Revolution.

Israelites scattered to be found today at every crossroad of the world. They were given a way to live even in exile (Jer 29:4–6). They were to marry, plant gardens, pray for all men so that they would lead a peaceable life, continue giving thanks, and make intercession with God for all people to come to know God. They were instructed to be light wherever they lived.

The churches were built and songs were sung to the God of Israel, but what was learned in synagogues was irrelevant to them. Children are prayed for with hope in the Messiah of Israel, but inside the synagogues, the ways of the church were irrelevant. His mercy covers everything we did not know to acknowledge, but his every plan to create a clean heart of unity in the One Humanity will be fulfilled. The gates of hell cannot prevail against this.

When John in Revelation saw a vast number of people from all nations, they are the people Jesus prayed would be one body on earth. Jesus said to his father, I want those you have given me to be with me in heaven so they will see my glory. He wants us to be with him. He wants us to be transformed fully by the glory we now only glimpse. Every knee will bow because of the staggering power of God's love poured on Jesus for all eternity.

OTHER PROBLEMS IN SEMANTICS[1]

by Shira Sorko-Ram

The word "church" in the New Testament has a different meaning than that ascribed to it today by most Christians. In the New Testament, "church" never meant "building." The word meant an assembly, group, or community of believers—the veritable body of Christ. Wherever human beings were with the indwelling God, there was the church. When Paul wrote to the church at Ephesus, he was certainly not writing to a building, but rather the little assemblies throughout the city which comprised the church. The same connotation is found in the term "church in the wilderness." Moses led the community of believers (i.e., Israel) through the wilderness.

But the Jew associates the word church with an idolatrous, heathen temple. For that reason, most Jews do not wish to visit a church.

"Missionary" is one of the most hated words in Hebrew. The Jewish person reasons as follows: "The Christians have tried to exterminate us for 2,000 years. Finally, we have found our way back to our own land with God's help, and what happens? The Christians follow right after us and tell us we should not be Jews anymore. We should convert to Christianity." The Jew feels this is an attempt to exterminate the Jewish race, and that it is as deadly as any form ever used. Occasionally, when an Israeli did become a born-again believer, he also, unfortunately, learned how to be a good Western Christian. Bacon and eggs began to taste better than gefilte fish. Soon he felt foreign to his land and his people. He, therefore, asked to immigrate to the United States or Europe.

Incidentally, Messianic Jews in Israel have substituted the word *shaliach* (pronounced shah-LEE-ah, with a guttural "h" on the last syllable) for the term *missionary*. *Shaliach* means a "sent one" and, in modern Hebrew, refers to an ambassador, emissary, or delegate. In the New Testament, *shaliach* is the only appropriate word available in Hebrew to translate the Greek word for apostle.

To a Jewish person, convert means to turn his back on his nation, people, God, and Scriptures and become a part of a Gentile religion. Thus, the term "converted Jew" is an anathema.

This connotation of *convert* is certainly not based on Scripture. The King James Version of the Bible uses the word convert in place of the exact

---

1. Sorko-Ram, "Other Problems in Semantics."

Hebrew and Greek words meaning repent. (The meaning of this word is more fully considered later.) For example, the phrase in Matthew 18:3, " . . . Except ye be converted . . . " is more properly rendered "unless you repent." In many modern versions of the Old and New Testaments, "convert" is replaced by the closer meaning "repent."

I would never use the word *convert* to a Jew, because he does not know the King James meaning of the word. Paul said that if meat offended his brother, he would eat no meat as long as the world stands (I Cor. 8:13). Surely we, upon realizing how a Jew understands this word, will not use it to confuse him and hinder him from finding God. I would hate to think that I kept someone from the kingdom of God because of my vocabulary.

In the sense that the Jewish person understands the word, he certainly must not convert—that is, stop being a Jew and go over to another religion. He must instead turn around and go back to the God of his fathers that he has left.

Furthermore, many Jews who have converted to nominal Christianity, usually to marry, have rarely repented of their sins. So, the meaning is further muddled. On the other hand, a believing Jew or Messianic Jew is one who has repented.

Many times when a Gentile speaks to a Jew of spiritual things, he sees the Jew as one of those who rejected Christ—with all it implies. The answer to that, of course, is: "Did the Gentiles as a whole accept Christ?" An overwhelming, tragic "no!" What percentage of Gentiles, even those of the Western world, have accepted Jesus as Savior and Lord of their lives? The percentage is small. In many countries, one would have to search far and wide to find even a few born-again believers. The truth is, man has rejected God; and Jesus died because of, and for, all mankind.

Church and Israel

WHAT I BELIEVE AND WHAT I REJECT[2]
by Rabbi Loren Jacobs

There is a consistent distinction in the Scriptures between Israel and the church. Israel and the nations, Jews and Gentiles, together make up Messiah's Holy Community. Jews remain Jews in the Body of Christ, and gentiles remain gentiles.

Messianic Jews serve as the bridge connecting Israel and the Church. We are part of Israel—the faithful remnant within Israel—and we are also part of the Church. We should strive to be part of our people as much as possible and, yet, never compromise our bold testimony. And we should be involved in the larger Body of Messiah and, yet, without assimilating our Jewish identity. Rabbi Paul commands Messianic Jews to not become uncircumcised (1 Cor 7:18), which means not to seek assimilation into the prevailing gentile culture but to continue their Jewish way of life.

The laws of Moses are still extremely valuable. The Torah continues to inform and guide the lives of the Jewish people. It teaches us the right things to do and gives us a good way to live. It helps us live an authentic Jewish lifestyle. It helps us remain part of the Holy People.

The issue of assimilation is a major problem for Messianic Jews. Historically Messianic Jewish families who make no effort to live a Jewish lifestyle or to be involved in Jewish evangelism will almost always assimilate and lose their Jewish identity within a couple of generations. The issue of assimilation is something that is addressed in the New Testament.

More than a Mosaic Covenant, all the word of God, including the New Covenant, is Torah because Torah literally means teaching or instruction. The early Messianic Jews were zealous to live in accordance with it, continuing to live a distinctly Jewish lifestyle for centuries after Messiah Yeshua arrived. All believers are in some sense to fulfill the teachings, but not everyone is obligated to the same requirements. For example, gentiles don't need to be circumcised. But no one can be saved without faith in Yeshua.

I accept the fact Messianic Jews who choose not to keep every aspect of the law, particularly ceremonial laws, do not lose their salvation. One of the main purposes of the Torah is to point us to Messiah. Those Messianic Jews who want to keep the customs and traditions of our people are free to do so, provided those customs and traditions do not contradict the

2. Jacobs, "What I Believe and What I Reject."

teaching of the Word of God. Many rabbinic customs and traditions are profound and are a blessing to Jewish life. But there is a danger. Jewish traditions and practices and forms can be over-emphasized so that Orthodox Judaism is unduly elevated in the minds of our people. The result is that non-Messianic Judaism starts being wrongly perceived as more genuine, authentic, and authoritative. Then some go on to abandon Messianic Judaism and deny their faith in Yeshua altogether. Also, the forms and traditions can become so important that Yeshua is crowded out; and he becomes little more than a bystander in our services or a footnote in our prayer books.

Messiah's teaching returns us to the Torah's original intent regarding issues such as a man being married to only one woman. I am against women being in the position of pastors and rabbis or being in positions of spiritual authority over men. It's clearly unbiblical. There was nothing ambiguous about Rabbi Paul's words to Timothy: "A woman must quietly receive instruction with entire submissiveness. But I do not allow a woman to teach or exercise authority over a man but to remain quiet" (1 Tim 2:11–12). "An overseer must be the husband of one wife" (1 Tim 3:2). God created an order among human beings. The man is the head of his family even if his wife is smarter than he is. God's Word, not our talent, is the determinative factor in family leadership or spiritual leadership.

Being the leader of a congregation is similar to being the leader of a family. A congregation is like an extended family. Just as the head of the home is the man, so the head of the congregation is reserved for male leadership. Just as the man is the head of the home and a home functions properly when the man is the leader, so the church functions properly in the same way. The church, for 1,900 years, rightly didn't allow women to be leaders. Several years ago our synagogue made it a policy that none of our representatives speak in a church that has a woman pastor in a position of authority over men.

Our sexuality is an integral part of who God made us to be, and it must not be perverted. Homosexuality defies the laws of nature and the laws of God. Homosexuality is a sexual perversion, harmful to those who engage in it, and destructive to the society that encourages it. It is a very serious sin and is treated as such in the Tenach (the Law, the Prophets, and the Writings) and the *Brit Chadasha* (the New Covenant). It is regarded as *toh-ay-vah*, an abomination, something that is extremely repugnant and detestable to the holy God. It is such a serious sin that, unless it is turned from, it results in loss of the Kingdom of God.

Homosexuals are not to be mistreated but, instead, to be shown compassion and love. But they also need to be told the truth—that they are misusing their sexuality and that, unless they turn away from the serious sexual sin which nature and God forbids, they will go to Hell. Our attitude toward homosexuals should be to love the sinner but hate the sin. We are to be tolerant toward homosexuals, but tolerance does not mean that you accept all ideas, religions, philosophies, worldviews, opinions, lifestyles, and practices as being equally true, valid, or beneficial. The church must never declare that homosexuality is acceptable to God or to the church. Those who do so, as have most of the Episcopal churches in the United States, have left the faith. States have left the faith.

HOLIDAYS AND FESTIVALS[3]

by Chosen People Ministries

To prepare for Pesach, a ceremony called *Bedikat Chametz* is performed in every traditional household in a final search for leaven throughout the house, gathering it together and burning it to make the home kosher. God instructed Israel to refrain from eating leaven for seven days and to clean their houses of it for the Pesach. Anyone eating leaven during this time would be cut off from Israel, whether a stranger or a native.

Paul used the practice to illustrate that leaven can be malice through the whole lump. Your glorying is not good. Purge out the old leaven because Christ, our Pesach, was sacrificed for us. At the time there was tolerance of immorality in Corinth and Paul compared sin to leaven permeating the congregation.

We cannot compartmentalize our lives and isolate sin in a particular area so that it does not affect the other areas of our lives. God created us as holistic people. Even small and hidden sins will permeate and corrode our entire being. Righteousness should be pursued because Messiah removed the *chametz* (leaven) from our lives. Paul describes people with leaven as depraved and wicked. People who are pure in motives have no leaven. The "unleavened" person does not have a hidden life. If we are serious about honoring God and having a healthy spiritual life, then we cannot tolerate the hidden and secret sins. In the spirit of Passover, let us remove the sin from our lives, so that we are kosher for Passover.

---

3. Chosen People Ministries, "Holidays and Festivals."

PAUL EMPLOYING LEVITICUS: SAME SEX INTERCOURSE CONSIDERED AMONGST TORAH COMMANDMENTS[4]

by Dr. Jon C. Olson

It is sometimes argued that because the New Testament writers set aside circumcision, food laws, Sabbath, biblical purity laws, and welcomed Gentiles, anything in the Old Testament ought to be set aside if unsuitable for the ekklesia (the called out, the church). The argument implies that because other laws from the Old Testament are set aside in the New Testament, Pauline passages that seem to use the Levitical prohibition of same-sex intercourse either (1) do not truly cite Leviticus, (2) allude to commands without intending they be taken as commands, or (3) are in contradiction to those other passages that set aside various Old Testament laws.

Scripture commands the people to be holy because the Lord is holy (Lev 11:44–45). Leviticus 18 begins and ends with a threefold admonition to follow God's ways rather than the abominations of other peoples, and the declaration: "I am the Lord your God." Leviticus 18:22 and 20:13 prohibit a male to lie with another male as with a woman (i.e. same-sex intercourse), characterizing it as *toevah* (abomination). In 18:22 male-with-male intercourse appears between burning one's child to Molech and bestiality; in 20:13 it appears between incest with a daughter-in-law and marrying both a woman and her mother.

Paul says homosexual behavior is God's punishment for idolatry. Punishment for turning away from God takes the form of allowing humans to follow their own passions to their own destruction (Rom 1:18–32). The result of Christian estrangement from Judaism is an inability to understand parts of the New Testament, one's place in the biblical story, one's relationship to Yeshua and to God, and whether certain sexual behavior is fitting for a follower of Yeshua. Paul remained steadfast within Judaism, implying that the Levitical prohibition of same-sex intercourse is a commandment to be obeyed by both Jewish and Gentile Yeshua-believers. Under the first assumption, 1 Corinthians 6:9 clearly uses Leviticus. One expects Paul to look in Scripture—including Torah commandments—when listing persons who will not inherit the kingdom of God. Paul urges Gentile Yeshua-believers to respect Jewish sensibilities by altering their own eating behavior (Rom 14).

Paul wrote, "I appeal to you, therefore, brothers and sisters, by the mercies of God, to present your bodies as a living sacrifice (singular), holy

4. Olson, "Paul Employing Leviticus."

and acceptable to God" (Rom 12:1). "You (plural) are God's temple and God's Spirit dwells in you (plural)" (1 Cor 3:16). Fornication with a prostitute is wrong because it defiles the body of Messiah (1 Cor 6:15). Giving priority to love, justice, reason, experience, science, and conseuentialism alone lead to conclusions different than the bible.

Same-sex intercourse is neither part of the original design for human sexuality given in the creation story, nor the biblical vision of restored humanity. Yeshua and Paul, by their table fellowship with outsiders, model how love of neighbor leads one to become "all things to all people." Yet Yeshua and Paul did not break or abandon the commandments of the Torah, though accused of doing so.

The debate about homosexuality is often carried out by parties living different paradigms. However, even here, the ekklesia's debate must no longer take place within an anti-Jewish theological paradigm antagonistic to the New Testament adoption of Torah commandments.

Most congregations have too little experience of God's power for transforming difficult situations to support homosexual persons who wish to pursue celibacy or the change that would enable heterosexual marriage. What kind of congregations could interpret Scripture rightly? What kind of congregations could offer a way of life that is more compelling to homosexual persons than one that included same-sex intercourse?

Immediately after Paul's denunciation of those Gentiles whom God gave up to a base mind and improper conduct (Rom 1:28), and who deserve to die (1:32), he announces that, "In passing judgment on him you condemn yourself" (2:1). Further, "all have sinned and fall short of the glory of God" (3:23). After listing those who will not inherit the kingdom of God, Paul reminds his readers what God has done for them. "And such were some of you. But you were washed, you were sanctified, you were justified in the name of the Lord Messiah Yeshua and in the Spirit of our God" (1 Cor 6:11).

The congregation ought to be a place "where all sinners are truly welcome and given the time, space, and love that will form them in [Messiah] and in . . . community—so that they might live whole and holy lives." This would include recognition of the activity of the Holy Spirit in the lives of people with same-sex attraction. The differences that lead to moral growth on the pattern of the incarnation, of Christ and the church, are those, as Gregory Nazianzen says, that turn our limits to our good. The differences that turn our limits to our good are those that cause us to need one another, since love can exist only as relationally possessed.

CHURCH AND ISRAEL

WHAT I BELIEVE AND WHAT I REJECT[5]

by Rabbi Loren Jacobs

Theological liberalism has been one of the main enemies of the faith for the past 150 years. It developed in the 1800s during the trend toward deifying human reason, science, and anti-supernaturalism. It excludes the supernatural from the faith, discounts clear biblical teaching such as a six-day creation, the flood, prophecies, and miracles, and often denies Messiah's virgin birth, his resurrection, and the existence of Hell. It teaches that Genesis 1–11 is not real history with real people and real events. But it is not possible to dismiss the supernatural aspects of the Word of God and leave intact the Faith that was "once for all delivered to the saints." Paul wrote to Timothy to avoid those who "hold to a form of religion but deny its power" (2 Tim 3:5). The bible is a supernatural book about a supernatural God who supernaturally intervenes in human history.

In their effort to eliminate the supernatural from the bible, theological liberals undermine faith in God and confidence in the bible. Francis Schaeffer observed, "Liberal theologians don't believe in content or religious truth. They are really existentialists using theological, Christian language." Liberalism has, in fact, destroyed the faith of millions and ruined entire denominations (particularly mainline churches, including many United Methodist, Episcopalian, and Presbyterian churches). The liberal churches are losing members and shrinking, as they should. I like the way Jackie Alnor put it: "Theological liberalism is under a curse for having taken away from the Word of God." Perhaps she based that statement on the following verses: You shall not add to the word which I am commanding you, nor take away from it (Deut 4:2). If anyone takes away from the words of the book of this prophecy, God shall take away his part from the tree of life and from the holy city (Rev 22:19). In other words, those who accept anti-biblical tenets of Liberalism have denied the faith. Theological Liberalism is apostate and heretical and must be rejected.

I believe that the Roman Catholic Church is a corrupt religious institution. I identify it as the woman who sits on the beast (Rev 17–18). It is connected to a great city that exercises political control over kings and nations. It is full of abominations and immorality, outwardly rich, and politically powerful, having exercised great political control over many governments.

---

5. Jacobs, "What I Believe and What I Reject."

It is a persecutor of the real saints and religiously corrupt. The Gospel it offers has been perverted and, consequently, will not save its adherents. It has added to the Word of God by acknowledging the Apocrypha as part of the Holy Scriptures. It has added to the Word of God by elevating Catholic traditions, laws, and decrees to the same status as the Word of God!

In addition, it has arrogantly declared the bishop of Rome to be the infallible leader of the entire church. It invented the doctrine of a non-existent place called Purgatory. There is no Scriptural support for traditions and practices, such as the sacrifice of the mass, transubstantiation, prayers and masses for the dead, indulgences, the worship of Mary, prayers to the saints, adoring a piece of bread, the use of icons in worship, holy water, rosary beads, and scapulars, a Roman Catholic priesthood, the demand of celibacy from these priests and nuns, and confession to priests to obtain absolution. It has developed a complicated system of salvation based on works and man-made teachings mixed with Scripture. It does not teach salvation by grace alone, or by faith alone based on the finished work of Messiah. It teaches another gospel which is a false gospel. I am terribly disappointed with those involved with "Evangelicals and Catholics Together" and want to keep my distance from them.

THE UNIQUE PLACE OF GENTILES IN MESSIANIC JEWISH CONGREGATIONAL LIFE[6]

by Rabbi Dr. Richard C. Nichol

Learn the value of grandfathering—for leaders who come to understand that the very nature of Messianic Judaism demands distinctions between Jews and Gentiles even within the four walls of our congregations, the transition can be difficult. As a general rule, it is best not to take privileges away that have already been offered, but to allow a transition time sometimes lasting a few years. Of the five non-Jewish men accustomed to wearing a talit at our synagogue at the time we made the transition to viewing the donning of a talit as the province of Jews, we made no demands of these good men. They knew about our transition, but were free to do as they chose. One kept wearing the talit. One saw the transition as the next step in our maturation as a synagogue and though he had a prominent role among us, willingly gave up wearing his prayer shawl. Another, a man with some Jewish lineage, stopped wearing his talit and later chose to enter the conversion process. The remaining two did leave the congregation for reasons tangential to this specific change in our policy, but related to the overall development of our congregation's bilateral outlook. The point here is that though transitions are never easy, a light touch clearly helped minimize damage to the community and was appreciated by a majority of those who were affected.

Take away, but give back—Robert Frost's poem is the source of the familiar phrase, "Good fences make good neighbors." An application in our context is this: once clarity comes to Messianic Jewish leadership regarding the rules guiding Gentile participation, great liberty and largesse can be expressed within those boundaries. Non-Jews can have important roles among us. Why should a qualified gentile not teach a Scripture study? Why not preach on occasion? Why not serve on a standing committee or lead an ad-hoc committee? Or, lead a musical group? It is the ambiguity of their status that creates the up-tightness in the community and prevents the relaxed, good-natured feeling conducive to creativity and joy. Identity confusion is the curse. Clear boundaries with love embody the blessing.

Explain, explain, explain—the other day I made my very first stock purchase on TDAmeritrade. It was a huge step because, though I enjoy

---

6. Nichol, "The Unique Place of Gentiles."

fund-raising, I have always viewed involvement in the market with the trepidation one might feel approaching the entrance of an interesting cave, but hearing a low animal growl from within. But there was assurance and help from the lady in the customer service department. She explained what an "option" was. Other terms which undoubtedly were as clear as water in a mountain stream to her and her colleagues went from completely murky to almost clear for me as she patiently answered my many questions.

We Messianic Jewish leaders sport a rich theological vocabulary and a glossary of in-house terminology. It is an act of love to explain transitions in the congregation's outlook clearly, simply and with great patience. Had the very wealthy proprietors of TDAmeritrade expected me to penetrate their world without that lady's patient help over better than an hour, I would likely have opted for the piggy bank. It just smiles and says "klink" with each investment! But there can be much gain with oxen (I mean TDAmeritrade!) so, explain, explain, explain, and the good people of your congregation will, for the most part, respond positively.

Appreciate and validate—looking back over thirty-plus years, I am filled with gratitude for many of the non-Jewish believers who have come among us. Ruach Israel has been enriched by such people. In fact, I would argue that without the presence of these selfless servants of the king, ours—and many other—Messianic Jewish synagogues might not have come into existence at all. These folks deserve our highest esteem and love. Once clear boundaries have been established it is fairly easy to show appreciation at every turn of the synagogue's life. Of course, such expressions of praise and appreciation should be "equal opportunity." Good hearted Jewish members contribute to the whole and these need to know that the rabbi thinks they are terrific, too!

Guard their futures—I am not referring to stock futures here, but the possible futures of Gentile members of our synagogues. We must help them cultivate love for the church while they sojourn with us. We don't want these folks to burn their bridges with their own religious roots because in time, many will feel the tug of their early childhood experiences and desire to move back into familiar territory. This can be a very healthy thing for all. Help them celebrate their re-entry to church so they can look back at their experience in the Messianic Jewish congregation as a time of growth—a wonderful God ordained step along the way. Help them return with a mandate to help their church love the Jewish people and especially the remnant of Israel.

Find a sympathetic church or two—particularly in the BA, but possible in the MA, it becomes very clear that most gentiles should belong to healthy churches. As noted, there are exceptions. Would it not be a good thing for the rabbi to locate a couple of churches in the area which supports the Messianic Jewish idea, have a regard for Israel and the Jewish people and could make a comfortable home for the non-Jew who, having spent some time in the Messianic Jewish congregation, is ready to move on? All these strategies intended to grow a healthy Messianic Jewish congregation, where a strong majority of Jewish members creates space, with real love for others, takes courage and determination. Where do these come from?

Not long ago, I spontaneously declared to our Board, "The one thing I dislike about my job (as Senior Rabbi) is having to protect our boundaries." I was referring to my role as center on the offensive line of our team ... so often called upon to protect the community's Messianic Jewish identity from patterns that will likely assure that we will lose our essence in the years to come. Some of these patterns that are clearly observable among our larger Messianic Jewish world have to do with the role of gentiles in our midst.

Being the gatekeeper is a role many of us would like to delegate (or theologize!) away. But, at what cost?

It seems to me that every Messianic Jewish rabbi should cultivate friendships among Christian pastors and, if possible, among mainstream rabbis. We leaders need a deeply-rooted set of convictions that arise from God's revelation so that we may be able to do the necessary "heavy lifting." Without such convictions the social pressure to conform to the usual patterns will be too great to bear in the long term. Additionally, in a culture which values egalitarianism ("we are all winners here" says the kid's soccer coach) it is hard to escape the nagging feeling that we as leaders are acting from unworthy motivations like prejudice, or ungodly exclusivism, when in fact, such sinful attitudes may not be the true story at all. We need sources of strength that take us to the very substructure of our callings.

BEIT HALLEL

A House of Praise

And nations will come to your light, And kings to the brightness of your rising (Isa 60:1–3)

9

Baruch HaShem (Blessed is God)

In my prayers I keep asking the God of our Lord Yeshua the Messiah, the glorious Father, to give you a spirit of wisdom and revelation, so that you will have full knowledge of him

(Eph 1:17)

Music lilting with minor keys harmonizes in buildings all over the world. It's a Saturday morning and the days are short. Evening falls early, snow blankets the earth, and the moon is dark. Chanukah comes in with a blaze of winter solstice anticipating the final victory out of the longest darkness. The leader of a congregation steps forward, draped in the traditional prayer shawl. Worshippers rise and proclaim, "*Shema Yisrael Adonai Eloheynu Adonai Echad.*" Hear O Israel, the Lord thy God, the Lord is One." The Messianic Rabbi says, "*Baruch ha Shem.*" Praise the Lord.

The Book of Acts records Jews by the thousands coming to faith in Yeshua HaMashiach and the struggles and persecutions of the first Messianic congregation in Jerusalem as they kept remembrance in the holidays while proclaiming the Messiah had come. God promised, "I will also make you a light to the nations, so my salvation can spread to the ends of the earth" (Isa 49:6).

Today Messianic congregations are gaining momentum in triumphal procession around the world carrying the foundation of the Christian faith to more than 332,000 Jews in hundreds of congregations.[1] The Jews in

1. Pfister, "Messianic Jews Worldwide."

Germany, for instance, were a community of survivors of the Holocaust. Seven times as many Jews had died as were born. At the end of the 1980s congregational membership was estimated to be about 27,000 in about sixty-five congregations. Messianic Jews began establishing congregations in the 1990s which grew to the turn of the century's 59 percent women and 41 percent men comprising more than 200,000 Jewish believers, some coming as believers from Russia, others finding faith while in the country. Chosen People Ministries acquired a facility just ten minutes from the place Hitler and his generals planned the Final Solution of extermination.

The ekklesia, still mostly Gentile, is gradually leaving behind the paternalistic notions that grievously quenched the Holy Spirit and tried to anglicize Jesus. Peter had explained there are letters that Paul wrote that are difficult to understand, letters which the untaught twist and give wrong meanings of other scripture because of their lack of knowledge (2 Pet 3:16). The apostles spent much time teaching about God in the Old Testament. They were the teachers Jesus spoke of, saying they were like scribes who brought new treasures as well as old out of their storerooms (Matt 13:52). In quiet respect they were listened to elders, who as grandfathers carried ancient knowledge that turned hearts to the living God.

The inclusion of the Gentiles was seen as fulfillment of prophecy. By you all the families of the earth will be blessed (Gen 12:3). The islands will put their hope in his teachings (Isa 42:4). He will gather the people of all nations and languages and they will see his glory (Isa 66:18). To you the nations will come (Jer 16:19).

Incomplete without each other, both the church and Israel have a mission of salvation. Both find their story in the prophetic meanings in the festivals that bring community together. This coming together of Jews and Gentiles in the first centuries brought Judaic law to influence the value of children in a society that promoted abortion and infanticide. They brought the compassion of the God of Israel to a people trapped in futility trying to please a diversity of stone-faced gods. An extraordinary movement by the Holy Spirit is again raising Jewish disciples to lead the way to the time of Messiah's return. The church, regardless of denomination or division, all intrinsically desire to return to the ideal of the first generation of believers.

At its foundation we are shown that the festivals through the year's cycle were a priority for Jesus to keep. His celebration of Chanukkah reflected the guiding plan of redemption for all nations. Chanukkah is an opportunity to learn the story of how living in a secular culture dominated by

Baruch HaShem (Blessed is God)

excessive consumerism and self-serving, God's family is called to prioritize the knowledge in scriptures. The shining lights of Chanukkah tell of men and women who were called out, who died to preserve the tradition given to them by God, and the victory of those struggling to honor the holiness of their covenant with God.

Chanukkah reminds the church that God is working on behalf of those he ordained to be distinct. The lights of the candles bear witness to the relationship between church and Jews through Jesus, a relationship intended to shine steadily in solidarity to bring about God's plan.

The Messianic movement is bringing them back together. They are listening to each other. They are finding understanding of the one new humanity through the biblical appointments that founded Israel. Like the Bereans, God finds this noble because they receive the word and search the scriptures to see if these teachings are true (Acts 17:11).

Chanukkah is observed for eight winter nights and days. Also called the Festival of Lights or the Feast of Dedication, the holiday begins with a single light that becomes many lights shining together. Chanukkah is a time light that ascends with one more candle added to the menorah each night as the new moon appears, commemorating the miracle of God empowering a small number of Jewish people to overcome the vast Syrian army. The shammus (servant) candle is lit first and held while the blessing is recited.

> *Baruch Ata Adonai Elohaynu Melech ha'olam,*
> *she-heh-cheh-ya-nu v'kee-y'mah-nu v'hi-gee-yah-nu laz-man ha-zeh!*
> Blessed are You O Lord our God, King of the Universe,
>   who granted us life, sustained us and permitted us to reach this season.

> *Baruch Ata Adonai Elohaynu Melech ha-olam, ah-sher nah-tan lah-nu*
> *chah-geem, meen-ha-geem, oo-mo-ah-deem l'sim-cha, l'hag-deel*
> *et dah-at Adonai, v'leev-note oh-tah-nu b'eh-muh-nah kee-doh-shah v'na-ah-lah.*
> Blessed are You O Lord our God, King of the universe,
>   who has given us holidays, customs, and times of happiness,
>   to increase the knowledge of God and to build us up in our most holy faith.

> *Baruch Ata Adonai Elohaynu Melech ha-olam, she-ah-sah nee-seem la-*
>   *ah-vo-tay-nu ba-ya-meem ha-hem baz-man ha-zeh.*
> Blessed are You O Lord our God, King of the universe,
>   who performed miracles for our fathers in those days at this season.

THE REAL MIRACLE OF CHANUKKAH[2]

by Rabbi Loren Jacobs

Before the service started, a couple confided to me that their pastor didn't want them attending our Chanukkah celebration—that there was something wrong, maybe even spiritually dangerous, about Christians celebrating Jewish holidays like Chanukkah. I want all my Christian brothers and sisters everywhere to know that Chanukkah is not spiritually dangerous! It's an important holiday that all of us should be aware of. It's mentioned by name in the New Testament in connection with some amazing statements made by the Messiah.

John tells us: Then came the Festival of Chanukkah ("Chanukkah" means "Dedication") at Jerusalem. It was winter, and Yeshua was in the temple courts walking in Solomon's Colonnade. The Jewish people who were there gathered around him saying, "How long will you keep us in suspense? If you are the Messiah, tell us plainly." Yeshua answered, "I did tell you, but you do not believe. The works I do in My Father's name testify about Me, but you do not believe because you are not My sheep. My sheep listen to My voice; I know them, and they follow Me. I give them eternal life, and they shall never perish; no one will snatch them out of My hand. My Father, who has given them to Me, is greater than all; no one can snatch them out of My Father's hand. I and the Father are one."

What great Chanukkah light we see shining from the Messiah! What a courageous statement of truth given by Messiah in Jerusalem, at the Temple, during the holiday of the Dedication of the Temple—Chanukkah.

Chanukkah is predicted in three prophetic passages in the Tenach—in Daniel 8 and 11 and Zechariah 9. In this amazing prophecy (Zech 9:11–17), God forewarned us that he would bring the Greeks into conflict with his people, and it would be a horrific time for the one nation on Earth that knew the Living God and the way of salvation. But he would miraculously deliver the Jewish people from one of the greatest threats we ever faced—the near destruction of our nation and our religion by the Greek empire.

Let's start with verse 11: As for you also, because of the blood of your covenant, I have set your prisoners free from the waterless pit. Waterless pits were used as prisons in this part of the ancient world. Joseph was thrown into a pit without water. To imprison him, Jeremiah was thrown

---

2. Jacobs, "The Real Miracle of Chanukkah."

Baruch HaShem (Blessed is God)

into a cistern that had no water, only mud. This description of prisoners in a waterless pit is used to describe the Greek occupation of our nation during the time of the Maccabees. How bad was it for us? Very, very bad. Around 175 BC wicked king Antiochus, one of the most evil men who ever lived, and a type of the future anti-Christ, ruled the Syrian part of the Greek empire. After he conquered Egypt in the south, he and his army went north and came to Jerusalem. He entered the Temple, even though only the cohenim, the holy sons of Aaron were allowed to enter, and took the golden altar, the golden menorah and all its utensils; the table for the bread of the Presence, the cups for drink offerings, the bowls, the golden censers, the gold decoration on the front of the temple; the other treasures of silver and the gold and departed to Syria.

Two years later Antiochus sent a tax collector who came to Jerusalem with a large force. He deceived the leaders of the city, promising he came in peace. After they allowed him to enter the city, he betrayed us and attacked and killed many Jewish people. He plundered the city, burned it with fire, tore down houses and surrounding walls, took captive the women and children, and seized the cattle.

Now that Jerusalem was under his control, like the future anti-Christ, Antiochus exerted complete political and spiritual control. He turned the Temple into a shrine for Zeus. A statue of Zeus was erected in the Temple, and not surprisingly, the face of the idol looked like Antiochus. An altar to Zeus was erected at the Temple and sacrifices of non-kosher animals, like pigs, were offered on the altar. This is the infamous "Abomination of Desolation" that Daniel the prophet mentioned. It happened in the past, and it will happen again in the future.

The king decreed that any Jewish person studying the Torah be put to death. Any Torah that was found was destroyed. Jews were forbidden to observe Jewish holidays. Anyone observing the Sabbath, Passover, Shavuot, or Sukkot was put to death. We were forced to eat non-kosher foods forbidden by Torah and to sacrifice on pagan altars which the king's officials built in every town in Judea. Anyone who didn't offer sacrifices to the Greek gods was put to death.

We were forbidden to circumcise our sons. The families of those who had their children circumcised, and those who circumcised them, were put to death. The Greeks hung the dead Jewish infants from their mothers' necks.

Month after month Jewish people who resisted these evil decrees were put to death. Many capitulated and abandoned their faithfulness to God.

This was one of the worst times in the history of the Chosen Nation. The Temple, the place where God revealed his principles of salvation, and revealed himself most clearly on Earth, was defiled. The Holy People, who were to bring God's salvation to the world, were on the verge of being annihilated. The Word of God was on the verge of being destroyed. We needed Chanukkah for there to be the First Christmas!

Zechariah's prophecy begins with the Creator telling us why he is going to help the Jewish people during this crisis. As for you also, because of the blood of your covenant, I have set your prisoners free from the waterless pit. The reason the Lord gives for rescuing us is "the blood of your covenant." God takes his covenants with his people, especially his blood covenants, very seriously.

Next, the Lord informs us that he will enable us to return to our stronghold, Zion. Return to the stronghold, O prisoners who have the hope; this very day I am declaring that I will restore double to you. God will so work that the Jewish people, who have become like prisoners because of oppression of the Greeks, will be able to return to Jerusalem, the strong city of our God.

The faithful remnant of the Jewish people are called "prisoners of hope" because they possess, through their blood covenant with God, a sure hope of salvation. And this is exactly what happened when the Greeks took over the capitol city, defiled the Temple and committed the Abomination of Desolation. After three years of amazing victories, the Jewish people who had the hope were able to return to our stronghold.

The Lord not only promised to get his people out of a waterless pit, and not only to restore Jerusalem to us, but also to reward us double for all our suffering. Again, that is exactly what happened. Because of God's grace, the faithful remnant was able to capture Zion, rededicate the Temple and establish an independent Jewish kingdom. This was a double blessing, because we did not have our own independent kingdom in centuries.

After the Jewish people are stirred up and supernaturally empowered to fight the Greek invaders, Adonai himself promised to come to Israel's defense. Then the Lord will appear over them, and his arrow will go forth like lightening; and the Lord God will blow the shofar, and will march in the storm winds of the south. The Lord will appear over his people, protecting and directing them. His arrow will go forth like lightening, which means that his empowered people will advance forward suddenly and strongly. The Maccabees did in fact develop a type of guerilla warfare which devastated the enemy with sudden, deadly violence. The Lord will blow the

Baruch HaShem (Blessed is God)

shofar, announcing that it is time to gather our forces together and fight. The shofar gives direction which way to march. In other words, we will fight together and fight strategically—which we did. The Lord will march at the head of his people like the storm winds of the south. They suddenly and powerfully sweep in from the Arabian or the Sinai deserts, overwhelming everything. In other words, the Lord will be a mighty, irresistible force leading his nation to victory.

The greatest force in the universe will defend his people in their battles against the Greeks. Adonai Tz'vaot, the Lord of Hosts, will defend them. The Lord of armies, so strong that no single army or combination of armies can defeat him—will fight for Israel and through Israel. This is exactly what happened. When the Jewish people were stirred up to fight against the Greeks, God miraculously empowered us. Even though we were not professional soldiers, in battle after battle against professional soldiers with superior weapons, our losses were minimal. The Lord enabled us to win battle after battle, even when the odds were as much as fifteen to one against us.

And they will devour, and trample on the sling stones; and they will drink, and be boisterous as with wine; and they will be filled like a sacrificial basin, drenched like the corners of the altar. Did our enemies expect to swallow us? The opposite will happen. We will devour the Greeks like hungry lions who kill and devour their prey. We will trample on their weapons as if they were sling stones lying uselessly on the ground. We will trample on the sling stones because when Israel is in a right relationship with God, no weapon formed against us will prosper. We will completely conquer the Greeks, and will drink and be boisterous—but drunk with victory, not with wine. Our enemies will fall as victims to divine justice. And they will be filled like a sacrificial basin. We will be more than conquerors, with tremendous successes that are compared to the sacrificial bowls which overflowed with the blood of the Temple sacrifices. They will be drenched in victory like the corners of the altar were drenched with the sacrificial blood smeared on it—symbolizing righteousness and closeness to God and success.

The Lord will save his covenant nation because the sons of Israel, when we are faithful to him, are like precious stones fit for a king's crown. They are as the stones of a crown, sparkling in his land. And, isn't every king committed to protect his crown jewels?

The miracle of Chanukkah is not about oil being multiplied for eight days. It's about God supernaturally saving his people from one of the worst men who ever lived—a type of the future anti-Christ; and saving his people from one of the worst periods in our long, and often painful, history. The real miracle of Chanukkah is that a small number of faithful and courageous Jewish people, supernaturally empowered by the God of Israel, were able to overcome the vastly superior Greek forces. The righteous few overcame the godless many; the weak who were loyal to the true God overcame those who were much stronger than they were. The faithful remnant of Israel won miraculous victory after miraculous victory until the Syrians were defeated, Jerusalem was captured, the Temple was cleansed and dedicated for the worship of the one true and Living God who alone can rescue fallen human beings from the real and utterly destructive forces of Satan, sin, the sin-nature, and death. The Word of God, which gives us the truth that sets us free, was preserved. The Chosen People were saved, so that 160 or so years later, the Son of David was able to be born among us as the Savior of the World. And there is more. Just as the Jewish people were oppressed and imprisoned, all human beings have been conquered and imprisoned by Satan, sin, the sin-nature, and death. God's message to you today is that, no matter where you are, even in the deepest and driest hole, God can rescue you from there!

Just as God committed himself to rescue the chosen nation because of the blood of the covenant we had with him, Messianic Jews and Christians from the nations have an even greater blood covenant today—Messiah's Covenant. Because of that covenant, God has bound himself to help us, deliver us, and protect us from all evil.

Just as the faithful remnant of Israel was compared to gems in a royal crown, all of God's children are like the crown jewels—valuable and precious and honorable in the sight of God. And just as the stones of a crown, which are of great value, are protected, so King of Kings protects those who are his.

We too are "prisoners of hope." Christians and Messianic Jews have a great hope, a sure expectation of salvation and eternal life and a great inheritance. That's why Simon Peter told us to fix our hope completely on the grace that will be brought to us when Messiah Yeshua is revealed.

If God does allow you to suffer for a time in a waterless pit, and if you remain faithful to him during that time of testing, you too will be doubly rewarded. That's why Rabbi Paul could write: "I consider that the sufferings of this present time are not worthy to be compared with the glory that is to be revealed to us." Our reward for faithful endurance will far outweigh any suffering we might experience in this life.

So, what do you think? Is Chanukkah spiritually dangerous? No.

Baruch HaShem (Blessed is God)

KEEPING A BALANCE FOR THE GENTILE MESSIANIC[3]

by Pastor Ross Clark

In most areas of our lives we have to be careful to walk in a balanced way. Too far to one side or the other can cause us to "fall off the tight rope" or be too extreme one way or the other. To find a balanced view we must study carefully the words of scripture. To do this we have to look at a number of scriptures and come up with a balanced view.

Apostle Paul declares at Caesarea that he was a circumcised Jewish Pharisee of the tribe of Benjamin. He continued to follow Jewish law. His habit was to worship on Shabbat and to attend the feasts as a believer, it is clear.

As his custom was, Paul went into the synagogue, and on three Sabbath days he reasoned with them from the Scriptures (Acts 17:2).

Paul had decided to sail past Ephesus to avoid spending time in the province of Asia, for he was in a hurry to reach Jerusalem, if possible, by the day of Pentecost (Acts 20:16).

But if we say that the Gentile church must follow the Law of Moses this implies there is no difference between Israel and the church. This is actually substitution theology.

The Apostle Paul wrote to the Gentiles believers in Yeshua in Colossians. This is in the bible!

Therefore do not let anyone judge you by what you eat or drink, or with regard to a religious festival, a New Moon celebration or a Sabbath day. These are a shadow of the things that were to come; the reality, however, is found in Messiah (Col 2:16).

Who was the "anyone" in this verse? Those who were false brethren/Judaisers who insisted all new converts must first be Jewish converts living a Jewish lifestyle. This verse doesn't say these Jewish things are wrong. It just says don't criticize a Gentile believer if he doesn't follow the following:

1. Kosher laws.

2. Attending religious festivals—IE Passover, Pentecost, Tabernacles, etc

3. New moon celebration—Feast of Trumpets (Rosh Hashanah)

4. A Sabbath day.

3. Clark, "Keeping a Balance."

But they are completely free to follow them if they wish. What does the bible say in Romans 11?

If some of the branches have been broken off, and you, though a wild olive shoot, have been grafted in among the others and now share in the nourishing sap from the olive root, do not boast over those branches. If you do, consider this: You do not support the root, but the root supports you (Rom 11:17–18).

The nourishing sap is the Spiritual blessings of Israel. This includes our salvation and our participating in the wonderful Shabbat and seven feasts of the LORD. We are allowed to "share in it."

In the Torah the Sabbath is not primarily about worship but rest. God decreed that the Sabbath day was to be Kaddosh or set aside from the other six days as a rest day for God's people.

Remember the Sabbath day by keeping it holy. Six days you shall labor and do all your work, but the seventh day is a Sabbath to the LORD your God. On it you shall not do any work, neither you, nor your son or daughter, nor your manservant or maidservant, nor your animals, nor the alien within your gates. For in six days the LORD made the heavens and the earth, the sea, and all that is in them (Exod 20:8–11) but he rested on the seventh day. Therefore the LORD blessed the Sabbath day and made it holy (Kadosh-separate).

The Sabbath was a reflection of God's creative work where after it was completed he rested. The Sabbath command also includes their servants/slaves, this points to when Israel as slaves was delivered from the burden of slavery in Egypt and had come to Mt. Sinai.

The Sabbath was Israel's sign of covenant with God. The ongoing regular weekly rhythm of work and rest was following God's pattern in an ever-renewed sign of their covenant with God.

Then the LORD said to Moses, "Say to the Israelites, 'You must observe my Sabbaths. This will be a sign between me and you for the generations to come, so you may know that I am the LORD, who makes you holy'" (Exod 31:21).

Actually God wants his people to worship him always not just on one day a week!

Hear, O Israel: The LORD our God, the LORD is one. Love the LORD your God with all your heart and with all your soul and with all your strength. These commandments that I give you today are to be upon your hearts. Impress them on your children. Talk about them when you sit at home and when you walk along the road, when you lie down and when you get up (Deut 6:4–7). Messiah Yeshua explains clearly the real purpose of the sabbath. The Sabbath is for man's benefit. As a blessing.

For in six days the LORD made the heavens and the earth, the sea, and all that is in them, but he rested on the seventh day. Therefore the LORD blessed the Sabbath day and made it holy (*Kaddosh*-set aside) (Exod 21:11). And he explains something. This is basically "a higher priority thing overides a lower thing." And so Yeshua himself is above the Sabbath! "Lord of the Sabbath." And it is lawful to do good on the Sabbath.

He answered, "Haven't you read what David did when he and his companions were hungry? He entered the house of God, and he and his companions ate the consecrated bread—which was not lawful for them to do, but only for the priests. Or haven't you read in the Law that on the Sabbath the priests in the temple desecrate the day and yet are innocent? I tell you that one greater than the temple is here. If you had known what these words mean, 'I desire mercy, not sacrifice,' you would not have condemned the innocent. For the Son of Man is Lord of the Sabbath." Going on from that place, he went into their synagogue, and a man with a shriveled hand was there. Looking for a reason to accuse Jesus, they asked him, "Is it lawful to heal on the Sabbath?" He said to them, "If any of you has a sheep and it falls into a pit on the Sabbath, will you not take hold of it and lift it out? How much more valuable is a man than a sheep!" Therefore it is lawful to do good on the Sabbath (Matt 12:3–11).

Then he said to the man, "Stretch out your hand." So he stretched it out and it was completely restored, just as sound as the other (Matt 12:13). Yeshua was clearly making a stand before them all. Yeshua does not want legalism on the Shabbat and doing good is allowed. But for Jews it is God's requirement as the sign of their Covenant with God. Gentiles are welcome to partake of the nourishing sap of the Shabbat too, but are not under the First Covenant as Jews so it is their choice, not obligation, as Col 2:16 says. For Messianic Gentiles who fellowship together with Messianic Jews the day of worship, of course, should be Shabbat, or Friday night.

The seven feasts listed in Leviticus 23 depict the whole redemptive story. Yeshua is actually there in them too. The Feasts of the LORD all point to him and God's purposes. Yeshua has already fulfilled the first three feasts (Passover as he is our Passover lamb, the First fruits as he is the first fruit of the resurrection, unleavened bread as he is pure of sin and Pentecost as the Holy Spirit has come to start the church).

The next three feasts to come are (Trumpets, Yom Kippur, Tabernacles) these point to major things to come in God's plan. The final day of the Lord as Yeshua returns for his people, the wrath of God on sinful mankind by the Messiah and the Millennial reign under the Messiah. Oh what a joy to joyfully participate in these biblical feasts not as a compulsion but willingly.

It is time for the church to discard the vestiges of the early church fathers' anti-Jewish bias. To embrace the God-given festivals and where possible worship at the same time as Jewish people do on the Sabbath. This is not "going under the law, ie. legalism." It is partaking of Israel's nourishing sap! This is part of the Jewish roots of the church that are its inheritance. Not to distain but to embrace.

Baruch HaShem (Blessed is God)

GENTILES WITHIN THE MESSIANIC JEWISH COMMUNITY[4]

by Rabbi Jeffrey A. Adler

It might help us in dealing with this issue to look back at the call of Israel. Abraham was called to leave everything he had known to follow the God he could not see to a place he had never been, abandoning all security for himself, his servants, and, even more, for Sarah. All this was done for the purpose of his being blessed and being a blessing—or, we might say, be blessed by being a blessing: "through you all the families of the earth will be blessed."

Abraham would represent his God, despite being without might or power of his own, yet having the intimate and personal oversight, protection, favor, and provision of the Creator of the Heavens and the earth. He would be the delegate of the Divine One to a broader world that since the Fall in the Garden had not a clue as to what to expect from the Holy God. In God's dealings with Abraham and his fledgling band, he established that he would show Mercy, Faithfulness, Rachamim (Parental Compassion), and Power, among other infinite qualities, to those willing to enter into a covenantal relationship of complete trust. The world, now made up primarily of a people to be known as Gentiles, needed to see the character of God acted out, demonstrated in real time and real events, and, so it happened. God showed his power and might through the events so eloquently portrayed on the pages of the T'nakh—the birth of Isaac, the wisdom given to Joseph, the plagues on Egypt and subsequent Exodus, the supply of manna and water from the rock, the parting of the Jordan, destruction of Jericho followed by the Conquest of the Land, the triumphs of David, etc. Even when the people turned away, God's "Soul could bear no longer the misery of Israel" (Judg 10:16). Hence, he raised up deliverers such as Barak, D'vorah, Gideon, Shamgar, et al. And, bearing in mind the stirring promises of passages like the great statements of Deuteronomy 7:6–9, "For you are a holy people to the Lord your God; the Lord your God has chosen you to be His own treasure out of all peoples that are upon the face of the earth. The Lord did not set His Love on you, nor choose you, because you were more in number than any people—for, you were fewest of all peoples—but, because the Lord loved you, and because the Lord would keep the oath which He

---

4. Adler, "Gentiles Within."

swore unto your fathers, has the Lord brought you out with a mighty hand, and redeemed you out of the house of bondage, from the hand of Pharaoh, king of Egypt. Know, therefore, that the Lord your God, He is God, the Faithful God, that keeps Covenant and Mercy with them that love Him and keep His commandments to a thousand generations . . . "

It should not surprise us if many who recognize this God as the God of the Jewish people would want to identify as closely as possible with his people. The texture of the world causes many of us to feel small, obscure, unimportant, unnoticed, and powerless. A God like the one just described is so appealing. What would it be like to be one of his very own?

Even the call to humility in passages such as Deuteronomy 8, "Beware lest you forget the Lord your God . . . lest when you have eaten and are satisfied, then your heart be lifted up, and you forget the Lord your God, Who brought you out of the Land of Egypt, out of the house of bondage . . . and you say in your heart, 'My power and the might of my hand has gotten me this wealth.' But, you shall remember the Lord your God, for, it is He that gives you the power to get wealth, that He may establish His Covenant which He swore to your fathers, as it is today" (Deut 8:11–18) could be understood to be telling Israel not to allow pride to obscure the role of the nature and character of the God of Israel from the eyes, not only of their own future generations, but, also, of the nations, who need to also trust in Israel's God.

Having said all this, we, as the Messianic Jewish community, must humbly realize that we, as an avant garde of the future believing Remnant of Israel, carry the standard and responsibility of serving as the collective witness of the faithful rule of the Lord before the greater world. As such, our response to the Gentiles among and around us, must be handled with some sensitivity and dexterity. The Gentile world, born again and not, still has a need to see the faithfulness of God to his Covenant in action. There is a very real danger that the survival of Israel will be perceived merely as the survival of culture and philosophy, rather than the rule of God over all. The use of the Pual stem, "*yulad*," in Isaiah 9:6, testifies to the demand for God to exert Divine force to carry out his plans, even in the gifting of Messiah's Birth. The real message of Israel is less cultural and religious tenacity than divine stamina and resilience. That message still desperately needs to be communicated.

Bearing in mind that the Messianic Jewish community has in the forefront of its collective consciousness the need and focus to reach our own Jewish community for Messiah Yeshua, we need to maintain a genuine

Baruch HaShem (Blessed is God)

Jewish expression of faith in Yeshua. Since the Jewish community is largely suspicious of our congregations as some sort of church-financed, church-directed, and church-controlled front that is not really Jewish at all, but, is merely some sort of sham with Jewish trappings meant to bait an evangelistic mousetrap, there is a genuinely felt need to maintain a viable Jewish face that has an integrity of real Jewish identity. Some feel a need to limit Gentile inclusion to a bare minimum. Some fear the temptation to welcome Gentiles for their financial and administrative support, rather than welcoming them sincerely as partners in ministry.

It is wise to recognize that, while many Gentile Christians might be interested in Messianic ministries of various sorts—because of a desire to reach Jewish friends, relatives, neighbors, business associates, etc., for Messiah; for personal enrichment of their faith through exploration of its Biblical, Jewish roots; due to a fascination with Jewish heritage, such as feasts and festivals; and the like—only certain ones would have a desire for long-term residential relationship with such ministries. It is here where we might wish to place our focus-on the issue of personal sense of calling.

First of all, we all recognize that not all of us in Jewish ministry have the same personality, temperament, skills, style, motivations, giftings, et cetera. Some work better with more traditional Jewish people, some with mixed marriages, some with professionals, and so forth. Some of us attract certain types of people, functioning better in particular types of settings and formats. Some need more of a team approach, at least in certain circumstances. This needs to be recognized as provision, even Fathering, by the sovereign Hand of the Lord. In this light, some of us are going to attract more Gentile teammates than others. Others of us are going to draw out Jewish people who might be frightened, uncomfortable—at least initially—by the presence of Gentiles, fearing this might be indicative of a less than Jewish identity should they decide to commit themselves to Messianic faith. These perspectives seem so natural to those in possession of them that it would almost seem that everyone should operate the same way. But, there is still that element of divine calling and equipping. All need to be reached, and so, God equips different individuals to reach the different types of Jewish people.

However, God is not so cold and calculating, even manipulative and mercenary, merely exploiting his children/servants in such ways. Psalms 37:4 says, "Delight yourself also in the Lord, and, He shall give you the desires of your heart." "Desires" here is a rendering of the Hebrew noun "*mishalot*," derived from the verb "*shaal*," to pray. It refers to cravings sent from God, cravings so intimate and personal that they become part of the relational context between himself and us that we find them at the core of our lives. It was these that caused Adonai to say to Jeremiah, "I have gifted you as a prophet to the nations," in spite of all that man's angst and trauma. It was the mishalot in Paul that led him to state, "Woe to me if I preach not the Good News," not that God would kill him, but, that he could not be himself if he failed to carry out his calling.

As servants of the Lord, we also have a role in helping the people who come to us determine their "mishalot," including the Gentiles. We need to help discern whether they have a sincere calling—a "mishalah"—to join us as true partners, or not. There are some who, having become disenchanted with their own identity, merely wish to dump it for another. Jewishness may look exotic and alluring, but, if their involvement is not Holy Spirit-directed, they will be a liability to themselves, as well as to the ministry. Their motivation is personal pain, not divine direction.

There are, however, Gentiles who genuinely find their sincere calling in involvement and identity within the Messianic Jewish community. Recently, one of our non-Jewish women was asked by an elderly Jewish woman why she, as a Gentile, was involved with a Messianic Jewish congregation. This Jewish woman had been given a very questionable response by another person, and was highly disdainful of us as a result. The non-Jewish woman responded that the God of Abraham, Isaac, and Jacob is God. The elderly woman was so impressed by the maturity and sincerity of the response that she has become very open to the younger one. This Gentile woman, with one statement, communicated the integrity of message of the Jewish scriptures in a way only a Gentile could.

When all has been said, there are avenues open to Gentiles in relating to the larger Jewish community not available to us who have been born naturally into the Jewish world. Paul had this in mind in his famous Romans 11:11 when he spoke of the ministry to Gentiles being a provocation to Jewish jealousy. While the exact meaning of this concept has been the topic of some debate and discussion, certainly, the love of Gentiles for Israel's people, heritage, and God would certainly expose a deficit of appreciation in the eyes of many Jewish people for their own heritage. That, against the background of so much anti-semitism by Gentiles down through the centuries, Gentiles loving Jewish people, culture, Jewishness itself, stands in stark contrast and can certainly grab attention, at least raising attention as to why and how this came about in this person.

Baruch HaShem (Blessed is God)

Ezekiel 47:21–23 makes a profound statement about the role of Gentiles in the Kingdom Age.

> "So, you shall divide this land unto you according to the tribes of Israel. And it shall come to pass, that ye shall divide it by lot for an inheritance unto you and to the strangers that sojourn among you, who shall beget children among you; and they shall be unto you as the homeborn among the children of Israel; they shall have inheritance with you among the tribes of Israel. And it shall come to pass, that in what tribe the stranger sojourneth, there shall ye give him his inheritance, saith the Lord God."

Here, Gentiles have obviously chosen to live among Israel, to the point of establishing their homes and rearing children. They submit themselves to the culture, economy, education—the very life of Israel. This could not be speaking of any or all Gentiles, but, those with a particular motivation to select such a life and home, to the point that God's statements here go so far as to protect their interests and rights. From a Biblical perspective, I believe we must refer to this motivation as a sense of divine calling.

In summation, I believe that we should recognize that not every Gentile is called to live among us, identifying with us and our lives and communities, and, that many who claim to wish to do this may well be desirous of an unhealthy escape from their own identity. Also, we should acknowledge that the Messianic community is not desirous of denigrating other cultures and ethnicities, instead recognizing that those other identities are just as gifted from Adonai as ours. Further, we also need to recognize that there are also people who have a genuine call, a "mishalah," if I may borrow the term from Psalm 37:4, to be among us as more than occasional visitors. If we were to deny them, we would, from a pastoral perspective, be doing them, as well as our ministries, even our communities, a great disservice.

We seek constantly to develop a viable strategy to carry out the tasks presented to us by the Lord. The danger, as the previously cited passages from Deuteronomy 7 and 8 warn, is in not giving priority to the supreme role of the Lord himself over our own perspectives.

If the divine composer has written parts for the instrumental gifts of Gentiles, not including them in the orchestra of the Messianic community, if not causing the sounding of some sour notes, would at least deprive the world, and Avinu, Malkeynu, of some of the sweetest notes of his symphony.

10

Mikveh (Immersion)

It's true that I am immersing you in water so that you might turn from sin to God (MATT 3:11).

The first command of the new covenant invites people to the water, calling them from their sins to turn toward God, for the Kingdom of Heaven is near! (Matt 3:2). A voice called from the desert summoning people through baptism in the flow of a river. When a Gentile is raised from the waters of the mikveh, his old man perishes and he becomes the seed of Abraham.

The last command in the new covenant tells us, "Come!" Let anyone who hears say, "Come!" And let anyone who is thirsty come—let anyone who wishes, take the water of life free of charge.

Life centers on God providing water.

Summer fills Jerusalem with hot clear skies from May to September and cooling nights as grapes ripen on vines. There is little rain on the people strolling the city streets in these months. An occasional *hamsin,* a dust storm, can bring in dry winds raising temperatures up to 104 F.

Because Israel depends so much on rainfall for water supply, Israelis welcome the wet season that begins in late autumn. Torrential downpours are known as "rains of blessing" and both young and old run outside to dance with joy, their faces turned up to the sky's raindrops. Sukkot is celebrated at summer's end, just before the rainy season, with rituals of water libation and the four species, especially the willow representing a plant

Mikveh (Immersion)

thriving on water. Sukkot is also known as Feast of Booths, Feast of Tabernacles, or Feast of the Ingathering. The celebration brings the *Sh'mini Atzeret*, the prayer for rain, recited at the conclusion of the Festival of Sukkot in a melody acknowledging the blessing of water and our deep thirst when rains don't come and there is famine and disease in the land.

Supplication is made to *masheev ha'rua'ch u'moreed hagashem*, "who causes the wind to blow and the rain to fall." There was a joyous ceremony of songs and dancing at the Temple involving pouring water, called the *Simhat Beit Ha'Shoeva*. The Mishnah (Sukkah 5:3) says every courtyard in Jerusalem was illuminated from the light of the water drawing ceremony at the temple.

The cantor recites the prayer for rain in six parts to our God and God of our ancestors, each part referring to water in the lives of Abraham, Isaac, Jacob, Moses, Aaron, and the Twelve Tribes.

> Remember Abraham who flowed to You like water.
>
> You blessed him like a tree planted by streams of water. You rescued him from fire and water.
>
> He passed Your test by planting good deeds by every source of water.
>
> For Abraham's sake, do not keep back water.
>
> Remember Isaac, whose birth was foretold when Abraham offered the angels a little water.
>
> You asked his father to spill his blood like water. In the desert Isaac dug and found wells of water.
>
> For Isaac's sake, do not keep back water.
>
> Remember Jacob, who crossed the Jordan's water. He bravely rolled the stone off the mouth of the well of water. He wrestled with an angel made of fire and water, And therefore You promised to be with him through fire and water.
>
> For Jacob's sake do not keep back water.
>
> Remember Moses, who was drawn in a reed basket out of the Nile's water. Who helped Jethro's daughters: He drew water and gave the sheep water. He struck the rock and out came water.
>
> For Moses' sake do not hold back water!
>
> Remember Aaron, the High Priest, who, on Yom Kippur, washed himself five times with water,
>
> He prayed and was sprinkled with purifying water, He kept apart from a people who were as unstable as water.
>
> For Aaron's sake do not hold back water.

Remember the Twelve Tribes whom You brought through the divided waters; For whom You sweetened bitter water; Their descendants' blood was spilled like water. Turn to us, God, who are surrounded by troubles like water.

For the Jewish people's sake, do not hold back water.

You are Adonai, our God Who causes the wind to blow and the rain to fall.

For blessing and not for curse. Amen. For life and not for death. Amen.

For plenty and not for lack. Amen.

Mikveh (Immersion)

BAPTISM[1]

by Rabbi Stephen Luft

The concept of baptism within the church is that it is an ordinance specific to and unique to the church. However, baptism is anything but new. I have a saying... there is nothing new in the New Covenant. Meaning that everything you read about are not new concepts, but are found throughout the Tenach, which is known as the Jewish Bible. This is also true for baptism.

When Yochanan the Immerser (John the Baptist) said, "I am immersing people in water, but among you is standing someone whom you don't know," (John 1:26), he was practicing an ancient culture that is still practiced today. In Hebrew immersion by water is known as mikveh. Mikveh means pool or gathering of water. Typically, it's a vessel that is constructed as a permanent structure to collect water. It cannot be filled by human hands, but gathers water naturally through rainfall. The concept originates in Leviticus 11:36, when the Jewish people were instructed to use only a spring or cistern for water that remains ritually clean without the assistance of human action.

Yochanan was performing mikveh in a natural body of water that was flowing which was permitted. No human hands were used to bring forth the water used for immersion. At the time of Yeshua there were some 500 mikveh vessels in Jerusalem alone. Meaning that immersion was performed at various times.

The origin of the mikveh began in Genesis when the earth was unformed and the Spirit of G-d hovered over the surface of the water. The first immersion was creation when the entire earth was covered by water. Out of the water came the land. G-d gathered the water together, called it seas, and let dry land appear. G-d said that it was good.

In these two verses you see a gathering of water or mikveh—"let the water under the sky be gathered" and out of the gathered water came the land—the second half of immersion. What did Adonai say at the end? He said that It was good. Meaning it was pristine, undefiled, without blemish.

The oral law of the Talmud, rabbis over the centuries teach that the Spirit of Adonai over the waters refers to the Spirit of Messiah. The Messianic age represents the final fulfillment of G-d's purpose in creation. Evil will be vanquished and good will reign over all mankind. The Spirit of

---

1. Luft, "Baptism."

Adonai directs all change and movement in a positive force, moving the world, his creation, back to its ultimate goal, which is its original state of perfection. This is the Messianic age.

These insights came centuries before Yeshua walked on the earth. So, the concept of Messiah was well engrained within the Jewish mind. Yochanan the Immerser is preparing the people to be immersed, cleansed in preparation for the Kingdom of Adonai.

At least three reasons compel a person to go through immersion: ritual purification to restore through washing for the purpose of entering the Mishkan, Temple, area. This is important because ritually unclean persons were not allowed to bring a sacrifice to the Mishkan. Consecration requires a mikveh. An example is Aaron and his sons being chosen to be kohanim and represent the people. Aharon and his sons were brought to the entrance of the tent of meeting and were washed with water (Exod 29:4). Conversion requires a mikveh. An example is Israel being set apart from all other nations. They were transformed into a nation for Adonai when they were instructed to wash their clothing and prepare for the third day when Adonai came down on Mount Sinai before the eyes of all the people and gave the Torah.

All three of these aspects are also the reasons why a believer is instructed to go through immersion, commonly known as baptism. Ritual impurity is a symbolic cleansing of our sinfulness (Matt 3:2). This concept of turning from your sins and turning to G-d in Hebrew is known as T'shuvah, what many understand as repentance. Consecration sets us apart to be citizens of the Kingdom of Adonai, the Kingdom of Heaven. In essence separating us from our old life and old nature. This is the same concept when Adonai consecrated Israel at Mount Sinai in Exodus 19. Conversion or Transformation. As believers in Yeshua, we have been transformed. Sha'ul says that we have received a new nature. By being immersed you are making the statement that I am "ritually unclean" one of sinfulness, that I have either ignored Adonai or never recognized him to begin with. You are willing to submit and be obedient to the smallest of instructions in order to be transformed. Coming out of immersion, you are consecrated and transformed. Separated from your past life and transformed into a new creation. Through acceptance of Messiah, we are identified as a new creation (2 Cor 5:17).

This is what is called being born again. For believers there is also another immersion, not of water but of the Spirit of Adonai (Matt 3:11). It is when we receive this second immersion that our lives forever change. The

Mikveh (Immersion)

statement, "you must be born again," in the encounter between Yeshua and Nakdimon (Nicodemus) is a well-known concept among Jews.

When someone converts to Judaism, they have gone through a born again experience. In Judaism, you have been transformed from a goy or gentile and into a person of the covenant of Adonai. This transformation for men would include physical circumcision. Likewise, coming to faith and trust in Yeshua as Messiah, requires a circumcision of the heart, performed by the one who created us. Yeshua answered, "Yes, indeed, I tell you that unless a person is born from water and the Spirit, he cannot enter the Kingdom of God" (John 3:5). Both Jewish conversion and accepting Yeshua as Messiah are born again experiences, whereby you are turning away from your past sinful nature and being made new. Both transformations include going through mikveh, which we spoke about in previous segments. This is the water that Yeshua spoke about. The Spirit is the heart circumcision.

Within Jewish understanding there are other born again experiences besides conversion. Getting married is a born again experience. Your previous state was as one of being an individual. When you get married, you are no longer seen as single but your life has been transformed and you are now part of something new. When you have a child, this is viewed as a born again experience. You have gone from being a couple to becoming a family. When one goes through the steps of training and finally becomes a rabbi, he has had a born again experience.

Although not called born again experiences in the Jewish culture today because it is associated with Christian proselytizing, it is a very Jewish idea that even Nakdimon should have known and ultimately did know when Rabbi Yeshua did what he does best—teach.

Before the born again experience can happen, there is another Jewish idea that must first occur—T'shuvah. Known as repentance, many teach that you are to turn from your sin. However, turning from your transgression is only half of T'shuvah from a Jewish perspective. The other part is to return to Adonai. Without emphasis placed on returning to Adonai, the potential to return from what you have turned away from is more likely because you have only changed direction, but not established a destination. The idea of T'shuvah can be found throughout scriptures. "But because I, Adonai, do not change, you sons of Ya`akov will not be destroyed. Since the days of your forefathers you have turned from my laws and have not kept them. Return to me, and I will return to you," says Adonai-Tzva'ot (Mal 3:6–7).

Returning to Adonai requires a repentant heart first, followed by action on our part to take the first step. When we do these two things first, Adonai says he will return to us. Yochanan the Immerser conveys the same principle when he is preparing the way for Yeshua who will convey the message of redemption. If you have really turned from your sins to G-d, produce fruit that will prove it! (Matt 3:8). True repentance requires two actions on our part, turning from our ways that are contrary to that of Adonai thus enabling us to return to him as our destination. Yochanan takes it a step further by stating that if you have done T'shuvah, there will be results that are tangible for others to see.

It is our transgression that separates us from Adonai. It is through T'shuvah—repentance, and trust in that what Yeshua has said and done that our redemption can be restored. T'shuvah isn't just lip service, but action with results. The concept of new birth Yeshua introduced can come only from above as G-d transforms a life. It is not the rebirth of a Gentile becoming Jewish or a Jew becoming part of a Gentile church, but an awakening of a kingdom of children born through the water.

Mikveh (Immersion)

SHIC'ZUR O T'CIYA?—RESTORATION OR REVIVAL?[2]

by Geoff Davenport

Yahveh is very clear when he speaks to Moshe, confirming his identity as the same God who appeared to Avraham, Yitz'chak, and Ya'akov as El Shaddai or God Almighty, a description of what he is, as well as who he is. To Moshe he introduces himself by name, Yud Heh Vav Heh or Yahveh, often mistranslated as "I am who I am" (Greek Tetragrammaton). The actual Hebrew translation (no not Aramaic, Yeshua's native tongue was Hebrew) is "I was, I am, I will be." Then he restates and re-confirms his covenants and promises to restore their inheritance, the land of Cana'an, to rescue them from oppression, and redeem them personally, to establish a personal relationship between them and himself forever.

They were simply looking for revival, a sudden burst of renewed energy to cope with everyday life as they knew it, a spiritual adrenaline fix, a virtual reality to escape to, in the midst of grinding oppression, human control, and poverty. Yet what they really needed was not a flashy quick fix that feels good but doesn't last, but a total restoration, a *Yovel* (Jubilee) that wipes the slate clean and gives them absolute freedom as they reclaim their original rightful inheritance as Yahvehs own nation of Y'israel.

Many people today are praying fervently for "revival," a term that generally refers to business as usual with a quick fix burst of energy, a specific period of increased spiritual interest or renewal in the life of a church congregation or a particular church denomination, either regionally or globally. Revival is a process of bringing something back to life that is near death with a jolt from a set of spiritual electric paddles, a process repeated many many times due to poor health of the "patient," a condition brought on by excessive punishment of the body, chronic disease, and severe malnutrition.

In the year 325 a breach birth took place in Nicaea of a counterfeit lifeless body called Christendom. Its father was Constantine 1st and its mother was a variety of pagan goddesses. Neither were Jewish, and all Jews were banned from attending the birth. It was used then and still is today to try and kill off and replace the Messianic Body restored by Yeshua ha Mashiach about 290 years earlier, a body with both spiritual and physical genetic links stretching back to the beginning of time. The good news of course is that,

2. Davenport, "Shic'zur o t'ciya?"

just like Moshe, we survived and thrived and today we are continuing to be fully restored as his true body that ironically includes the gentiles who have worked so hard to wipe us out.

So do I want revival? No! Am I praying for it? No! Why on Earth would I want this present day Frankenstein-like monster of cobbled together religious body parts revived even once, let alone over and over again in a regurgitated politically correct multitude of new identities and disguises? What I want, what I really really want, is complete restoration, a "Back to the Future" scenario that strips back the multiple layers of blatant lies, religious propaganda, and age old superstitions and finally reveal the actual, one true, real live, Body of Yeshua Ha Mashiach. Complete and undivided with him as its head uniting both halves, Jew and Gentile grafted together as one into his Olive tree. A tree that produces genuine "good fruit" both in season and out of season, a tree that enables us to love one another and forgive one another unconditionally.

Many will say, "that's impossible," but I say a miracle is making the impossible possible, making a way where there is no way. The body began life with both halves and will only function properly when both halves are restored as one, as we go forward together in unity.

Will the tentacle-like multinational religious organizations step aside, finally repent and admit the truth? Sadly probably not, no! Why? Because their very existence hinges on their existing power bases, and depends on denying the truth by continuing to live the lie. But just like Goliath they will fall, taken down by the small smooth stones of truth delivered by an army of seemingly insignificant "Davids" who understand that it's not by power, nor by might, but by Yahvehs spirit, the spirit of truth, led by the Spirit of Truth, the Ruach ha Kodesh that will defeat the enemy and remove its head.

So finally what's the difference for us personally between revival and restoration? Aren't they just the same thing? Absolutely not! Revival is merely a temporary fix, an adrenaline shot, a respite from the inevitable. It's like putting a band aid on the hull of the Titanic, or slapping yet another coat of paint onto a crumbling decaying house. You are only covering the decay and delaying the inevitable. Restoration on the other hand is the act of bringing something back to its original condition, like an ancient building stripped back to its original framework and foundations and then fully rebuilt following the exact original blueprints until it is duplicated and completely renewed and ready to carry out and fulfill its original purpose.

Mikveh (Immersion)

So we have an inheritance. We are not "slaves." We simply need to reclaim our original rightful deed of covenant whose terms of the inheritance are outlined and made very clear. Our responsibilities to carry out and administer our side of it are equally clear. Please spend time studying and rereading your copy, then start fulfilling its terms and conditions as you put them into practice. Torah (both halves) are a living covenant that is just as relevant today as the day it was written, but you have to translate it into action on a daily basis. No one else can or will do it for you, no one else can claim your inheritance or fulfill your responsibilities.

Ask the Ruach to give you an ear (spiritual) to hear what he is telling you and then follow the maker's instructions, his directions. After all, he has promised to lead you into all truth hasn't he? As it says in 1 Corinthians 2:19, "As the Tanakh says, no eye has seen, no ear has heard and no one's heart has imagined all the things that Yahveh has prepared for those who love him."

And we love him right? But remember it is a spiritual inheritance we seek. Anything physical "enough" is an added bonus designed to keep us functioning on a daily needs basis. So trust and remember to pray for restoration, not revival (we are already alive and kicking), and for redemption not conversion. Redemption rescues me from slavery and restores me to my rightful place in Abba's family. Conversion just tries to turn me into something I'm not, like converting money, dollars to euros or lire, or transforming me from Jew to Gentile, or "Christian."

So be bold, claim your full inheritance Abba's way. We think that just because eternal life is a gift, we have no obligations at all. But the word Yarash is an active verb, not a passive acceptance. It means "to take possession of, to drive out, to dispossess" the enemy. The gift is there, thanks only to Yahveh, but we have to go into battle to possess it. We have to displace the enemy who occupies our territory. We have to drive out those who would prevent our full enjoyment of Abba's goodness. We have to make the gift our own. The land will remain dormant, until we, his people, arrive and take control of our inheritance. It will not be given to others. It will wait until we step up and fulfill what he asks of us when he says. "Go into the inheritance I have given you and occupy it." All of it. So trust, be bold, be strong, be obedient, today.

Shalom Yarash—Take Possession Shalom.

11

Sukkot (Feast of the Ingathering)

> Finally, everyone remaining from all the nations that came to attack Yerushalayim will go up every year to worship the king, ADONAI-Tzva'ot, and to keep the festival of Sukkot
>
> (ZECH 14:16).

Sukkot begins with the full moon spilling light from its overflowing cup on the fifteenth of the seventh month, in the very middle of the month, six months after Passover. Sukkot is the seven-day harvest festival set aside for Adonai to enjoy with his people

Building a sukkah is a family event and great fun for children to decorate with branches, flowers, the fruits of harvest, and dwell in when the weather is warm enough. The people are to live in a sukkah in remembrance of the forty years in the wilderness when Israel lived in temporary shelters and God himself tabernacled them (Lev 23:42–43). The holiday is a full week celebrating the bounty of the harvest, giving thanks to the God of Israel for blessing another year, for land to grow foods, seeds to plant, sun to shine on them, rain to water them, and strength to harvest them. The four plant species used to rejoice before the Lord are an etrog, which is a citron fruit, the beautiful foliage of a lulav, which is a palm branch, two aravot, which are willow, and three hadassim, myrtle branches. The branches are bound together and the etrog is held separately. The blessing is recited and the species are waved east, west, north, south, up toward heaven, and down toward earth because God is sovereign everywhere. The end of Sukkot celebrates the conclusion of the annual cycle of Torah readings and the beginning of a new cycle.

Sukkot follows Yom Kippur, which begins the Day of Atonement ten days after the new moon in early autumn. Coming home on this evening the people do not eat dinner. It is a time to fast. The Day of Atonement ended when the high priest entered the Holy of Holies and confessed the collective sins of the nation of Israel and offered sacrifice. Mercy calls back the estranged and all that God spoke of through his prophets and teachers is remembered. It is a day the corporate failings of the body of the Messiah can be confessed.

Traditionally the books of judgment are reflected on to consider the deeds of the past year. Every name is written in these books, whether in the wicked, the righteous, or those wavering between. It is a time of repentance. The ceremony of Tashlikh symbolically casts off sins. After the morning service of Yom Kippur, the people gather to a body of water, an ocean, lake, or river, where they pray. They take bread from their pockets and throw it into the water for the water to carry it away, representing the letting go of transgressions.

> Who is a God like you, pardoning the sin and overlooking the crimes of the remnant of his heritage? He does not retain his anger forever, because he delights in grace. He will again have compassion on us, he will subdue our iniquities. You will throw all their sins into the depths of the sea. You will show truth to Ya'akov and grace to Avraham, as you have sworn to our ancestors since days of long ago (Mic 7:18–20).

Sukkot, the Feast of Tabernacles, follows with a season of joy under the commandment to rejoice before the Lord. On the last day the water ceremony was observed using water from the pool of Siloam where Jesus healed a blind man. In the Temple the court of the women was illuminated with lights placed on candelabra's seventy-feet high. Each candelabra had four branches. At the top of each branch there was a large bowl. Four young men bearing ten gallon pitchers of oil would climb ladders to fill the four golden bowls on each candelabra. The oil in the bowls was ignited and flames blazed toward the sky and illuminated the court of the women.

Flutes were played leading the priest who was sent for the water. The flutes continued with the Israelites singing songs of praise (Ps 118) as the procession went back to the Temple through the east gate, the water gate. A trumpet sounded as the priests enter. The priest poured out the water onto the altar as a drink offering to the Lord.

It was at this high altar service that Jesus was moved to cry out, "If anyone thirsts, let him come drink of me!"

Prophetically, Sukkot speaks of a future exodus from the nations to be gathered back to the promised land, spoken of by Jeremiah about the end of the ages. The observance of the Feast of Ingathering and its relationship with the future exodus is considered to be the greatest Messianic prophecy. God will dwell with his people and be known.

In the wilderness time, the tabernacle was erected a year after the first Passover when God instructed Moses to "make a sanctuary for me, and I will dwell among them" (Exod 25:8). A tent was constructed to travel with and set up in the center of the twelve tribes wherever they camped.

A white linen curtain seven and a half feet high, 150 feet long, and seventy-five feet wide surrounded the area. There was one outer gate and it faced east. The entrance was thirty-feet wide and seven and a half feet high, hung with linen in a colorful blend of white, blue, purple, and scarlet.

The gate entered into the outer court where there was the altar for a sacrifice offered for mercy. A bronze wash basin stood between the altar and the curtain to the Holy Place. Only priests could enter. In the Holy Place, the gold menorah was placed on the left. On the right was the table with twelve loaves of the Bread of the Presence. In the back was the gold altar of incense, then the veil of the *Kodesh HaKodashim* (the Holy of Holies). The gilded wooden Ark was kept here, containing the tablets with the ten commandments, Aaron's budded rod, and the golden jar of manna. Above them, the pillar of cloud by day and the pillar of fire by night taught the Israelites to watch and follow God.

A curtain of white linen woven with blue, scarlet, and purple led into the fifteen-by-fifteen foot square of the Holy of Holies. Only the high priest could enter here until Jesus died, when the veil in the Temple was torn from top to bottom. "I am the gate; whoever enters through me will be saved" (John 10:9). Before this, non-Jews could not walk in beyond the outer wall when the Israelite people could go into the courtyard. The wall separated Jews and Gentiles, initially calling out the Jews to come into relationship with God that they would take to the nations. Because of Jesus, they both now have access to God.

When Jesus establishes his tabernacle in Jerusalem, the entire world will come and celebrate. "And I heard a loud voice from heaven saying,

Sukkot (Feast of the Ingathering)

"Behold, the tabernacle of Elohim [is] with men, and He will dwell with them, and they shall be His people. Elohim Himself will be with them [and be] their Elohim" (Rev 21:3). Sukkot is the last of God's annual feasts, acknowledging the mountain of the Lord's house to be the highest of hills where all people will stream. Many Gentiles will go and say, "Come, let's go up to the mountain of ADONAI, to the house of the God of Ya'akov! He will teach us about his ways, and we will walk in his paths" (Mic 4:1–2).

The Lord God, who gathers the dispersed of Israel, declares, "Yet others I will gather to them, to those already gathered" (Isa 56:8).

THE MEANING OF SUKKOT[1]

by Rabbi Stephen Luft

He did not leave them in the desert to die, they were not abandoned or orphaned. Just as Yeshua made a similar promise. "I will not leave you orphans" (John 14:18). Specific instruction is given that you are to be joyful during this time. That means no heavy hearts, no grieving, no sadness.

The command to come and rejoice with the Lord is so important to God that he gave instruction to those who are traveling far distances and can't bring their tithe of harvest with them. Every year the people are to take a tenth of their harvest and eat it in the presence of Adonai in a place he chooses. If too far away to carry it to that place, people were to convert their harvest into money and take the money with them, then exchange it for any harvest they choose and join the celebrating in the presence of Adonai (Deut 14:22–26).

Eating in the presence of Adonai in essence is having a meal together that ultimately reaffirms the covenant. Many people don't realize the significance of Sukkot and its future impact for all nations and believers in Yeshua. Within the framework of Sukkot, created by Adonai, there is an element that pertains to the nations as well as Israel.

In Numbers 29, Adonai gives instruction regarding the sacrifices that were to be done during the seven days of Sukkot and also the eighth day. On the first day of Sukkot, there were thirteen bulls to be offered. The next day it was twelve, the next day it was eleven until they got to the seventh day when seven bulls were offered. The total number of bulls offered was seventy. When we look at Genesis 10, we are told of the number of nations that existed. The number of nations that existed after the flood was seventy. There was an eighth day where a single bull was offered. Israel was not present at the time of Genesis 10 when Adonai had conveyed who the seventy nations were. What the nations don't know or even what believers don't understand is that Adonai, through Israel, has been interceding for the nations for centuries.

The time of Sukkot is significant to the future of all nations and believers. Zechariah prophesied that all the nations that had once attacked Jerusalem would finally go up every year to worship the king, Adonai-Tzva'ot,

---

1. Luft, "The Meaning of Sukkot."

Sukkot (Feast of the Ingathering)

and to keep the festival of Sukkot. If any of the peoples of earth do not, they will have no rain on their land (Zech 14:16–17).

When you consider some of the bad teachings today where people are being taught that the feasts are no longer valid or have been done away, there is prophecy that has yet been fulfilled that speaks of a future time where the King of Israel, whom we know is Yeshua, and is identified here as Adonai-Tzva'ot, the Lord of Hosts, is requiring everyone from all nations who came to attack Yerushalayim, to keep the festival of Sukkot. I can hear it now... "well that applies to others, not us." Believe it or not, as a believer and follower of the King of Israel, it is understood that you will already be keeping Sukkot.

Sukkot is the back drop for some of the most powerful and significant teachings of Yeshua. In relation to Messiah, this feast will be a celebration like no other in history. Yeshua was continually challenged by religious leaders who threatened to arrest him. He persevered to perform miracles during this feast that would establish his identity without confrontation. The Feast of Tabernacles was nearing and his brother said he should to go Judea. Yeshua told them to go, his time had not yet come. But he went to the Temple in secret and taught on the last day of the great feast. This is when he stood up and said if anyone thirsted they should come to him. He spoke to them again saying he was the light of the world and anyone following him will never walk in darkness but have light that gives life (John 8:12).

It is Yeshua who not only created the light that exists but is the light, the hope of anyone who believes in him. The light of the future new heaven and new earth will be him. During Sukkot was also the time where he conveyed being the River of Living Water, thus connecting him to Adonai in the wilderness with Israel.

SUKKOT: MESSIAH AND THE WORLD TO COME[2]

by Rabbi Joshua Brumbach

The sukkah is a reminder of our human frailty and mortality. When dwelling in the sukkah, we find ourselves exposed to the elements, eating our meals without certain familiar comforts, and spending time in a shelter that at any moment could be brought down by weather. Like the sukkah, our earthly bodies are also temporary dwelling places that at any time could be brought down. This reality forces us to recognize our dependence upon HaShem, who daily causes us to live.

But a sukkah carries even greater imagery in both biblical and rabbinic thought. Jewish tradition has long understood the connections between Sukkot, Messiah, and the Messianic Age. That is why the image of a sukkah is used multiple times throughout our prayers and is even used as an image for Messiah himself! For example, in the evening service, at the end of a prayer called Hashkivenu, we pray: Spread over us your sukkah of peace. Blessed are You, Adonai, who spreads a sukkah of peace over us, over all your people Israel, and over Jerusalem.

According to Zechariah 14, the Haftarah reading for the first two days of Sukkot, in the Messianic Age all the nations will be gathered together in Jerusalem at Sukkot to worship the one true God. That is why Sukkot is also known as Chag Ha'Asif—the Festival of Ingathering. God's desire to reconcile humanity back to himself is mirrored most vividly in the festival of Sukkot because God's desire has always been macro—to reach all of humanity, beginning with Israel. That is why the Jewish people are called to be Or l'Goyim—a Light to the Nations. It is also why seventy bulls were offered as sacrifices during Sukkot, corresponding to each of the seventy nations of the world (Gen 10). Because, according to our rabbis, this was a prophetic act of intercession for the nations.

The imagery of a sukkah is also used as an allusion to Messiah. In Birkat HaMazon, the blessing after the meals, we add a special line during the festival of Sukkot:

The Merciful One, he will raise up for us the fallen sukkah of David.

What is the "fallen Sukkah of David?" Most commentators (Targum, Maharal, Malbim) understand this phrase from Amos 9:11 to refer to the rejuvenated Davidic dynasty. The Talmud, playing on the word for "fallen"

2. Brumbach, Joshua, Sukkot.

(nafal), even refers to the Messiah as a Bar Nafli, the fallen son: R. Nachman said to R. Isaac: "Have you heard when Bar Nafli will come?" "Who is Bar Nafli?" he asked. "Messiah", he answered. "Do you call the Messiah Bar Nafli?" "Yes," he responded, as it is written, "on that day I will raise up the fallen sukkah of David" (Sanhedrin 96b–97a).

According to the Maharal of Prague, the Davidic line cast as a sukkah and not as a house is a precise and purposeful formulation—for the sukkah's flimsiness allows it to be rebuilt. This allusion to resurrection fits perfectly with our own Messianic Jewish understanding of Messiah. When we pray this line in Birkat HaMazon we can, and should, understand this reference Messianically (and in doing so we are in good company).

Using the imagery of a sukkah in reference to the Messiah is not unique to rabbinic tradition. In fact, this is precisely the imagery behind the Greek of John 1:14: For the Word became flesh and tabernacled (or sukkah-ed) among us, and we beheld his Shechinah.

The Greek word used is skeno'o, which literally means to "tabernacle" or "to dwell." Therefore, the image of the sukkah is not restricted only to Sukkot, but rather because of its powerful allusions, is also used to refer to the Messianic Age, Messiah, and the presence of HaShem dwelling among us.

WHEN WAS YESHUA BORN?[3]

by Rabbi Stephen Luft

Within the church, Yeshua's birth is recognized on December 25th yet there is no evidence to support this date. You even have within the church impassioned justification for this time with staunch supporters and poetic catch phrases "remember the reason for the season."

You have yet another camp that will claim that there isn't enough information to truly know when Yeshua was born. We tend to look for the *p'shat*, the plain and simple meaning, however when it isn't written out for us, we will tend to follow the crowd and recognize what other people believe. I am here to tell you that the information is before you and has been there all along. You just didn't know what to look for, or understand the heritage from which Yeshua was birthed. What is even more ironic is that the beginning of our journey is read every Christmas, yet it is missed year after year.

Why is this missed year after year? It is missed because they involve the feasts for which the church in general believes are for the Jewish people only and are not relevant to the church.

In the days of Herod, king of Y'hudah, there was a cohen named Z'kharyah who belonged to the Aviyah division (Luke 1:5). His wife was a descendant of Aharon, and her name was Elisheva. This verse gets read every year yet is the starting point for our journey. If you are not familiar with Israel, the Jewish people, the Temple, the Priesthood, and prophecy then you will be lost before you even start. First ask, who are Z'kharyah and Elisheva? They are the parents of Yochanan the Immerser, John the Baptist, the one who would come before Yeshua.

Z'kharyah, a Levitical priest, is part of the Aviyah division. When you understand the division of the Levitical priesthood, this piece of information will make perfect sense. Each division would serve at the Temple twice a year, according to their division. In addition to their division service, all priests were required to serve during the three pilgrimage feasts—Passover, Shavuot, and Sukkot (1 Chr 24). A priest would serve in the Temple five weeks out of the year. The remainder of the time, they were the spiritual leaders and judges of the communities where they resided. The Aviyah division for which Z'kharyah belonged was the eighth division, meaning that

3. Luft, "When was Yeshua (Jesus) Born?"

Sukkot (Feast of the Ingathering)

seven other divisions of priests would serve before them. With this additional information and the fact that the religious year began at Passover, we know that all the priests served in the Temple for one week. In addition to Passover, Shavuot would occur seven weeks after Pesach, thus meaning all the priests would be serving. Z'kharyah served in the Temple on the tenth week, from the start of Pesach. This would have been during the Jewish month of Sivan, which relates to the May to June time frame. This is when Z'kharyah was in the temple and the angel appeared to him. It would have likely been shortly after his time in the Temple that Elisheva would have become pregnant (Luke 1:13).

Miryam's conception occurred in the month of Kislev, the November to December time frame and occurring around the time of Hanukkah, the Festival of Light. The Messiah was conceived during the Festival of Light. It makes more sense than any other scenario. When Miryam heard the news that she would become pregnant by the Ruach ha Kodesh, without delay she went to the hill country of Judah where Z'kharyah and Elisheva lived. Elisheva was six months pregnant.

At the time of Passover there is great expectation of the coming Messiah. During the Passover seders of today, a young child will be instructed to open the door for Eliyahu, based on Malachi: 4. Yochanan was born during Passover. Six months later, during Sukkot, Yeshua entered the world. The common traits that Passover and Sukkot share are that they are both eight days in length and incorporate the first day and the last day of the feasts as Sabbaths and Holy Gatherings or convocations.

On the eighth day after his birth, when it was time for his b'rit-milah, he was given the name Yeshua, which is what the angel had called him before his conception. On the eighth day of Sukkot, Yeshua was brought into the covenant of Avraham, Yitzchak, and Ya'akov by being circumcised and receiving his name. When the time came for their purification according to the Torah of Moshe, they took him up to Yerushalayim to present him to Adonai (Luke 2:22). Many believe this time of purification happened at the same time as Yeshua's circumcision and naming, however, without knowing the scriptures in their proper cultural context, they are in error. This time of purification is called *pidyon-haben* and takes place after the son is forty-one days old (Lev 12:4).

I pray that these last several segments have opened your eyes to just how important and relevant cultural context is when applying it to scripture. Not only will it reveal truths that only appear to be hidden, but will also keep you on that narrow path that leads to righteousness. It is a narrow gate and a hard road that leads to life, and only a few find it (Matt 7:13).

I have great concern for the church as it is today. The great deceiver has done a masterful job in blinding the church of the truth. He already knows what his final outcome is and therefore, his primary goal is to take as many people with him as he can, in the time he has remaining. Our Messiah was never part of what we know as Christmas, and for that matter never will be. Just think about the endless lies told by parents to keep the myth of Santa Claus and Christmas alive. There are millions of people who believe this is harmless. The information is before you. That has to stop now.

When our Messiah was speaking to the woman at the well, regarding worship of God, his reply is, "You people don't know what you are worshiping; we worship what we do know, because salvation comes from the Jews. But the time is coming—indeed, it's here now—when the true worshipers will worship the Father spiritually and truly, for these are the kind of people the Father wants worshiping him. God is spirit; and worshipers must worship him spiritually and truly" (John 4:21–24).

The time is at hand where the return of our Messiah is close and can happen at any time. He is coming for his bride—his spotless bride. It is time for the church to remove it's spots, and prepare for the coming of its bridegroom. As a believer, when you stand before our Messiah at his judgment seat and you are asked, "why did you celebrate these pagan feasts in my name?"

What will your answer be?

Sha'ul was the first evangelist to deal with pagans who were coming into the new faith, he too wrote about their attempts to maintain their old festivals. Paul reminded the Galatians that they once had no knowledge of God, but now that they do, how is it they went back again to their old ways keeping days, months, fixed times, and years. Paul penned that he was in fear his time teaching them was to no purpose (Gal 4:10).

Sukkot (Feast of the Ingathering)

IS CHRISTMAS SCRIPTURAL?[4]

by Graeme Purdie

The Christian celebration of Christmas had nothing to do with birth of Yeshua the Jewish Messiah who is clearly portrayed in the Gospel of Luke as having been born when the shepherds were in the field, guarding their flocks by night, which indicates that Yeshua was born either late summer or early autumn. In the northern hemisphere this time falls around mid to late September or, in a scriptural leap year, as late as mid-October, but definitely not as late as the 25th of December. None of the Gospels define the exact day on which Yeshua was born, nor do even remotely suggest the date was on or near the 25th of December. Hence, in recent years many commentators have written extensively on the matter of the origin of the Christmas celebration, with a general consensus that the date set down by the fourth-century Christian Church was nothing more than an attempt to win many converts from among the polytheistic (pagan) communities of the Roman Empire, who already had their own celebrations on or around the 25th of December.

Secular history suggests that throughout Roman Europe of the first to fourth-centuries CE, there were many (polytheistic) pagan religious cults, which celebrated the winter solstice calling it *"Dies Natalis Solis Invicti,"* (the Birthday of the Unconquerable Sun), which on the Julian calendar, fell on the 21st December. During that same period there was widespread cultic worship and feasting in favour of Saturnalia, (Golden Age of Saturn), the god of sowing and husbandry, with the celebrations taking place between the 17th to 23rd of December. In addition many historians have suggested, that the 25th of December was the celebration of the birthday of Mithras, a Persian deity whose worship penetrated the Roman world in the first century BCE. The cult of Mithras was brought to Rome by the military. Therefore, in the midst of all that cultic worship and festivity, the fourth-century Christian Church having been ordained as the official State religion of Rome by Emperor Constantine, deemed it was necessary to have its own festive celebration sometime within the month of December. So, what better event to celebrate than the birth of their Christ? The result was that yet another festival was added to the Roman celebratory mix.

4. Purdie, "Graeme The Origin of Christmas."

Throughout the last 1,600 years the Roman and Orthodox Churches have gone on to embrace many of more national customs from communities who had ties back to Roman times. Since the Christian Reformation, until the nineteenth-century it would have been difficult to find any "Protestant Christians" who embraced any of the cultic pagan feasts and practices of Roman Europe. But, since the ninteenth century, Christmas practices have become the norm even for most "Protestant" churches, and woe to anyone who speaks against them.

A broad element of English Christianity considered the Christmas celebration a pagan blasphemy. The Puritans, Baptists, Quakers, Presbyterians, Calvinists, and other denominations brought this opposition to early New England and strong opposition to the holiday lasted in America until the middle of the eighteenth century. Indeed, many Protestants abhorred this pagan day until recent times. Henry Ward Beecher, a Congregationalist, wrote in 1847:

> "To me Christmas is a foreign day, and I shall die so. When I was a boy I wondered what Christmas was. I knew there was such a time, because we had an Episcopal church in our town, and I saw them dressing it with evergreens, and wondered what they were taking the woods into the church for; but I got no satisfactory explanation. A little later I understood it was a Romish institution, kept by the Roman Church."

Anyone who has the inclination can soon find out for themselves that "Christmas" is a totally non-scriptural festival—with its origin, its trappings, and in all its traditions centred in the cultic practices of the pagan world. No honest person can deny these truths!

How then should we, as Talmidim of Yeshua respond to this non-scriptural pagan festival? The answer lies in Jeremiah 10:1–4, which gives specific instructions to Isra'el in relation to the use of what later became known as the "Christmas Tree" where it says:

"Hear the word YHVH speaks to you, house of Isra'el! Here is what YHVH says: "Don't learn the way of the Goyim (nations), don't be frightened by astrological signs, even if the Goyim are afraid of them; for the customs of the peoples are nothing. They cut down a tree in the forest; a craftsman works it with his axe; they deck it with silver and gold. They fix it with hammer and nails, so that it won't move."

Instead of following such practices, we should always look to YHVH Elohim for guidance through his Torah by embracing the cycle of his seven

Sukkot (Feast of the Ingathering)

Moedim (designated times of YHVH) as commanded in Leviticus chapter 23. We can also acknowledge, through the celebration of Hanukkah and Purim, that YHVH honours those who were and still are faithful to His Torah. By observing these festivals alone we begin to acknowledge Yeshua HaMashiach (Messiah), as the true light of the world. Further, Luke chapters 1 and 2 strongly indicate that he was born on the first day of Sukkot, in the year 2 BCE, which would have been mid-September in the Julian calendar. So, we have no reason at all to embrace the 25th of December as the time of his birth.

WHAT I BELIEVE AND WHAT I REJECT[5]

by Rabbi Loren Jacobs

I don't for one moment believe that those who celebrate Christmas or Easter or who make Sunday their day of assembly and worship are guilty of engaging in paganism. Did you know that a book of the Bible is named after Ishtar, a goddess of sexuality? But now the name "Esther" is used by Jewish people and Christians with the highest regard. Did you know that one of the Jewish Biblical months is named Tammuz after an ancient Babylonian god? Did you know that the name of another Jewish hero of the Faith, Mordecai, most likely comes from another pagan deity, Marduk? But Mordecai is now a name that is used by the Jewish people with the greatest respect. Do you really suppose that, by using the names Esther, Mordecai, and Tammuz, the Jewish people are pagans? No! The Jewish people have taken pagan names and over time removed the original pagan connotation. Should it bother us that a Christian holiday (Easter) is also called by this name? I don't think so.

    The early Christian leaders tried to remove paganism from their culture by replacing false gods with the true God. They tried to bring Christ into their culture. Instead of Sunday being the day of the Sun, they made it a day for the Son of God, who is like the Sun of Righteousness. Instead of a holiday dedicated to Saturn near the winter solstice, they replaced Saturn with Messiah, the Light. Instead of a day devoted to Ishtar, they focused on the resurrection of Messiah. I don't believe these early leaders sinned. I believe that Christmas, Easter, and Sunday worship are legitimate traditions and that people have a right to observe traditions that are meaningful to them without being derided for it—as long as the traditions don't contradict the Word of God. Messiah Yeshua himself observed some extra-biblical Jewish traditions—like drinking more than one cup of wine at the Last Supper, which was a Passover Seder, and like celebrating Chanukah. (John 10).

    There are some pagan practices that do stand in contradiction to the Word of God and should not be used at all. For example, many pagans had shrines with idols in which they prayed to their gods, including a mother-goddess figure. Instead of giving up this idolatry, some nominal Christians simply renamed them Mary and the saints. Praying to fellow human beings who have died or using statues and icons as part of worship are practices

---

5. Jacobs, "What I Believe and What I Reject."

that are incompatible with biblical worship. I also find the "Sacrifice of the Mass" and the doctrine of Transubstantiation to be pagan if it is taught that the literal body and blood of the Messiah are being eaten and drunk, since the Torah forbids cannibalism and the consumption of blood.

It is the presence of the Holy Spirit, making people holy and transforming them into the image of Messiah, that purifies. I believe in two ordinances for the Church—Baptism and the Lord's Supper. I believe that ideally baptism should be done by full immersion to someone who has made his or her own decision to follow Messiah, but that does not prevent me from having fellowship with those who sprinkle and engage in infant baptism. The Lord's Supper is a memorial, a symbol of our union with the Risen Lord, who is united to the Father. Transubstantiation is error, but that does not prevent me from having fellowship with those who believe in *Con*substantiation.

I do not believe in Baptismal Regeneration. I believe that baptism is symbolic of the inward renewal that takes place at the moment that saving faith is generated in a human heart and the Holy Spirit is given to that individual. Baptism is the first thing that should be done after a person comes to a saving knowledge of the Lord. It shows commitment and public identification with the God of Israel, with Messiah Yeshua, and the New Covenant Community. Baptism is the initiation of our life with God. The Lord's Supper helps us sustain our life with the Lord and maintain unity with his people. Therefore, a person must be baptized before he or she is allowed to participate in the Lord's Supper. I believe that the community of believers can observe the Lord's Supper as often as they assemble or when they choose to do so. Our community celebrates the Lord's Supper once a month on the first Sabbath of the new Jewish month. I believe that the bread can be either leavened or unleavened bread (except during Passover when we will use matzah).

12

Tikkun Olam (Repairing the World)

For Tziyon's sake I will not be silent, for Yerushalayim's sake I will not rest, until her vindication shines out brightly and her salvation like a blazing torch.

(Isa 62:1)

The people of God accepted the Torah as they stood in the shadow of a high mountain and God descended to bring his mercy, as he always does, to a humble and contrite people who are not strong in their own strength. Every Jewish man, woman, and child, an estimated three million people, heard God speak that day and testified of the words to their descendants.

The Israelite nation grew believing in the redemption of all nations. The Torah tells that life has purpose. There is a Creator who put this world in place and set each of us on a mission to repair what has been broken as we move toward the Messianic age. We are his instruments beautifying his garden to bring out the flowers and the fragrance of his presence. Believers carry sparks of light that began with God wanting relationship with Adam and Eve to share in his care for each other. The process ever since has multiplied the sparks with creation's longing for Israel and the church to be consummated in the Lord.

Cumulative forces erupting sparks everywhere are an integral part of bringing this about. The Messiah does not bring about his age in a moment. It's a result of thousands of years and billions of souls contributing their part

Tikkun Olam (Repairing the World)

and God doing the rest. Elijah asked the woman what she had and she said all she had was a jar of oil. David had only a sling. The 5,000 hungry people had only a boy with his two fish and five loaves. The servants at the wedding had only water to bring to Jesus for him to turn into wine. The church and Israel each bring their part to the work that God weaves together in unity. Jesus said, but if you greet only your brothers, what are you doing more than others? (Matt 5:46). That's what the Gentiles were doing. The division left both Jew and Gentile incomplete with no combining of gifts to offer to God to empower with his Spirit.

For although darkness covers the earth and thick darkness the peoples; on you *Adonai* will rise; over you will be seen his glory (Isa 60:2). Seven-hundred years before Jesus walked earth, the prophet Isaiah wrote the description in Hebrew saying, Who has believed our report? And to whom has been revealed the Zeroah? (Isa 53:1) God created the universe by the Zeroah. God saved his people out of Egypt by using the same Zeroah. Then God showed salvation to the entire earth through the Zeroah. The bone of the lamb present at Passover is called the Zeroah. Jesus is the Zeroah, a man of sorrows, who created the universe, brought people out of bondage, and healed them by his own wounds. This power of God's arm to reach is retold in the seven annual festivals each time earth spins under the seasonal sky.

The heavens declare the glory of God, the dome of the sky speaks the work of his hands (Ps 91:1).

Jesus has fulfilled the four spring holidays.

Pesach. When the first full moon of spring brings Passover, a feast of salvation because he is our Passover lamb whose blood was shed.

Chag Hamotzi. The day after the Pesach begins the days of Unleavened Bread, the body of Jesus, the bread of life, unleavened as he is pure of sin.

Yom habikkurim. On the day after the Sabbath that completes Unleavened Bread, the Israelites hold the feast of First Fruits. Acknowledging the fertility of the land, they brought early crops from spring planting and wave sheaves before the Lord, representing the resurrection of Yeshua and the restoration of the people.

Shavu'ot. Seven weeks after Pesach, Pentecost marks the summer harvest with an offering of two baked loaves made with leaven, representing adding the Gentiles into the people of God. The Holy Spirit came during Pentecost to begin the church.

These festivals were the first coming of the Messiah. Jesus was crucified on Passover, buried on Unleavened Bread, raised on First Fruits, and sent the Holy Spirit on Pentecost. We remain in the church age of Pentecost until the trumpet sounds, the next of the three feasts to come in autumn when the figs are ripe in Israel and the pomegranites burst with seeds. Trumpets usher in the days, followed by Yom Kippur and Tabernacles.

Yom Teru'ah, the Day of Trumpets, (Lev 23:23–25, Num 29:1) comes at the new moon, a time the light is present again. Longing for the illumination, we don't know when the moment will be that the light will appear and Jesus will resurrect the dead and gather them to himself. No man knows the hour or day (Mark 13:32).

Trumpets, known as Rosh Hashanah, was given to Moses and the nation of Israel while in the desert wilderness at Sinai. The people were told to have a holy convocation and a day for remembering when the crescent of this new moon appeared, announced with blowing the shofar on the first day of the seventh month. The feast was held when the high priest blew the horn to bring in the people. They would stop harvesting the fields and put down their tools. When the trumpet sounds from heaven to call the church, the church will end its harvesting. When he comes there will be a hush on all creation as all the nations gather before him. He will answer the call for justice to billions of people because the desire for justice is innate in all cultures. The sound of his voice will be heard. This is Yeshua, who we sinned against, whose blood the world despised.

Rosh Hashanah is also called Yom Harat Olam, the birthday of the world, acknowledging when creation was first made and our role as partners with God in creating each other's lives.

TIKKUN OLAM: REPAIRING THE WORLD[1]

by Stan Meyer

Tikkun olam has become a favorite Hebrew catch phrase to describe social activism, opposition to injustice, and efforts to improve society and repair the world. Non-Jews have also appropriated the term: Former U.S. president Bill Clinton used tikkun olam to describe his social agenda. Where did the term originate? The meaning of the phrase went through four iterations. It began as a verb meaning "to make straight" in the Hebrew Scriptures. Rabbis used the term in legal discussion in the Talmud. In the Middle Ages it was used to describe a Kabbalistic concept of cosmic repair. Finally, American Jewry appropriated the term in the mid-twentieth century to describe modern social activism.

Repairing or Making Straight.

The Hebrew verb *T.K.N.* is only found four times in the Scriptures (Ecc 1:15, 7:13, 12:9, and Dan 4:36). It means to make straight, establish, arrange, or repair. In Ecclesiastes 7:13 the writer said, "Consider what God has done: Who can straighten [*Takkan*] what he has made crooked?"

    The concept that we have a moral duty to society originates in the Torah. In Deuteronomy 16:20 God commanded Israel: "Follow justice and justice alone." The Hebrew prophet Amos condemned Israel's disregard of the widow, orphan and alien. He declared: "Seek good, and not evil, that you may live . . . Hate evil, and love good, and establish justice in the gate . . . let justice roll down like waters, and righteousness like an ever-flowing stream!" (Amos 5:14–15, 24).

Improving Society.

The rabbis put the words *tikkun* (repair) and *ha-olam* (the world) together to create a term for "improving society": *tikkun ha-olam*. The phrase is found thirty times in the Babylonian Talmud, eight times in the Palestinian Talmud, and a few times in the Midrashim. Tikkun ha-olam in this sense referred to rabbinic interpretation of biblical law that provided a way for

---

1. Myer, "Tikkun Olam."

Torah to be carried out while protecting those who could not defend themselves. The phrase was extended to describe fairness in business practice. For example, physicians could not be held liable for accidental malpractice. Because these moral rulings improved society or made the world straight, they were called tikkun ha-olam.

Repairing the Universe

Then the term underwent a third iteration. The *Zohar*, a book of Jewish mysticism, which first appeared in Spain in the late thirteenth century, used tikkun olam to describe the cosmic benefits when a Jew performs mitzvot. An entire philosophy called *kabbalah* sprung up around this book. It postures how through the fall of Adam, the universe was "ruptured" in both the physical and spiritual realms. When a Jew carries out the *mitzvot* (the 613 commands in the Torah), cosmic repairs are made in the invisible spiritual world. The benefits then "flow down" into the physical world and slowly repair the damage done on earth by the sin of Adam. Later Kabbalists elaborated on this philosophy by claiming that at the time of the fall, God's presence was scattered in the same way a clay pot is shattered and the shards scattered. These pieces were called "divine sparks." Famed Kabbalist Isaac Luria (1534–1572) explained that the Jews were dispersed throughout the world in order to "elevate" these sparks and restore the unity of God's presence.

Repairing Our World

Tikkun olam underwent its fourth iteration in the mid-twentieth century. While Jews struggled to make sense of the horrors of the Holocaust, a handful of theologians said that the tragic event gave the Jewish people a right to be heard. The Jews, they maintained, had earned a platform to speak out against hatred and injustice wherever it reared its ugly head.

Emil Fackenheim (1916–2003), rabbi, professor of philosophy, and Holocaust survivor, postulated that world history follows an ontological cycle: "rupture" and "repair" (tikkun). The Holocaust (rupture) was followed by the creation of the State of Israel (repair). It is incumbent on the Jewish people to lead the way toward repairing the rupture created by the Holocaust through acts of tikkun olam.

Tikkun Olam (Repairing the World)

Repairing World Peace

With the establishment of the State of Israel in 1948, our Jewish people hoped to design a society founded on moral values led by a government that protected freedom of speech and religion and cared for the outcast, the orphan, and the widow. Moreover, many Jewish people believed that having a sovereign state won the right for us to advocate for tikkun olam on an international scale.

Sadly, the years that followed have not borne out this optimistic vision. Conflicts between Israel and her neighbors have erupted into regional wars. After each Middle East peace agreement, war erupted again over a new issue. Since the Holocaust, the world has come to the brink of nuclear holocaust. Ethnic genocide has been repeated numerous times against other peoples. Tikkun olam is elusive.

Tikkun HaLev (Repairing the Heart)

Any attempt to repair the world must take into account that society is made up of flawed people who are moved by their heart. The motivations of the heart can be fraught with problems. Although the Hebrew prophets charged Israel with the task of tikkun olam, they also condemned the human heart as sick, wicked, and ill-equipped to carry out that mission: "The heart is deceitful above all things, and desperately sick; who can understand it?" (Jer 17:9).

While it is our moral duty to pursue peace, establish justice, and care for those who cannot protect themselves, not until our own hearts are repaired can we repair the world. As long as we are at war with our own evil inclinations, we will be at war with those around us. That is why I believe we need the agent of peace God has provided. Isaiah wrote of the Messiah who was to come:

Surely he has borne our griefs and carried our sorrows; yet we esteemed him stricken, smitten by God, and afflicted. But he was pierced for our transgressions; he was crushed for our iniquities; upon him was the chastisement that brought us peace, and with his wounds we are healed (Isa 53:4–5).

This Messiah came to mend our hearts by dying in our place for our wrongdoing, thereby wiping our slate clean and giving us *shalom* with God. Those of us who are Messianic Jews maintain that Y'shua (Jesus) was that one.

The *Aleinu* (third century CE), a Hebrew prayer recited at the conclusion of the Shabbat service, looks forward to a day of complete tikkun olam when God himself will mend the world:

> And therefore we hope to You, Lord our God, that we may speedily behold the splendor of Your might, to banish idolatry from the earth—and false gods will be utterly destroyed; to perfect the world [le-takken Olam] under the sovereignty of the Almighty. All mankind shall invoke Your Name to turn all the wicked of the earth to you.

Tikkun Olam (Repairing the World)

THE FEAST OF TRUMPETS[2]

by Tom Martincic

Yahweh has not yet had Messiah fulfill everything the Feast Days represent. When we were in bondage, he revealed himself. He set us free. He saved us by the blood of the lamb, led us into the wilderness where we are now. He gives us his Torah. That was at Pentecost he gave the Torah. So there are two feasts: The Feast of Unleavened Bread and Passover, and then we have Pentecost, or Shavuot, or Feast of Weeks. So he gave us his spirit, which brings us forgiveness of sin for having broken the Law and leads us to keeping his commandments and places that Law right here in our hearts. And now, what are we waiting on? We are in the wilderness. We are waiting on Yahushua's return. And there is this vast length of time between the third month and the seventh month. There is a four month time period approximately, a little less than four months, that we are waiting now for the Feast of Trumpets to be fulfilled.

The Feast of Trumpets is held in the moon of Ethanim, which is the seventh new moon, or seventh month, that is when they gathered. "Ethanim" means "to endure with strength." And it is the seventh moon that we are all waiting on, really. Spiritually, we are waiting on that seventh moon. If we are not living in such a way that we would be accepted by him if he were to return tomorrow, then we are walking a very dangerous line. And so, our goal is that we would all be ready and prepared, because: Behold, I tell you a mystery: We shall not all sleep, but we shall all be changed, in a moment, in the twinkling of an eye, at the last trumpet. For the trumpet will sound, and the dead will be raised incorruptible, and we shall be changed (1 Cor 15:51–52).

This Feast of Trumpets, which is the first day of the seventh month of Yahweh's calendar, Yahweh never just comes right out and explains what this feast is really all about. He just says "in the seventh month, on the first of the month" you are going to go and get your trumpets out, your shofars, and you are going to blow the shofar. Or, he says, you can also shout because the word "teruah" means "shout" also. They both make a very similar sound (Lev 23:24).

YAHWEH spoke to Moses, saying: Make two silver trumpets for yourself; you shall make them of hammered work; you shall use them for

---

2. Martincic, "The Feast of Trumpets."

calling the congregation and for directing the movement of the camps. When they blow both of them, all the congregation shall gather before you at the door of the tabernacle of meeting. But if they blow [only] one, then the leaders, the heads of the divisions of Israel, shall gather to you. When you sound the advance, the camps that lie on the east side shall then begin their journey (Num 10:1–5).

So there is one long blast. One blast, and then there is this "sound the advance." Interesting. There are different kinds of sounds that could come from a trumpet. With one trumpet, that is one blast, the princes, which are the heads of the thousands of Israel, they would gather themselves. And if they blow an alarm, then the camps that lie on the east part would go forward. So there are two different kinds of sounds. And then we have the alarm. There would be seven short blasts. And it is kind of an alarming sound. So when they heard this "teruah," this advance, then they knew what that meant and what they were supposed to do. So it says:

> When you sound the advance the second time, then the camps that lie on the south side shall begin their journey; they shall sound the call for them to begin their journeys. And when the assembly is to be gathered together, you shall blow, but not sound the advance. The sons of Aaron, the priests, shall blow the trumpets; and these shall be to you as an ordinance forever throughout your generations (Num 10:6–8).

And then it says: When you go to war in your land against the enemy who oppresses you, then you shall sound an alarm with the trumpets, and you will be remembered before YAHWEH your Elohim, and you will be saved from your enemies (Num 10:9).

These were the two silver trumpets that were used by the priests. The priests would blow these trumpets, and it says "to sound an alarm" with these trumpets, and when they did so, Yahweh would deliver them from their enemies. I have wondered sometimes, whenever you need Yahweh's work to fight for you, maybe a time of temptation or a time where you need his victory over the enemy in some area of your life you are being attacked, what might happen if you got the ol' shofars out and just started blasting these things, the alarm sounds? Because we know that even back then the battle was Yahweh's, and the battle was actually a spiritual battle.

Also in the day of your gladness, in your appointed feasts, and at the beginning of your months, you shall blow the trumpets over your burnt offerings and over the sacrifices of your peace offerings; and they shall be a memorial for you before your Elohim: I [am] YAHWEH your Elohim. (Num 10:10).

It is something that Yahweh must see as significant in his eyes. And so, imagine. This would be a normal sound they would hear in Israel at the temple service, especially during the Feasts. They would be hearing this sound all the time because these trumpets were blown over all the offerings. And so, whenever there was an offering done, trumpets would be used. And maybe that is why even during our Feast of Tabernacles that we host here in Missouri, along with our praises to Yahweh, we have people who bring shofars. Now many believe, as I do, that this feast is symbolic of the time of Yahushua's return and our own advance toward the promised land when he will move us. We will meet him in the air. He will move us and we will gather to him from the east, the west, the north and the south. And so, along with our trumpet blowing, when we give praise to Yahweh, you might hear a lot of shouting at the Feast of Tabernacles in Missouri. And there is significance to this.

Also, notice in Joshua chapter 6:1–4, the "walls of Jericho that came tumbling down." Jericho was securely shut up because of the children of Israel; none went out, and none came in. "You shall march around the city, all [you] men of war; you shall go all around the city once. This you shall do six days. And seven priests shall bear seven trumpets of rams' horns before the ark. But the seventh day you shall march around the city seven times, and the priests shall blow the trumpets."

These were actually the rams' horns. They were not the silver trumpets.

> It shall come to pass, when they make a long [blast] with the ram's horn, [and] when you hear the sound of the trumpet, that all the people shall shout with a great shout; then the wall of the city will fall down flat. And the people shall go up every man straight before him (Josh 6:5).

There is a striking parallel here between Joshua leading Israel into the promised land and giving them victory over their enemies. You may not know this, but the word "Jericho" is actually pronounced "Yericho." The word actually means "its moon." "Yerach/yareach" in Hebrew means "moon." Now when Moshe led the children of Israel out of Egypt into the wilderness, of course he spent a lot of time teaching the people his Torah, his Law, but we know that not even Moshe himself was allowed to enter the promised land. Why? Because he himself was a sinner. And this is a picture of our own walk because we know Yahweh saved us by the blood of the Lamb. Likewise, at Passover, he saved them by the blood of the lamb.

And he led them through the Red Sea. And there is a New Testament scripture that says they were baptized into Moshe, or Moses, in the sea and in the cloud. So there is the water baptism and the baptism of the Spirit. And when they got to the other side, the sea fell down and the old men who were of the enemy died, right? The men of Egypt died. And in that is a picture of our own baptism. The old man, that was Yahweh's enemy, perishes in the water, and the new man, Yahushua the Messiah, rises up through us.

He brought them through this wilderness land, this land that was not their own, and he taught them his Torah, his Law. He taught them the way of righteousness. However, Moshe, who taught them the Law, was not able to bring them across the Jorden. And in that is a picture of us. We are strangers and sojourners, and we cannot rely upon Moses and the Law to lead us across the Jordan. The name "Joshua" in the Hebrew—he was the one who actually led them across the Jordan—the name "Joshua" in the Hebrew actually is pronounced "Yoshua" or "Yahushua." He carries the exact same name as the Messiah. Joshua, or Yoshua, is the same name. Joshua is just another way of saying Yahushua because there is no "J" in Hebrew.

So he led them across the Jordan. And what did he do in this town called "its moon?" They shouted and the first city fell, and that was the sign that Yahushua was going to destroy every enemy. And this was the beginning where he destroyed every enemy. And he brought forth a new nation. And, likewise, Yahushua. We need to rely upon him, not Moses. Moses can't take us there. We need a man named Yahushua to take us across the Jordan and into the promised land.

The seventh month, this Feast of Trumpets, we see in the New Testament it talks about the Messiah coming at the last trump. This is all a picture of what the children of Israel went through, because, remember, the Feast of Trumpets takes place on the "seventh moon." Seven times the children of Israel went around this city called "its moon." The seventh time around it they shouted and they blew the trumpets and the city came down and the kingdoms of that world became the kingdoms of Yahweh. And so, likewise, with the shout of an archangel and the trumpet of Elohim, the Messiah will return. And the earthly, temporary, shaky, wobbly foundations and walls of the kingdoms of this world that people have relied upon for their protection will come tumbling down.

Tikkun Olam (Repairing the World)

Then the seventh angel sounded: And there were loud voices in heaven, saying, "The kingdoms of this world have become [the kingdoms] of our Master and of His Messiah, and He shall reign forever and ever!" (Rev 11:15).

And all the things that we think are important in this age will suddenly mean nothing. Wouldn't it be wonderful if the church kept this Feast as a yearly testimony to the world that a Savior is coming to rescue us from the hole we are digging ourselves into, and there is hope, there are answers, there is a Kingdom coming that we are all invited to. And if the people of the churches would just realize, "Look, this Feast has not been fulfilled?" It cannot have been fulfilled. Yahushua is coming with the sound of the trumpet, but for some reason, in traditional Christianity, "Ahh . . . dismiss it. Ahh . . . just Jewish stuff. We don't do that." So I say, "Let's sound the trumpet!"

Sometimes we just have to be like little children who want to learn and be obedient to our Father and His will, set aside our own traditions and be willing to do it. And Yahweh expected that of them. He expects that of all of us. A lot of times when we begin to practice the things that He tells us to practice, we get to learn a lot of the reasons why we are doing it. It is not about practicing Judaism. It is about using these Feast Days to call our attention to the things that Yahweh wants to get our attention with. And we are called to be watchmen.

In Israel of old, another reason for the blowing of the trumpet was to announce a new king. "There let Zadok the priest and Nathan the prophet anoint him king over Israel; and blow the horn, and say, '[Long] live King Solomon!' They are blowing the trumpets to announce the new king. Then you shall come up after him, and he shall come and sit on my throne, and he shall be king in my place. For I have appointed him to be ruler over Israel and Judah" (1Kgs 1:34–35).

So when this last trumpet sounds, the world is going to be under a rule that it has never known or seen before unless they are believers. He is already our King. But the ruler and the king of this world will be dethroned, and Yahushua will sit on the throne. And He will be the King that we all submit to, that we all seek. And Micah 4:2—Many nations shall come and say, "Come, and let us go up to the mountain of YAHWEH, To the house of the Elohim of Jacob; He will teach us His ways, And we shall walk in His paths." For out of Zion the law shall go forth, And the word of

YAHWEH from Jerusalem. So the Law will still be there. It will not have been abolished.

He shall judge between many peoples, And rebuke strong nations afar off; They shall beat their swords into plowshares, And their spears into pruning hooks; Nation shall not lift up sword against nation, Neither shall they learn war any more (Mic 4:3).

When He gathers the outcasts, we have to be willing to be outcasts. We have to be willing to be afflicted and be among those who are looked down upon and thought to be nothing by the world. Let's be ready to hear that shout of the archangel, that midnight cry to meet the Bridegroom, having our lamps filled with oil, our hearts filled with the service of love, being filled with Yahweh's Spirit of love, joy, peace, kindness, faithfulness, goodness, self-control, faith.

Bibliography

Adler, Jeffrey A. "Gentiles Within the Messianic Jewish Community." In *Borough Park Papers*, Lederer Books. Web. http://www.chosenpeople.com/symposium/page8.html?time=12345678.

Brumbach, Joshua. "Sukkot: Messiah and the World to Come." In *Ahavat Zion Synagogue*. Web. http://www.umjc.org/sukkot-messiah-and-the-world-to-come/.

Chosen People Ministries. "Holidays and Festivals." Web. http://chosenpeople.com/main/index.php/holidays-and-festivals/595-removal-of-the-leaven.

Clark, Ross. "Keeping a Balance for the Gentile Messianic." In *Perth Messianic Assembly*. Web. http://www.pma.org.au/uploads/3/4/2/7/3427709/keeping_a_balance_for_the_gentile_messianic.pdf.

———. "Why All Christians Should Celebrate Pentecost." In *Perth Messianic Assembly*. Web. http://www.pma.org.au/new-articles.html.

Cox, Brian. "Let Us Reclaim Our Family." *The Living Church Foundation*, March 16, 2012. Web. http://livingchurch.org/let-us-reclaim-our-family.

Dauermann, Stuart. "Inconvenient Truths: The One New Man." In *The Messianic Agenda: A Messianic Judaism Media blog*, April 29, 2011. Web. http://www.messianicjudaism.me/agenda/2011/04/29/inconvenient-truths-the-one-new-man/#comment-22103.

Davenport, Geoff. "A Challenge to Believers." *The Way—Haderech Messianic Community in New Zealand*. Web. http://thewaycentral.org.nz/the-way-the-truth-the-life/.

———. "Shic'zur o t'ciya?—Restoration or Revival?" January 16, 2016, *The Way—Haderech Messianic Community in New Zealand*. Web. http://thewaycentral.org.nz/wp-content/uploads/2016/02/restoration-and-revival.pdf.

Eliezer, Pirkei deRabbi. "The Course of the Moon." In *Pirkê de Rabbi Eliezer: (The Chapters of Rabbi Eliezer the Great)*. Web. https://archive.org/stream/pirkderabbieli00frieuoft/pirkderabbieli00frieuoft_djvu.txt.

Jacobs, Loren. "The Real Miracle of Chanukkah." *Congregation Shema Yisrael*, November 30, 2013. Web. http://www.shema.com/category/messianic-judaism/judaica/holidays/.

———. "Shavuot, the Feast of Weeks." In *Congregation Shema Yisrael*. Web. http://www.shema.com/shavuot-the-feast-of-weeks-168/.

———. "What I Believe and What I Reject." In *Congregation Shema Yisrael*. Web. http://www.shema.com/about/what-we-believe/.

Bibliography

Lazarus, David. "Why Jews Don't Like Evangelicals." In *Beit Immanuel* Messianic Jewish Congregation. Web. http://archive.constantcontact.com/fs103/1101937328142/archive/1119052402393.html.

Lowinger, Frank. "The Jewishness of the Gospels." In *Congregation B'rith Hadoshah* http://www.shalombuffalo.org/about-us/the-jewishness-of-the-gospels/.

Luft, Stephen. "Baptism." *Kehilah Portland*. Web. http://www.shalommaine.com/messianic_perspectives/mpepisode12-Mikveh.pdf.

———. "The Meaning of Sukkot." *Kehalah Portland*. Web. http://www.shalommaine.com/messianic_perspectives/mpepisode61-Sukkot.pdf.

———. "New Covenant Writings." *Kehilah Portland*. Web. http://www.shalommaine.com/messianic_perspectives/mpepisode22-New_Covenant_Writings.pdf.

———. "The True Origin of Easter." *Kehilah Portland*, Maine. Web. http://www.shalommaine.com/article_index_pdf/trueoriginofeaster.pdf.

———. "Understanding Messianic Judaism." *Kehilah Portland*, Maine. Web. http://www.shalommaine.com/article_index_pdf/what_is_messianic_judaism.pdf.

———. "When was Yeshua (Jesus) Born?" *Kehilah Maine*. Web. http://www.shalommaine.com/article_index_pdf/when_was_Jesus_born.pdf.

———. "Yom Hashoah." *Kehilah Portland*. Web. http://www.shalommaine.com/messianic_perspectives/mpepisode80-Yom%20Hashoah.pdf.

Martincic, Tom. "Exposing the Elitist, Sectarian Spirit." *EliYah.com*, March 23, 2013, Web. http://www.eliyah.com/transcripts/html/20140802.html.

———. "The Feast of Trumpets." *EliYah.com*, August 15, 2015. Web. http://www.eliyah.com/transcripts/html/20150815.html.

Myer, Stan. "Tikkun Olam: Repairing the World." *Jews for Jesus*. Web. http://jewsforjesus.org/publications/issues/v20-n03/tikkun-olam-repairing-the-world.

Nichol, Richard D. "The Unique Place of Gentiles in Messianic Jewish Congregational Life." *Borough Park Papers*, Lederer Books. Web. http://www.chosenpeople.com/symposium/page8.html?time=12345678.

Olson, Jon C. "Paul Employing Leviticus: Same-Sex Intercourse Considered Amongst Torah Commandments." *Kesher: A Journal of Messianic Judaism*. Web. http://www.kesherjournal.com/index.php?option=com_content&view=article&id=159:paul-employing-leviticus-same-sex-intercourse-considered-amongst-torah-commandments&catid=88888900:issue-27&Itemid=451.

Ontario Consultants on Religious Tolerance. "Two millennia of Jewish Persecution." Web. http://www.religioustolerance.org/jud_pers1.htm.

Pason, Pat. "Any Other Name Would Still Be a Jew." *Congregation B'rith Hadoshah*, March 27, 2014. Web. http://www.shalombuffalo.org/blog/rabbi-shaul-name-still-jew-part-1/.

Pfister, Stefanie. "Messianic Jews Worldwide." *Pasche Institute of Jewish Studies*, Mishkan Issue 58 (2009) 7. Web. http://caspari.com/new/images/stories/archives/Mishkan/mishkan58.pdf.

Purdie, Graeme. "The Origin of Christmas." January 18, 2012, *Talmedei Yeshua Messianic Ministry of New Zealand*. Web. http://www.messianic.org.nz/origin.php.

Rubin, Barry. "Messianic Judaism Gaining Momentum in Israel." *Charisma News*, December 1, 2014. Web. http://www.charismanews.com/world/46304-messianic-judaism-gaining-momentum-in-israel.

Sedaca, David. "In what ways did Jesus live as a Jew?" *Celebrate Messiah*. Web. http://celebratemessiah.com.au/jewish-roots/245-in-what-ways-did-jesus-live-as-a-jew.html.

Bibliography

Seif, Jeffrey. "Gentiles and Jews Together in Ancient Rome and North African Carthage." *Borough Park Papers*, Lederer Books. Web. http://www.chosenpeople.com/symposium/page8.html?time=12345678.

Shalom Messianic Congregation Northern Ireland. "What is the Role of the Church?" Web. http://shalommessianiccongregation.weebly.com/smc-articles.html.

Sorko-Ram, Shira. "I Became as a Jew." In *Moaz. Inc.* Web.http://baruchhashemsynagogue.org/?p=2535.

Stokes, Bruce H. "Gentiles in the Messianic Movement." In *Journal of the Union of Messianic Jewish Congregations* 1997. Web. http://www.hbrucestokes.com/images/Gentiles_in_the_Messianic_Movement.pdf.

Suitt, Chris. "Covenant of Salt: You Gotta Serve Somebody." Torah Class. Web. http://torahclass.com/archived-articles/1036-featured-article-sp-940659465.

Tepe, Nette. "Coming Home to My Jewish Messiah." In *Celebrate Messiah*. Web. http://celebratemessiah.com.au/personal-stories/569-coming-home-to-my-jewish-messiah—by-netty-tepe.html.

Volman, Ben. "Jewish Roots." In *Chosen People Ministries*. Web. http://chosenpeople.com/main/index.php/jewish-roots/264-why-is-it-thought-that-jewish-followers-of-jesus-are-no-longer-jewish-is-this-true.

www.ingramcontent.com/pod-product-compliance
Lightning Source LLC
Chambersburg PA
CBHW070323230426
43663CB00011B/2202